From the library of:
Jimmy Rodriguez

Through the Church the Song Goes On

Through the Church the Song Goes On

Preparing a Lutheran Hymnal for the 21st Century

Edited by

Paul J. Grime
D. Richard Stuckwisch
Jon D. Vieker

COMMISSION ON WORSHIP
THE LUTHERAN CHURCH—MISSOURI SYNOD

THE COVER ART portrays the ancient song of the pilgrims in Jerusalem as they welcomed Christ into the holy city on Palm Sunday, singing a psalm of the Old Testament church: "Blessed is He who comes in the name of the Lord" (Ps. 118:26; Matt. 21:9). So the church of the New Testament has sung these same words in the Sanctus of the Lord's Supper, proclaiming the coming of Christ today in His body and blood, given His people to eat and drink. Photo by Otto Munch.

This book was underwritten by a generous grant from Aid Association for Lutherans (AAL).

The Scripture quotations in this book marked NIV are from the HOLY BIBLE: NEW INTERNATIONAL VERSION, © 1973, 1978, 1984 by International Bible Society. Used by permission of Zondervan Publishing House. All rights reserved.

The Scripture quotations in this book marked NKJV are from the New King James edition, copyright © 1979, 1982. Used by permission.

Luther's Small Catechism © 1986 Concordia Publishing House.

Art work for section headings from Art of the Word, copyright by Concordia Publishing House. Used with permission.

Technical Editor: Jon D. Vieker
Cover Design: Steve Teson
Proofreader: Annette Schroeder

ISBN 0-9671169-0-2

Copyright © 1999 The Lutheran Church—Missouri Synod
1333 S. Kirkwood Rd.
St. Louis, Missouri 63122-7295

All rights reserved. No part of this publication may be reproduced, stored in a retrieval system, or transmitted, in any form or by any means, electronic, mechanical, photocopying, recording, or otherwise, without the prior written permission of the Commission on Worship of The Lutheran Church—Missouri Synod.

Table of Contents

Abbreviations... viii
About the Authors.. ix

Introduction 1

Beginning 3
Theology of Worship... 5
    JOEL A. BRONDOS

Lectionary.. 9
Sacrament of the Word: Reclaiming the
    Church's Historic Lectionary 11
    LEE A. MAXWELL
A Three-Year Lectionary for the New LCMS Hymnal.............. 24
    DEAN D. PITTELKO
Doing 'Our Own Thing' with the Lectionary.................... 34
    D. RICHARD STUCKWISCH

Eucharistic Prayer... 43
A Defense of Eucharistic Prayer in the Evangelical
    Lutheran Liturgy: And a Concern That Now
    May Not Be the Time to Introduce One 45
    BRUCE E. KESEMAN
The Usage of a Eucharistic Prayer:
    Theological and Pastoral Concerns 51
    WILLIAM E. THOMPSON
Eucharistic Prayer: The Middle Ground........................ 57
    WILLIAM C. WEEDON
The Celebration of the Lord's Supper with Thanksgiving:
    Worship Statement No. 32 from the
    Lutheran Church of Australia 68

The Future of Hymnals 73
Do Hymnals Have a Future? 75
    Robert M. Zagore
Why a New Hymnal Now?: 'And Everyone Did
    What Was Right in His Own Eyes'. 86
    Larry A. Peters

Liturgy, Music and Culture 109
Holy Ground and Countercultural Music:
    Or, Save the Polkas for Saturday Night 111
    Daniel A. Zager
The People's Song: What Distinguishes a Hymn
    from a Liturgical Song? 122
    Kent A. Tibben
Liturgy and Culture: Can the Liturgy Be Made
    to Reflect a Particular Culture? 127
    Naomichi Masaki

Variety in Worship 145
Responding to the Call for Variety in the Church's Liturgy 147
    Kevin J. Hildebrand
Psalmody 155
    William M. Ickstadt

Assisting Ministers 161
Serving at the Altar: Retaining the Role of
    Assisting Ministers as Defined in the Rubrics
    of *Lutheran Worship* 163
    Mark A. Waldron
Serving at the Altar Reconsidered:
    The Role of Assisting Minister in *Lutheran Worship* 169
    Thomas M. Winger

Miscellanea 183
Liturgical Texts: Ecumenical Translations and
    Doctrinal Concerns 185
    Robert A.D. Clancy

Holy Absolution: Extolling and Rejoicing in the Gift............193
    BRENT W. KUHLMAN
Confirmation: Living and Rejoicing in the Sacramental Life.......203
    KENT J. BURRESON
Boolean Worship 212
    JAY S. LEMANSKI

Ending...219
Unified in Act and Song....................................221
    RONALD R. FEUERHAHN

Bibliography 227

Abbreviations

AE	*Luther's Works,* American Edition.
BSLK	*Die Bekenntnisschriften der Evangelisch-Lutherischen Kirche.*
CPH	Concordia Publishing House.
ELCA	Evangelical Lutheran Church in America.
ILCW	Inter-Lutheran Commission on Worship.
LBW	*Lutheran Book of Worship* (1978).
LCMS	The Lutheran Church—Missouri Synod.
LW	*Lutheran Worship* (1982).
LWHP	*Lutheran Worship: History and Practice* (1993).
SBH	*Service Book and Hymnal* (1958).
Tappert	*The Book of Concord: The Confessions of the Evangelical Lutheran Church.* Translated and edited by Theodore G. Tappert (1959).
	AC—Augsburg Confession
	Ap—Apology of the Augsburg Confession
	SC—Small Catechism
	LC—Large Catechism
	FC Ep—Formula of Concord, Epitome
	FC SD—Formula of Concord, Solid Declaration
	SA—Smalcald Articles
TDNT	*Theological Dictionary of the New Testament.*
TLH	*The Lutheran Hymnal* (1941).
WA	*Luthers Werke* [Weimar Edition].
WA Br	*Luthers Werke, Briefwechsel* [Weimar Edition].

About the Authors

Rev. Joel A. Brondos is headmaster of Zion Lutheran Academy, Fort Wayne, Ind. He also serves on the editorial board of *Logia*.

Rev. Kent J. Burreson is pastor of St. Peter Lutheran Church, Mishawaka, Ind. He is a doctoral candidate in liturgical studies at Notre Dame University.

Rev. Robert A.D. Clancy is pastor of Holy Trinity Lutheran Church, Garfield, N.J. He is a doctoral candidate in liturgical studies at Drew University.

Rev. Dr. Ronald R. Feuerhahn is professor of historical theology at Concordia Seminary, St. Louis, Mo. He is a member of the Commission on Worship and served on the liturgical subcommittee of *Hymnal Supplement 98*.

Rev. Dr. Paul J. Grime is executive director of the Commission on Worship.

Kevin J. Hildebrand is director of music at St. Luke's Lutheran Church and School, Mount Clemens, Mich.

William M. Ickstadt is director of music at Immanuel Lutheran Church and School, Valparaiso, Ind.

Rev. Bruce E. Keseman is pastor of Christ Our Savior Lutheran Church, Freeburg, Ill.

Rev. Brent W. Kuhlman is pastor of Trinity Lutheran Church, Murdock, Neb., and is pursuing a doctor of philosophy degree at Concordia Seminary, St. Louis, Mo.

Rev. Jay S. Lemanski is pastor of Immanuel Lutheran Church, Cleveland, Ohio.

Rev. Naomichi Masaki is pursuing a doctor of philosophy degree at Concordia Seminary, St. Louis, Mo.

Rev. Dr. Lee A. Maxwell is pastor of St. John Lutheran Church, Maryville, Ill. He is the author of the *Altar Guild Manual*, recently published by CPH.

Rev. Larry A. Peters is pastor of Grace Lutheran Church, Clarksville, Tenn.

Rev. Dean D. Pittelko is pastor of St. Mark Lutheran Church, Janesville, Wis., and is pursuing an advanced degree in liturgics at St. John University, Collegeville, Minn.

Rev. D. Richard Stuckwisch is pastor of Emmaus Lutheran Church, South Bend, Ind. He is a doctoral candidate in liturgical studies at the University of Notre Dame.

Rev. William E. Thompson is associate pastor of Our Savior Lutheran Church, Hartland, Mich.

Rev. Kent A. Tibben is pastor of Trinity Lutheran Church, Danville, Ill.

Rev. Jon D. Vieker is assistant director of the Commission on Worship.

Mark A. Waldron is Assistant Director of Development and Kapelle and Wind Symphony Coordinator at Concordia University, River Forest, Ill.

Rev. William Weedon is pastor of St. Paul Lutheran Church, Hamel, Ill.

Rev. Dr. Thomas M. Winger is a lecturer at Westfield House in Cambridge, England.

Rev. Robert M. Zagore is pastor of St. Paul Lutheran Church, Niles, Mich.

Dr. Daniel A. Zager is music librarian and professor of music at the University of North Carolina at Chapel Hill.

Other participants at the forum:

Mark Bender*
Barbara Bradfield*
Rev. Dr. Scott Bruzek
Rev. Steven Everette*
Rev. Henry Gerike
Rev. Matthew Harrison
Joseph Herl
Rev. Dr. Arthur Just
Rev. Dr. John Kleinig
Janet Muth*

Rev. Dr. Norman Nagel*
Donald Petering
Rev. Dr. Roger Pittelko*
Rev. John Pless
Rev. Richard Resch*
Rev. Harold Senkbeil
Rev. Stephen Starke
Mark Thoelke
Elizabeth Werner*

*current or past member of the Commission on Worship

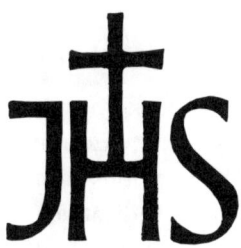

Introduction

Iesu, iuva

ON FEBRUARY 19–21, 1998, THE COMMISSION ON WORSHIP hosted a forum for worship leaders in the The Lutheran Church—Missouri Synod. The purpose of the forum was twofold. First, the commission desired to become better acquainted with a number of pastors and musicians in the Synod who have demonstrated an interest in liturgy, hymnody, and church music. To that end, approximately 25 people were invited to give presentations to the members of the commission. Other pastors and seminary professors who have served the commission in past years were also invited as respondents.

The second purpose of the forum was to explore some of the issues the Commission on Worship will need to examine as it begins work on a thorough revision of the Synod's hymnals, *The Lutheran Hymnal* (1941) and *Lutheran Worship* (1982). Presenters at the forum were invited to select from a predetermined list of topics and to present brief essays that explored these critical issues. The essays in this volume are essentially the same as were presented at the forum.

From the outset, it is important to understand that the essays vary greatly in length and depth. Because the essayists were given few parameters, each developed his assignment differently. In order to assist the reader, the essays are grouped according to topic (in an order similar to their presentation at the forum). A brief preface is provided for each section in an effort to provide background and context. Because of the exploratory nature of the essays, the Commission on Worship does not necessarily endorse all of the positions contained in them. The essays are, in effect, a first step and are indicative of the extensive research that will be required of the committees working on the new hymnal.

As the Commission on Worship begins the mammoth undertaking of preparing a new hymnal for the congregations of our Synod, it does so with a profound sense of humility and catholic circumspection. Echoing the words of the well-known paraphrase of the *Te Deum*, "Holy God, We Praise Your Name" (*TLH* 250; *LW* 171), the title chosen for this book suggests that the church's worship is no new creation of each generation, but rather one which draws on the ancient, ongoing and eternal song of the church from every time and every place. For the church at worship today is neither a repristination of some past, golden age nor a capitulation to the fast-changing demands of modern culture. Rather, it is, in the best sense of the word, a *catholic* endeavor, as faithful expressions of the Word of God from the past, the present, and from every part of our world, are assembled to serve as our spoken and sung confession of the faith.

The 1998 forum as well as the costs for the production of this book were underwritten by a generous grant from Aid Association for Lutherans (AAL).

Beginning

Theology of Worship

Where one begins will often determine where one ends up. The Introduction to *Lutheran Worship* takes stock of this fact when it theocentrically begins, "Our Lord speaks and we listen." And then, "The rhythm of our worship is from him to us, and then from us back to him." In other words, what happens in worship happens best when it is "begun, continued, and ended" with the Lord.

So it is with the theology of worship. The essay which follows seeks to explore the theological presuppositions associated with the German word *Gottesdienst* ("the service of God"). With this word and its heritage, the uniquely Lutheran understanding of worship, with its thoroughgoing emphasis on God's gifts given and received, finds renewed and relevant expression.

> *Direct us, O Lord, in all our doings with your most gracious favor, and further us with your continual help that in all our works begun, continued, and ended in you we may glorify your name and finally by your mercy obtain eternal salvation; through Jesus Christ, your Son, our Lord, who lives and reigns with you and the Holy Spirit, one God, now and forever. Amen.*

Theology of Worship

JOEL A. BRONDOS

THERE ARE A NUMBER OF FOLK IN OUR SYNOD TODAY WHO, LIKE Jephthah and the Gileadites taking the fords of the Jordan (Judg. 12:5–6), challenge all passers-by with a shibboleth. That shibboleth is *Gottesdienst* (the meaning of which may be as foreign to many as the word "shibboleth" itself).

Gottesdienst has been translated as "the service of God." The question arises whether the "of God" is an objective or a subjective genitive; that is, are we serving God, or is God serving us? Those who wield it most frequently and fervently are those who understand it as the latter: God's service to us—or more particularly, the Divine Service, in which the Lord serves us with His Word purely preached and the Sacraments rightly administered.

This distinction might well be understood in the context of an antipathy toward anything egocentric, self-centered, or synergistic. We have anathematized that belief which understands salvation as part God's work and part man's work (*partim partim*). It should come as no surprise that we would be similarly-directed in worship, so that *Gottesdienst* is not something self-centered, our works for God (Law), but rather Christ-centered, God's work for us (Gospel).

If one looks to the writings of Luther, however, one is hard-pressed to find him using the term *Gottesdienst* in this way. Almost exclusively, *Gottesdienst* is used to describe man's work for God, and that in a qualitative/quantitative sense (including references to "highest" or "best" work, allowing for lesser services of God). I have yet to discover when and how *Gottesdienst* came to be used in the way that many are using it today—namely, as God's service to us.

In whatever way we might trace the denotative and connotative lines of *Gottesdienst*, it is not sufficient when countering synergism merely to extol its opposite: monergism (God does it all). That leaves one open to the entrapments of a fatalistic, deterministic God; that is, "God does it, you gotta take it," or, "You've got to take the bad with the good as long as God is doing it." A balance is found in Luther's early *theologia crucis* ("theology of the cross"). But like *Gottesdienst, theologia crucis* is used today in a way that Luther never used it, even though he most clearly expounds the "theology of the cross" in opposition to a "theology of glory."

It isn't necessarily Gospel to say that God is doing it, any more than it would be Gospel to say that we have a part in doing something for God. (*Gottesdienst* is not a raw *opus Dei*.) What, then, is to be gained by asking, "Who is doing what?" in worship? Let us suggest that there is much more to be lost by asking such questions. If worship is divvied up into what God does for us, and then our response, a great divorce has ensued. A view that promotes, "God does this, now we do that," separates us from God in a way that can hardly be called a communion. At whatever point worship becomes our response to God, then Immanuel ("God with us") has become "the God up there." *Koinonia* ("communion") is threatened, if not actually broken. As Vilmos Vajta writes,

> Worship is inseparable from the God who revealed himself in Christ. It is much more than a form of response to God. That would imply a certain freedom on the part of man, as though man were independent of God and could decide at leisure whether or not he wanted to have any sort of worship. But worship is given wherever we speak of God. Revelation and worship constitute one and the same reality: fellowship between God and man on the earthly level.[1]

What will prevent the divorce from occurring between God and man in worship? If one thinks of *Gottesdienst*, then let one think of the cross. There is one time and place where man (the Man) serves God and God serves man: Christ crucified. And yet, that one place and time are given to all places and all times in Holy Baptism, Holy Absolution, and Holy Communion. Vajta again:

> In *De Servo Arbitrio,* Luther distinguishes between the revealed God and the hidden God. Only the God who revealed himself in Christ is our God. It is he who wants to deal with us. Luther calls the revealed God (*Deus revelatus*) also

---

[1] Vilmos Vajta, *Luther on Worship: An Interpretation,* trans. and condensed by U.S. Leupold (Philadelphia: Muhlenberg Press, 1958), 15.

the God who is preached (*Deus praedicatus*) and the God who is worshiped (*Deus cultus*). The God revealed is the God of pulpit and altar. Not the God who is hidden in eternal majesty and glory, but the God who is revealed is adored. As the God who is worshiped, God is clothed in the earthly media of the Word, of Baptism, and of the Lord's Supper, wherein he reveals himself. For only here is Christ present and active. By revealing himself in Christ, God himself instituted a definite form of worship. In the incarnation he humbled himself to meet us on the earthly level and clothed his gift to us in earthly forms. Thus there can be no fellowship between God and man except through the means of grace which belong to God's revelation in Christ.[2]

Whether we consider the term *Gottesdienst* in particular, or worship in general, we must inquire what sort of person would divide things into parts done by God and parts done by man. Such an approach would never come to the mind of the tax collector (Luke 18:10–14) or the woman at the well (John 4:4–42).

To break *Gottesdienst* into God's part, and then subsequently to consider what our response might be, is to create an impassable chasm. To proceed on this basis throws the door wide open to that antithesis of the Gospel called "self-actualization," everyone responding to God's work in his or her own way. Better to think of gifts given and received, *beneficium*, not *sacrificium*. Even thanksgiving and praise do not come from within, but from God: "O Lord, open my lips, and my mouth will declare your praise" (Ps. 51:15).

An orthodox theology of worship does not go the way of all other "-ologies." It does not derive from man's study of God, but from God's revelation of Himself to man through His means.

As we proceed with the production of a new hymnal, its hymns, prayers, and liturgies, we must not be moved by what is merely historic, nostalgic, aesthetic, marketable, or ecumenical, but by that one and only *Gottesdienst* that is not *partim partim*, not our work (or response) subsequent to God's work, but a communion that is Christ crucified, coming to us in gifts given, God with us in the flesh. That is the worship that benefits both the publican and the woman at the well. That worship sends people home justified—and they might even go home happy. That

---

[2]Ibid., 14–15.

is worship in spirit and in truth. Then we will have a *Gottesdienst* which is not work, not deeds to be done, but rather, a holiday (as Luther describes it in the Large Catechism, Third Commandment). And there is always more.

Lectionary

Sacrament of the Word

A Three-Year Lectionary

Doing 'Our Own Thing'

IN A 1997 SURVEY, nearly 90 percent of congregations in the The Lutheran Church—Missouri Synod indicated that they currently use the three-year lectionary contained in *Lutheran Worship*. In the years since its introduction, various revisions have been made to this lectionary. At present, a majority of Protestant churches in the United States have adopted the 1992 *Revised Common Lectionary* (*RCL*).

One of the first issues to resolve in preparing a newly revised hymnal is that of the lectionary. The choice of lectionary will affect nearly every part of the hymnal, including the psalter, the propers, and hymn selections.

The three essays that follow offer varying perspectives. The first invites a reconsideration of the traditional one-year lectionary. The second speaks from the perspective of following the more recent practice of using a three-year, common lectionary. Finally, the suggestion is given for "doing our own thing." Each of these perspectives raises valid concerns that will require careful thought before a final lectionary is adopted.

Sacrament of the Word
Reclaiming the Church's Historic Lectionary

LEE A. MAXWELL

"So [Jesus] came to Nazareth, where He had been brought up. And as His custom was, He went into the synagogue on the Sabbath day, and stood up to read. And He was handed the book of the prophet Isaiah. And when He had opened the book, He found the place where it was written: 'The Spirit of the Lord is upon Me, because He has anointed Me to preach the gospel to the poor; He has sent Me to heal the brokenhearted, to proclaim liberty to the captives and recovery of sight to the blind, to set at liberty those who are oppressed, to proclaim the acceptable year of the Lord.' Then He closed the book, and gave it back to the attendant and sat down" (Luke 4:16–20).

So runs the account of one of the first deeds of Jesus' public ministry according to the Gospel of St. Luke. It was a scene not unlike many others in that day and age. After the confession of faith with the words of the *Shema* ("Hear, O Israel . . ."; Deut. 6:4) and some prayers comes the focal point of the synagogue service: the reading of the Word of God. First the appointed *parashah* ("division") from the Pentateuch, and then a reading from one of the scrolls of the prophets, as our Lord Himself did.

But now a new order is on the horizon. The Word of God is enfleshed. With His life, suffering, death, and resurrection, He would show those whom He had gathered around Himself how all things written in the Law of Moses and the Prophets and the Psalms concerning Him had to be fulfilled (Luke 24:44). And then He would send His Spirit on the chosen twelve to continue the work He had begun, calling a people to Himself to be a "chosen generation, a royal priesthood, a holy nation, His own special people" (1 Pet. 2:9). Through His Word and Spirit, the twelve, along with St. James and St. Paul, would testify by mouth and by pen to the fulfillment of God's promises in the Word-become-flesh.

"Our Lord speaks and we listen. His Word bestows what it says. Faith that is born from what is heard acknowledges the gifts received with eager thankfulness and praise."[1] The Lord gives His Word to His servants. They testify to Him and speak what has been given to them. Through their testimony and their speaking of His Word, His Spirit "calls, gathers, enlightens, and sanctifies the whole Christian church on earth."[2] The Word of the Lord creates and sustains the Lord's own people. Without the Word, there is no people of God. This conviction the church has received from the Spirit Himself. Therefore, the Word is central when the people are called and gathered. It is read and preached and sacramentally given. It is received and believed. It is praised, prayed, and sung.

Since her beginning, the church has recognized the centrality and importance of the Word of God in the Divine Service. Over a period of centuries, a system for reading that Word developed. That system is called a lectionary; and the most ancient and venerable of those systems is today called the historic lectionary. *The thesis of this essay is that the "deficiencies" in the historic lectionary are not so deficient, and that the "advantages" of other lectionary systems are not so advantageous.*

Which Historic Lectionary?

In the practice of the early church, not much new was happening. The Christians continued the tradition of the synagogue with regular readings for each weekly gathering. What was new, however, was "the newness of the Gospel preached as promise fulfilled and not merely awaited."[3] "And they continued steadfastly in the apostles' doctrine and fellowship, in the breaking of bread, and in prayers" (Acts 2:42). As the apostles passed on to glory, their written testimonies were collected and added to the readings heard every week.

---

[1] *LW*, 6.
[2] *Luther's Small Catechism* (St. Louis: CPH, 1986), 15.
[3] Charles J. Evanson, "The Lectionary" (Typed doc., unpublished paper, 1990), 2.

The development of the lectionary, then, was tied very early to the development of the canon. Justin Martyr testifies to what seems to be selections from both the New and Old Testaments: "And on the day called Sunday, all who live in cities or in the country gather together to one place, and the memoirs of the apostles or the writings of the prophets are read, as long as time permits."[4] Justin's comment also seems to indicate that there was yet no order to the readings. According to the *Apostolic Constitutions*, in and around Antioch a fourfold selection was read: the Law, the Prophets, the Epistles, and the Gospels.[5] In Constantinople, in the fourth century, there was a threefold selection: Prophets, Epistles, and Gospels.[6]

Along with the development of the canon, the evolution of the church year also had an impact on the formation of the lectionary (particularly in the western church). In the early church the first day of the week was celebrated because it was the day when Christ rose from the dead. But there soon emerged an historical awareness leading to the annual observances of major salvific events. Very early was the yearly commemoration of Good Friday and Easter. This was soon followed by the season of Lent and the festival of Pentecost. Christmas was observed by the fourth century and Advent by the sixth. By the end of the first millennium the calendar of the church year was firmly in place.[7]

The appointment of particular lessons gradually replaced the system of *lectio continua* inherited from the synagogue.[8] This development

---

[4]Justin Martyr, *The First Apology*. English translation in *The Ante-Nicene Fathers* (Grand Rapids, Mich.: Eerdmans Publishing Co., 1980), 1:185–86.

[5]Gerhard Kunze, "Die Lesungen," in *Leiturgia: Handbuch des evangelischen Gottesdienstes* (Kassel: Johannes Stauda-Verlag, 1955), 2:135.

[6]Ibid., 139.

[7]Note again that this refers to the calendar of the *western* church. The development of the church year and lectionary in the eastern church took a different route.

[8]On the history of the development of the lectionary see, besides Kunze, K. Dienst, *Die Religion in Geschichte und Gegenwart*, 3rd ed. (Tübingen: J.C.B. Mohr, 1961), s.v., "Perikopen"; and John Reumann, "A History of Lectionaries: From the Synagogue at Nazareth to Post-Vatican II," *Interpretation* 31 (1977): 116–130.

appears to have taken place already in the fourth century.[9] At first, specially selected readings were assigned for Easter and Pentecost, then for the Christmas cycle and other days as the calendar evolved. For the Sundays after Pentecost, a biblical writing was read in successive sections.

The first historical reference to a fixed system of readings comes from the fifth century. The *Comes* (or "Companion") indicates readings from the Old Testament, the Epistles, and the Gospels for particular days. This list is apparently what the redactor of the Würzburg Codex (mid-sixth century) found and adapted. About two centuries later, Alcuin, the court theologian of Charlemagne, made some further revisions, fixing even more readings on certain days. By this time, two distinct changes had taken place: the reading of the Old Testament was discontinued (except on a few days when it replaced the Epistle), and *lectio continua* was dropped (except for some traces in the Epistles on the Sundays after Pentecost). About a century after Alcuin, a monk by the name of Theotinchus organized the lectionary once more (with minor changes), resulting in what could essentially be called the historic lectionary.[10]

At the time of the Reformation, the lectionary system of the western church varied from place to place, but really with no great divergences. Luther himself used a lectionary similar to the one developed by Alcuin without changing it. Lutheran churches, for the most part, followed Luther in using the historic lectionary until the mid-1970s. The historic lectionary was made the norm by Rome at the Council of Trent and appeared in 1570 in the *Missale Romanum*. This lectionary, which differed only slightly from the one used by Lutherans, remained in use until the appearance of the *Ordo Lectionum Missae* in 1969.

What's Wrong with the Historic Lectionary?

Although ancient and honored, the historic lectionary was not without its critics. Luther himself, in the *Formula Missae*, expressed his concern:

---

[9] J.G. Davies, ed., *The New Westminster Dictionary of Liturgy and Worship* (Philadelphia: Westminster Press, 1986), s.v., "Lectionary."

[10] Kunze, 154.

> Certainly the time has not yet come to attempt a revision here, as nothing unevangelical is read, except that those parts from the Epistles of Paul in which faith is taught are read only rarely, while the exhortations to morality are most frequently read. The Epistles seem to have been chosen by a singularly unlearned and superstitious advocate of works. But for the service those sections in which faith in Christ is taught should have been given preference. The latter were certainly considered more often in the Gospels by whoever it was who chose those lessons. In the meantime, the sermon in the vernacular will have to supply what is lacking.[11]

In the Roman Church there were no choices. The Council of Trent codified the lectionary so that all Roman congregations throughout the world had the same readings on the same days. In the Lutheran churches, however, it was different. During the 19th century, a number of alternative lectionaries were offered in both Germany and Scandinavia. In the Synodical Conference of North America in the early 20th century, another alternative lectionary was drafted.[12] These lectionaries were not meant as replacements for the historic lectionary, but as an occasional alternative to the usual system of readings.

With the changes implemented by the Second Vatican Council, however, Lutherans followed Rome in beginning to point to so-called deficiencies in the historic lectionary and calling for change. Herbert Lindemann criticized the historic lectionary by calling its "Trinity Season" too long with little order in it.[13] The Inter-Lutheran Commission on Worship (ILCW) alleged that the exegetical principles with which certain readings were chosen were no longer defensible, and that some readings could be misunderstood (as suggesting, e.g., anti-Semitism).[14] James

---

[11]Martin Luther, "An Order of Mass and Communion for the Church at Wittenberg (1523)," trans. Paul J. Strodach, rev. Ulrich S. Leupold, AE 53:23–24. Other inconsistencies are evident also. This is probably due to the fact that the Gospels in the historic lectionary are of Roman origin, while the Epistles can be traced back to a Gallican system. See Dienst, "Perikopen."

[12]The "Synodical Conference Series" listed in *The Lutheran Liturgy* (St. Louis: CPH, n.d.), 434–435.

[13]Herbert Lindemann, *The New Mood in Lutheran Worship* (Minneapolis: Augsburg, 1971), 91.

[14]The Inter-Lutheran Commission on Worship, *The Church Year: Calendar and Lectionary*, Contemporary Worship Series, no. 6 (Minneapolis: Augsburg Publishing House, 1973), 17. Hereafter, CW6.

Brauer, in his article on the church year in *Lutheran Worship: History and Practice*, contends that customs and practices associated with certain readings are no longer observed in the church.[15] Another criticism noted that certain verses or pericopes that should be heard in the Divine Service were omitted in the historic lectionary, such as John 3:16, Matthew 11:25–30, and Luke 15:11–32.[16]

What is one to make of these criticisms? Are they accurate? Are they compelling enough to abandon the historic lectionary for something completely new and different? Here the caution of Gerhard Kunze is appropriate: "The person who is against the ordering of the pericopes in the historic lectionary should ask the question: What should we put in its place?"[17]

Why Not Have a New Lectionary?

Many Lutherans concurred with the criticisms of the historic lectionary. They were prepared to abandon it in favor of a system closely resembling the *Ordo Lectionum Missae* of Vatican II. However, in the literature discussing the lectionary problems and solutions, almost no articles questioning the abandonment of the historic lectionary are found.[18] The crucial question is: concerning a series of readings that has served the church for over 1,000 years, why has no one seriously objected to its disposal?

The answer to that question lies in the many so-called "advantages" of the new three-year series. Brauer has listed a number of them, but they can be summarized under three types: the new lectionary is ecumenical; it is more inclusive of Scripture; and it offers more opportuni-

---

[15]James Brauer, "The Church Year," in *LWHP*, 150.
[16]See Wayne E. Schmidt, "*Lutheran Book of Worship*: A Perspective," *Concordia Journal* 3 (May 1977): 101.
[17]Kunze, 179.
[18]See Fritz West, "An Annotated Bibliography of the Three-Year Lectionaries. Part I: The Roman Catholic Lectionary," *Studia Liturgica* 23 (1993):223–244; and ibid., "An Annotated Bibliography of the Three-Year Lectionaries. Parts II–IV," *Studia Liturgica* 24 (1994): 222–248.

ties for preaching.[19] These are the reasons for abandoning the historic lectionary. Yet, while they do express the positive aspects of the new lectionary, they do not consider the negative results of abandoning the historic lectionary.

The Lutherans in Europe did not find sufficient reasons for disposing of the historic lectionary.[20] They objected both to the idea of completely breaking with the traditional pericopal system and to the principles that guided the selection of new texts. At the heart of the issue was the very understanding of the Word of God. According to the view of the Commission for Worship and Spiritual Life of the Lutheran World Federation, "Lutherans understand the life and renewal of the church to be built on a qualitative rather than a quantitative approach to Bible use. The lectionary texts are understood to serve as 'boundary lines and sign posts of Biblical proclamation,' and not least because of their yearly repetition of assigned readings and the regular course of preaching on familiar texts."[21]

Questions About the Old and the New

With a paucity of critical literature on either adopting a new lectionary or relinquishing the historic lectionary, some questions should now be raised. The first set of questions has to do with the so-called "advantages" of the new lectionary. Are these "advantages" really advantages? And do the benefits of the Lutheran three-year series make up for the losses incurred in abandoning the historic lectionary?

Proponents of the three-year lectionary underscore the claim that it is more ecumenical. The ILCW considered whether conformity with

---

[19]Brauer, "The Church Year," *LWHP*, 151. He lists the following: (1) it widens the range of Scripture heard by congregations; (2) it increases the scope, comprehensiveness, and variety of Scripture; (3) it promotes historical knowledge of the Bible; (4) it offers opportunity for treating larger units, even entire books in their historical setting; (5) it expresses solidarity with church bodies close at hand rather than to share a less immediate fellowship with European Lutherans in the cycle of readings; (6) it enriches the church's worship and preaching.

[20]See Karl-Heinrich Bieritz, "The Order of Readings and Sermon Texts for the German Lutheran Church," *Studia Liturgica* 21 (1991): 37–51.

[21]Evanson, 6.

world Lutheranism or agreement with Rome and other North American churches is more important.[22] The ILCW decided in favor of the second option. But from the start, agreement was incomplete. According to the ILCW's own report in *The Church Year: Calendar and Lectionary*, published in 1973, almost 20 percent of the readings in the Lutheran version of the three-year lectionary differ from those in the *Ordo*.[23] Now where does that figure stand with the appearance of the *Revised Common Lectionary* (*RCL*)? With the adoption of the *RCL* in the ELCA, the only church body using the Lutheran three-year lectionary of the Missouri Synod is—well, the Missouri Synod.

A more serious issue, however, is the criterion of ecumenicity itself. Is ecumenicity to be determined on formal or material grounds? That is to say, is it truly ecumenical to agree on a purely quantitative criterion (How many church bodies share the lectionary?) or on a qualitative criterion (Are churches of the same confessional fellowship in line with each other and in continuity with the practice of the historical church?)?[24]

Striving after ecumenicity on the basis of quantitative criteria has had the following results:

> [T]he rationale offered for this change is that the RCL, being the basis of Roman Catholic and Reformed tradition lectionaries, brings the ELCA into closer communion with those bodies. While this is indisputably true, such closer communion with both Roman Catholic and Reformed churches will come (as it always seems to come) at the expense of closer communion with our sister Lutheran bodies. . . . [O]n any given Sunday after Pentecost within these three Lutheran bodies (ELCA, LCMS, ELCIC) there might well be three different Old Testament lessons read—and absolutely no commonality between ELCA and LCMS readings. In short, Lutherans will have lost their common lectionary.[25]

---

[22]It seems to this author that the ecumenical question had not been seriously, but rather facilely considered. Reumann (p. 130) formulates it more comprehensively: "Does 'ecumenical' in this case mean agreement with one's geographical neighbors, confessional family or worldwide fellowship, or with the continuity of centuries, or some combination of these factors coupled with the needs of today?"

[23]CW6, 20.

[24]See note 22 above.

[25]Tom Shelly, "The Revised Common Lectionary," *Bride of Christ* 19, no. 3 (Pentecost 1995): 5.

Another "advantage" of the three-year lectionary is that more Scripture is read in the churches. But is more always better? At the heart of the issue lies a Lutheran understanding of the Word of God. Lutherans have a qualitative understanding of God's Word, as opposed to a quantitative understanding (which is Reformed). It is not *how much* of the Word that is read and heard, but *which* Word. Continual changes of the Word that are read and preached will certainly not help the parishioner to "mark, learn, and inwardly digest" the Word.[26] Perhaps what Luther said about selectivity of theological books also applies to the reading of Scripture in the Divine Service: "Many books does not make one learned, nor much reading either; rather to read a good thing and to read it often, regardless of how little it is, that makes one learned in the Scriptures."[27]

The third alleged advantage of the three-year lectionary is that it "enriches the church's worship and preaching." In conjunction, consider Brauer's second point: "Not the least among the selling points was the greater number of texts on which to preach."[28] Rather than being an "advantage," however, that "selling point" is alarming. A preacher has three texts for each of the three years. Theoretically, if he rotates the text he preaches on, he could go nine years before preaching the same text. And with an older average age of seminarians, a preacher, theoretically, over the course of his ministry, may preach the same particular text only four times. As with the quantitative approach to the Word of God, one wonders if this approach really reflects a Lutheran understanding of preaching.

The answer is, "No, it does not." The readings in the Divine Service are not read for their own sake, as salutary as the reading and hearing of God's Word might be. For Luther, the importance of the readings was found in their connection to the Sermon. "[T]he emphasis was on preaching, as one can already see in the brief passage from the *German Mass*. The lectionary for the mass was above all motivation for preaching,

---

[26]See Wilhelm Gundert, "Das neue katholische Meßlektionar," *Lutherische Monatsheft* 8 (1969):599, who makes this very point. Gundert's article is one of the few questioning the wisdom of climbing aboard the *Ordo* bandwagon.

[27]Luther, WA 6:461.

[28]Brauer, 152.

for proclamation which actualizes the Word. Luther was suspicious of the mere reading of Scripture which was not followed by preaching."[29]

A second set of questions has to do with the so-called "deficiencies" of the historic lectionary. Does the three-year series correct these deficiencies? Admittedly, in some cases it does. It does, for example, balance the "ethical" sections of the Epistles with more readings from the "doctrinal" sections. Former omissions, such as John 3:16 and Luke 15:11–32, are now included. On the other hand, the three-year series does not really provide a more "sensible order" in the course of the church year.[30] For the Sundays after Pentecost, the Gospels are simply *lectio continua* (as are the Old Testament readings in the *RCL*). And for the Sundays in Lent, the historic lectionary's clear progression of baptismal themes is lost in the three-year series (curiously, the restored Vigil of Easter now emphasizes these).

Could anything be done to correct the deficiencies of the historic lectionary without abandoning it? The answer is yes. But the correction is not to be found in the *LW* "one-year series," essentially a new lectionary in which about two-thirds of the readings are different.[31] A better version of the historic lectionary, one more faithful to it, is the lectionary revised by the Lutheran World Federation under the impetus and guidance of the German churches and used by Lutheran churches throughout the world (except in North America).[32] The changes made by the German Lutherans are very conservative; yet, they do correct some of the deficiencies of the historic lectionary, such as the problem with the Epistles and the omission of important texts.

Quo Vadamus Hinc? (Where Shall We Go from Here?)

It is clear that there are theological problems with the three-year lectionary, particularly with the assumptions made in pushing for its adoption, but also with the criteria used in arguing for its acceptance. The

---

[29]Bieritz, 37.
[30]See note 13 above.
[31]Brauer, 155.
[32]This lectionary can be found, e.g., in the *Evangelisch-Lutherisches Kirchengesangbuch* (Hannover: Selbständige Evangelisch-Lutherischen Kirche, 1988): 34–209, of the Selbständige Evangelisch-Lutherische Kirche (SELK).

benefits of the historic lectionary are simply too great to be lost. Perhaps by adopting the lectionary of German Lutheranism those advantages could be regained. But once changes have been made, it is extremely difficult to undo the damage. A theological argument can be made for using the historic lectionary, but the practical problems associated with its reception by the Missouri Synod might be hard to overcome.

One problem stems from the worship resources offered by the Synod. Although a "one-year lectionary" is included in *LW*, would using this lectionary be a viable option? All the resources provided by Concordia Publishing House (regardless of their relative merit), including *Proclaim*, *Creative Worship*, bulletin inserts with the propers, and bulletin covers, are designed to support the three-year series. If a pastor chooses to use a one-year lectionary of any kind, he is on his own. A twofold reason is given for CPH's lack of resources for the one-year series: there is no demand, and it is not "cost-effective." The latter should not ultimately be determinative for the Synod's publishing house when it comes to materials needed by the Synod. And if supply were there, perhaps demand would increase.

A second practical problem (related to the first) pertains to the curricula for parochial schools and Sunday schools. Wherever these materials reference the liturgy, they are geared to the three-year series. A pastor choosing to use a one-year series will face (potential) conflict with school and/or Sunday school teachers. This is a legitimate concern. If the purpose in using liturgically-oriented materials in schools and Sunday schools is to reinforce what takes place in the Divine Service, then it becomes counter-productive to use a different lectionary. CPH's rationale in focusing exclusively on the three-year series in educational materials is the same as its rationale for worship resources.

A third problem is with preaching resources, particularly *Concordia Pulpit Resources* and the *Concordia Journal's* "Homiletic Helps." Many parish pastors in the Synod do use or consult these resources to some degree. Yet, again, all are geared to the three-year series.[33] However, if a

---

[33]Except in the three years of the *Concordia Journal* from November 1982 to September 1985. The studies, however, were based on the one-year series of *LW* and not the historic lectionary.

pastor chooses to use the historic lectionary, he can consult older works (as in the *Concordia Pulpit* series prior to 1976), he can turn to German studies (like the *Homiletische Auslegung der Predigttexte,* by Gottfried Voigt), or he can simply do his own exegetical and homiletical studies.

A final difficulty in reviving the use of the historic lectionary concerns the homiletical and liturgical training of the Synod's seminaries. In both homiletics and worship classes, it is assumed that students will be using the three-year lectionary.[34] If students are trained in this way of thinking, how likely are they to consider the historic lectionary of the church, especially with the practical problems enumerated above?

What can be done to return to the historic lectionary? First, the confessional principle needs to be remembered: "It is not necessary for the true unity of the Christian church that ceremonies, instituted by men, should be observed uniformly in all places" (AC VII). The use of a lectionary, as with many other aspects of the liturgy, certainly belongs to that category of "ceremonies." Nevertheless, a proper understanding of Lutheran theology, especially as it pertains to the Word of God and worship, will influence our choice of lectionary.

The solution is really quite simple. Returning to the use of the historic lectionary necessitates the following: 1) The Synod in all its aspects, but especially through the Commission on Worship, needs to promote the historic lectionary. Promoting means not just a passing mention but demonstrating its viability and feasibility. To that end, 2) Concordia Publishing House needs to offer quality resources in the historic lectionary for congregations to use in the Divine Service and in their educational endeavors; and 3) the Synod's seminaries need to emphasize and promote the historic lectionary in training their students in homiletics and worship classes. If all of these steps are taken, the historic lectionary may well be received and restored in the congregations of the Synod.

A final thought from one of our Lutheran fathers—from Wilhelm Loehe's "Three Books on the Church," in a chapter titled "Your Preaching":

---

[34]Credit needs to be given to Daniel Reuning at Fort Wayne, who at least discusses the SELK lectionary (see footnote 32) as a good option and has provided his students with some resources to use it.

> [The preacher] rejoices in the ancient pericopes and would not, even if he could, base his sermon in the Divine Service on free texts or continuous portions of Holy Scripture instead of those pericopes. Preferably he keeps [as his sermon text] for the Divine Service the Gospels, and leaves the Epistles in their place in the order of the service, and he will not become weary in preaching on the Gospels. As the people love to hear them, so to him they will become richer and fuller the more he speaks on them. He learns, the more he treats them, the great wisdom of the homilitician to create access through the known to the unknown and to show all the teachings of the church in the familiar texts. The person who switches the texts every year is not fit as a preacher of the people, let alone, one may say, of the church. That which is always different and new, without a connection to the familiar texts, makes it hard for people to understand, but each person easily and gladly accepts new thoughts when they appear as freshly recognized depths of ancient wisdom.[35]

Conclusion

Inevitably there will (and should) be changes in the church's lectionary. New problems and circumstances arise among the people of God, and new emphases have to be made in response to those situations. At the same time, the age-old problem of sin is constant, and the eternal remedy of God's grace in Christ remains the same. For this reason, the argument here is not so much that the historic lectionary be retained in its present form. But it *has* served the church well for many centuries; its deficiencies are not so great, and its advantages transcend the peculiar needs of time and place. Any changes in the historic lectionary should thus be made only with caution and careful deliberation.

Before any lectionary changes are made for the congregations of the Missouri Synod, and before any other system of lectionary usage is considered, it would be wise to discuss lectionary issues with other Lutheran churches, particularly with our sister churches, those of the International Lutheran Conference. As with the liturgy, the lectionary belongs to the entire church (at all times and in all places) and should be subject to as few idiosyncratic usages as possible. Any further tampering with the lectionary could be confusing (at best) or sectarian (at worst).

---

[35] Wilhelm Löhe, *Drei Bücher von der Kirche*, 4th ed. (Gütersloh: C. Bertelsmann, 1904), 117.

A Three-Year Lectionary for the New LCMS Hymnal

DEAN D. PITTELKO

LECTIONARIES, AS A SYSTEMATIC READING OF THE HOLY SCRIPTURES IN worship, have been important in both Judaism and the Christian church.[1] In Judaism, a series of weekly readings began in the synagogue, possibly as a substitute for the sacrifices of temple worship.[2] It is probable that a schedule of continuous readings (*lectio continua*) from the Torah was established for Sabbaths and festivals (and also for Mondays and Thursdays, which were market-days in Jerusalem) already in the century before Christ.[3]

Two different lectionaries developed in Judaism. The Palestinian cycle divided the Pentateuch into 154 sections, to be read over a three-year period.[4] The Babylonian cycle divided the Pentateuch into 54 sections, to be read over the course of a year.[5] Though the Babylonian system is of more recent origin, it became more prevalent as a cycle of readings.

In the early Christian church, Justin Martyr (ca. 100–165) records that, on the Lord's Day, the "memoirs of the Apostles or the writings of all the Prophets are read for as long as time allows."[6] In the early cen-

---

[1] John Reumann, "A History of Lectionaries: From the Synagogue at Nazareth to Post-Vatican II," *Interpretation* 31 (1977): 116.
[2] Reumann, 118. Here he cites the Mishnah as his source.
[3] Reumann, 119.
[4] Lucien Deiss, *God's Word and God's People* (Collegeville: The Liturgical Press, 1976), 102.
[5] Ibid.
[6] Lucien Deiss, *Springtime of the Liturgy: Liturgical Texts of the First Four Centuries* (Collegeville: The Liturgical Press, 1979), 102.

turies "there seems to have been considerable latitude in the selection of the readings, which were interspersed with psalms."[7]

The development of various lectionaries from the fourth through 16th centuries is evident in the copious amount of manuscript materials. These include the notation of various pericopes in the margins of Bibles, lists of pericopes, and pericopes written out fully and assembled in a book (lectionary) or written out fully in conjunction with the other propers of the day (missal).[8] A full treatment of the history and discussion of extant manuscripts from the patristic period through the Tridentine lectionary is to be found in Cyrille Vogel's *Medieval Liturgy: An Introduction to the Sources*.[9]

It has been said that Alcuin (ca. 735–804) was responsible for standardizing the lectionary for the mass from existing local lectionaries: the Gallican for the Epistles and the Roman for the Gospels.[10] It is interesting to note, however, that lectionaries and missals varied among the dioceses until 1570, when a single order and lectionary was prescribed for the entire Roman church.[11] In the Lutheran Church, the German church orders retained the historic lections.[12] But in some Lutheran regions, an alternative series of preaching texts developed alongside the one-year series of readings.[13]

The Three-Year Series

With respect to the lectionary, the work of the Second Vatican Council began "the most radical change in the 1,500 years during which

---

[7]Philip H. Pfatteicher, *Commentary on the Lutheran Book of Worship: Lutheran Liturgy in Its Ecumenical Context* (Minneapolis: Augsburg Fortress, 1990), 132.

[8]Herman A.J. Wegman, *Christian Worship in East and West: A Study Guide to Liturgical History*, translated by Gordon W. Lathrop, (New York: Pueblo, 1985), 157.

[9]Cyrille Vogel, *Medieval Liturgy: An Introduction to the Sources*, revised and translated by William G. Storey and Niels Krogh Rasmussen (Washington D.C.: The Pastoral Press, 1986), 291–355.

[10]Pfatteicher, 132.

[11]Ibid.

[12]Pfatteicher, 133.

[13]Ibid.

the annual series of traditional gospels and epistles had developed."[14] The Constitution on the Sacred Liturgy placed much importance on the use of the Holy Scriptures in worship (see Articles 23, 33, and 35).[15] Article 51 of the CSL states that the "treasures of the Bible are to be opened up more lavishly, so that richer fare may be provided for the faithful at the table of God's Word. In this way a more representative portion of the Holy Scriptures will be read to the people over a set cycle of years."[16]

The result was the *Lectionary for Mass* (*Ordo Lectionum Missae*), published in 1969, a three-year cycle of readings with three lections appointed for each Sunday. The selections of Scripture to be read kept the traditional church year calendar.[17] The new lectionary took "its christology from Easter, which it regards to be the center of the liturgical year and understands in terms of the paschal mystery."[18] In general, the "Gospels reflect the events of the Christian year," with the first readings (from the Old Testament, or from the Acts of the Apostles on the Sundays of Easter) "more or less dependent on" the Gospel.[19] The second reading (from the Epistles or Revelation) is generally independent from these readings, often read in a semi-continuous manner (*lectio continua*).[20] The *Lectionary for Mass* received a great deal of attention and, "with alterations, was introduced in the Episcopal church beginning with *The Church Year: Calendar and Lectionary* (1970), in another form in the Presbyterian *Worshipbook* (1970), and in the Lutheran churches in North America in *Contemporary Worship 6: The Church Year: Calendar and Lectionary* (1973)."[21]

---

[14]Reumann, 128.

[15]Ibid.

[16]*Sacrosanctum Concilium*, Article 51 in Walter M. Abbott, ed., *The Documents of Vatican II* (New York: Guild Press, America Press and Association Press, 1966), 155.

[17]James L. Brauer, "The Church Year," *LWHP*, 150.

[18]Fritz West, *Scripture and Memory: The Ecumenical Hermeneutic of the Three-Year Lectionaries* (Collegeville, Minn.: Liturgical Press, 1997), 12.

[19]James F. White, *Introduction to Christian Worship*, rev. ed. (Nashville: Abingdon Press, 1990), 82.

[20]Ibid.

[21]Pfatteicher, 134.

The Lutheran Three-Year Series

The Inter-Lutheran Commission on Worship (ILCW) favored a three-year series of readings, and by September of 1970 the lectionary committee set out to do the following: 1) to produce a revision of the historic, one-year pericope series by Advent 1971; 2) to draft a multi-year system to be completed by the end of 1972; and 3) to assemble a series of preaching texts, independent of either lectionary, that addresses contemporary needs."[22]

The readings were selected for both the one-year and three-year lectionaries "with a view to the classic pattern of the chief service of proclamation and sacrament."[23] The major source of the Lutheran three-year series was the *Lectionary for Mass* and its revisions by other churches.[24]

The guiding principles used by the ILCW lectionary committee were as follows:

1) That the readings be chosen for their "congruity with the gospel," that is, "the good news of God concerning the redemption of man" (not simply the appointed Gospel for the day).[25]

2) The issue of "preachability": determining whether a passage can be "expounded meaningfully today," including "the clarity of a passage, textual problems in Hebrew or Greek which may render its meaning uncertain, literary form," as well as the balance between "law ... and gospel."[26]

3) That the "whole counsel of the Word of God" be reflected, so that the appointed readings would "set forth as fully as possible the truths of the scriptural witness to God's revelation in its totality."[27]

4) The issue of "canonical catholicity" was of great importance, but it

---

[22]Inter-Lutheran Commission on Worship, *The Church Year: Calendar and Lectionary,* Contemporary Worship Series, no. 6 (Minneapolis: Augsburg Publishing House, 1973), 15. Hereafter CW6.
[23]Ibid.
[24]Ibid., 16.
[25]Ibid.
[26]Ibid.
[27]Ibid.

was "not considered necessary to use excerpts from each and every book of the Bible or to give a biblical book prominence in proportion to its length."[28]

5) Readings were chosen "to exhibit passages bearing on the classic topics of the Christian faith," and to "reflect the Lutheran confessional stance without pressing it to the exclusion of other scriptural themes."[29]

6) A final principle was "consonance," or the "interlocking" nature of the appointed readings for a day. Although the three readings do not always form a unity, at least one reading "was chosen to reinforce another." The ILCW committee notes that as the readings were chosen, the hermeneutic of "Scripture interpreting Scripture" proved to be true time and again as "various parts of the Bible were aligned."[30]

The Lutheran three-year lectionary prepared by the ILCW committee corresponds with the *Lectionary for Mass* "completely about half the time."[31] Minor changes were made within some pericopes, "adjusting the beginning or stopping points or including or omitting verses between these points."[32] "In about one-sixth of the readings a totally different passage is substituted . . . often in the same book."[33]

The ILCW three-year lectionary appears in *Lutheran Book of Worship*.[34] The three-year lectionary of *LW* includes few alterations to that of LBW.[35] "Where there are changes, they are usually tiny adjustments in where to start or end."[36]

The *Revised Common Lectionary*

In 1978, the Consultation on Common Texts (CCT) invited 13 North American churches to participate in addressing concerns about the

---

[28]CW6, 17.
[29]Ibid.
[30]Ibid.
[31]Ibid., 20.
[32]Ibid.
[33]Ibid.
[34]Brauer, "The Church Year," *LWHP*, 151.
[35]Ibid.
[36]Ibid.

A Three-Year Lectionary

Lectionary for Mass.[37] The chief concern was over the lack of Old Testament historical narratives.[38] Along with this concern was a perceived weakness that "the Christological approach of the Old Testament lessons, which are chosen to relate to the Gospel Reading, frequently does an injustice to the Old Testament lessons by presenting them in a foreign context."[39] The theological presupposition of the CCT was that "the history of Israel was not seen to move inexorably toward Jesus Christ, [but] its patterns were understood to anticipate the emergence of Christianity."[40]

The draft version of the Common Lectionary was published in 1983. In this adaptation of the *Lectionary for Mass*, the Sundays after Pentecost included Old Testament readings "chosen independently from the gospel selection, some of which formed cycles selected on a semi-continuous basis."[41] Thus, the primacy of the appointed Gospel "no longer reigned absolutely over the other readings."[42]

To accommodate the variable length of the non-festival half of the church year, the readings are adjusted immediately after Pentecost.[43] That is to say, unlike the Lutheran three-year series prepared by the ILCW, which drops the propers for the Sundays at the end of the church year. The Common Lectionary omits the propers at the start of the second half of the church year.[44]

In 1992, the *Revised Common Lectionary* (*RCL*) was published.[45] The *RCL* is in reality two lectionaries, since it includes two full sets of alternative Old Testament readings for the second half of the church year.[46] One set of Old Testament readings is for those churches in which the

---

[37] West, 16.
[38] Pfatteicher, 134.
[39] White, 82.
[40] West, 13.
[41] Ibid., 17.
[42] Ibid., 16.
[43] Ibid.
[44] Ibid.
[45] Ibid., 17.
[46] Ibid.

Eucharist stands at the center of worship, who thus desire that the "readings be unified around the paschal mystery as it is proclaimed in the gospel reading."[47] A second set of readings follows a "Protestant liturgical paradigm" and "creates carefully crafted narratives extending over all twenty-five" Sundays in the latter half of the church year.[48]

While the *RCL* is markedly different in some of its appointed readings, it is still a derivative of the *Lectionary for Mass*.[49] The *RCL* was developed as a solution to the problem of too few readings from Old Testament narrative. However, even its proponents recognize its shortcomings.[50]

The *Revised Common Lectionary* is now being used by all publications of Augsburg Fortress for Sunday worship (inserts with propers for the day, etc.), so that the *RCL* has been "unofficially" adopted by the Evangelical Lutheran Church in America. In the February 1996 issue of *Currents in Theology and Mission*, former Lutheran School of Theology (Chicago) professor Jay Rochelle published a comparison of the Lutheran three-year series as found in *Lutheran Book of Worship* and the *RCL* as it is being used by Augsburg Fortress.[51] In his article, Rochelle notes that the changes in the readings are not highly significant, and that a number of repetitions of regular readings are omitted.[52] His conclusion is that not much "is lost by the ELCA's adoption" of the *RCL*, and that "the interrelationships between textual materials across the lectionary readings for each week have been improved."[53]

Conclusions

The three-year series of readings found widespread acceptance among Lutherans, even before the publication of *Lutheran Book of*

---

[47] *The Revised Common Lectionary: Report from the Consultation on Common Texts* (Nashville: Abingdon Press, 1992), 18.
[48] West, 18.
[49] Ibid., 168.
[50] Ibid., 177.
[51] Jay C. Rochelle, "Notes on the Revised Common Lectionary," *Currents in Theology and Mission* 23 (1996): 29.
[52] Ibid., 37.
[53] Ibid.

A Three-Year Lectionary

Worship.[54] The advantages of the three-year series are noted in *Lutheran Worship: History and Practice*:

1) "It widens the range of Scripture heard by the congregations."
2) "It increases scope, comprehensiveness, and variety of Scripture."
3) "It promotes historical knowledge of the Bible."
4) "It offers opportunity for treating larger units, even entire books in their historical setting."
5) "It expresses 'solidarity with other church bodies close at hand rather than share a less immediate fellowship with European Lutherans in the cycle of readings.'"
6) "It enriches the church's worship and preaching."[55]

The pedagogical value of the one-year series has been recognized.[56] However, the fact that a series of preaching texts developed alongside the one-year series of readings in some areas of the Lutheran Church is indicative of its shortfalls.[57] More recent German lectionary work has continued this tradition of including a series of preaching texts alongside the one-year lectionary.[58] Some have perceived and complained that too many sermons use the appointed reading(s) as a "pretext" for whatever a pastor wants to say to his congregation on a given Sunday. The temptation to do so is only made worse by the sole use of a one-year series of readings.

In the volume, *Studies in Lutheran Hermeneutics*, Arland Hultgren contributes a chapter on "Hermeneutical Tendencies in the Three-Year Lectionary," in which he is rather critical of the *Lectionary for Mass* and the work of the ILCW.[59] Despite his criticisms, however, Hultgren notes

---

[54]Philip H. Pfatteicher and Carlos R. Messerli, *Manual on the Liturgy: Lutheran Book of Worship* (Minneapolis: Augsburg Publishing House, 1979), 30.

[55]Brauer, "The Church Year," *LWHP*, 151. Point #5 is a quote from *Manual on the Liturgy: Lutheran Book of Worship*, 30.

[56]Reumann, 127.

[57]Pfatteicher, 133.

[58]Reumann, 127.

[59]Arland Hultgren, "Hermeneutical Tendencies in the Three-Year Lectionary," in John Reumann, ed., *Studies in Lutheran Hermeneutics* (Philadelphia: Fortress Press, 1979), 145–173.

the use of traditional Lutheran hermeneutics in the preparation of the Lutheran three-year series:

1) That the lectionary employs a hermeneutical principle of Martin Luther, one that "preaches Christ and makes him real."[60]

2) That the Roman Catholic committee which prepared the *Lectionary for Mass* (which was the starting point for the Lutheran three-year series) had as its express aim "to assemble texts that set forth the history of salvation."[61]

3) That there is a tendency in the lectionary to harmonize Old Testament and New Testament texts; it "is assumed that Scripture interprets Scripture and that such a principle should be made explicit in a lectionary."[62]

4) That salvation history is presented through a "display of moments of promise and fulfillment determined by the Gospel for the Day—not a presentation of the epochs of salvation history in sequence."[63]

5) That an "essential unity of the Scriptures as a witness to Christ is frequently affirmed in the lectionary."[64]

As previously indicated, the intent of the ILCW was that the three-year lectionary "let the gospel serve as an overall standard of selection" for the readings (the "gospel" here referring to "justification or reconciliation").[65] This is good!

The work of the ILCW in adapting the *Lectionary for Mass* was sound, and its results are Lutheran. The Lutheran three-year series of readings has served as an excellent tool in opening up the Word of God, the Gospel in particular, to congregations since 1973.

The LCMS Commission on Worship should seek to revise the three-year series of readings found in *LW*. A look at the *Revised Common Lectionary* in the form that is being used by the ELCA is warranted. We must deal with the issue of whether or not to include more narrative sec-

---

[60]Hultgren, 152.
[61]Ibid., 148.
[62]Ibid., 149.
[63]Ibid.
[64]Ibid.
[65]CW6, 65.

tions from the Old Testament. If changes are made along the lines of the *RCL,* then the primacy of the Gospel (justification) *and* the Gospel of the day must remain operative in a lectionary prepared for the congregations of The Lutheran Church—Missouri Synod. The committee established to work on a new lectionary must begin with a sound set of hermeneutical principles, according to which all decisions will be made in the selection of readings.

We have a sound model in the ILCW's work, especially as it has been slightly revised in *LW.* Now we must fully develop that model for the next hymnal.

Doing 'Our Own Thing' with the Lectionary

D. Richard Stuckwisch

It is with a certain amount of fear and trepidation that I set forth and defend the proposal that we should "do our own thing" with the lectionary. Not the least of all because I do have my own qualms (as a matter of principle) about any suggestion that would seem to advocate a sectarian departure from the church catholic. But also because I am well aware of the strong feelings that many of my fellow pastors have both for and against this or that lectionary. Those who defend the "historic" one-year series are surely sincere and (I daresay) passionate in their defense. And those who have embraced the three-year series are typically impressed and persuaded by its modern ecumenical significance. Thus, to suggest another (new) alternative runs the risk not only of sectarianism but also of provoking the wrath of my colleagues.

At the same time, no matter how strongly we pastors and theologians may well feel about the lectionary, it remains a veritable "non-issue" for the typical layperson. Even a well-catechized layperson might be genuinely surprised by any fears or trepidation in approaching this topic. After all, what's the big deal? The readings each Sunday all come from the Bible, and those for certain days (like Christmas and Easter) seem rather obvious. But beyond those observations, the lectionary as such remains more or less invisible to the congregation. The pastor gives attention to the public reading of the Holy Scriptures (or, perhaps more often than we care to admit, the publishing houses do so by way of their bulletin inserts). Few (if any) others are even vaguely aware of the order that determines what ought to be read when, to say nothing of the theological significance underlying this order.

Yet, the lectionary remains foundational for the Divine Service and the liturgical life of the church—even in those situations where there is no thought given beyond a standing order for bulletin inserts. For if the clichéd slogan, "sola Scriptura," means anything at all, it certainly does (and ought to) mean that the Scriptures read and proclaimed in the Divine Service on any given Sunday are the determinative authority for everything else that happens in the context of that particular liturgy: for the hymnody and other musical selections, for the preaching of the Gospel, and for the perspective with which one receives the Holy Communion. Indeed, we may go even further to say that one is catechized not only for the Holy Communion but for the daily life of the entire week ahead by the Scriptures ringing in his or her ears from one Sunday to the next. It *is* a big deal. It *does* matter.

At the present time, there are basically three (or four) lectionary options available to the Missouri Synod—each of them already being used to some extent. These options may be identified as the "historic" one-year series (as found in *TLH*), the *LW* one-year and three-year series, and the *Revised Common Lectionary* (*RCL*), now being used by default, if not by choice, in those congregations that purchase bulletin inserts from Augsburg Fortress. Each of these lectionaries has its own strengths and merits, and it is not my task or intention to identify those here. But suffice it to say that I am no longer convinced that any one of these current options is the way to go.

The "historic" one-year series, to begin with, is not nearly so "historic" as one is sometimes led to believe. For one thing, it is almost exclusively western, and basically medieval (not ancient). Much of its development took place in a rather haphazard, accidental fashion. A good deal of its character derives from the influence of numerous minor festivals that we no longer observe, and from its relationship to the daily office, which is all but non-existent in our congregations. As a consequence, it does not include such ancient practices of the early church as an Old Testament Reading and the continuous reading of the prophets, apostles, and Gospels.

Another option (already mentioned) is the *Revised Common Lectionary*, growing rapidly in popularity among Protestants in this country (and now adopted for use by the ELCA). In most respects, it follows closely the various and sundry redactions of the three-year series, which may be seen as its greatest strength. Unfortunately, where it differs from its predecessors, it has been driven and shaped by a modern liberal agenda. Thus, for example, it was heavily influenced by feminist and liberationist critiques. But its most significant contribution is found in its selection of Old Testament readings for the Sundays after Pentecost, the single most important factor in its development. It was the clear and explicit intention of those who crafted the *RCL* to avoid the correlations between the Old Testament and the Gospel, because it was felt that these correlations were insulting to the integrity of the Old Testament in its own right.*

In any case, knowing the agenda behind the *RCL* would make it impossible for some pastors to support its adoption by the LCMS or to make use of it in their congregations. If our Synod does make this choice, I'm afraid that many of these pastors would be compelled to go their own way with respect to the lectionary. Certainly, one should not expect any greater uniformity of practice than we have at the present time, but rather less.

The other two options currently available are those included in *LW*: the one-year series or the three-year series. (It should be either-or, not both.) But of these two, the *LW* one-year series is itself an innovative compromise. And to adopt this option would be to do "our own thing" in a way that is not satisfying in a number of respects.

Many good things could be said about the *LW* three-year series. Among these, it does have the advantage of being more or less in continuity with both the Roman *Lectionary for Mass* and the *RCL*. It is also essentially the same as the lectionary published in the new hymnals of

---

*Ironically, complaints about this approach to the Old Testament—from Lutherans, Roman Catholics, and Episcopalians—led the developers of the *RCL* to include two complete sets of Old Testament readings [and Psalmody] for the Sundays after Pentecost. One set is a semi-continuous reading of Old Testament books, and the other a slight modification of the Old Testament readings already in use in the predecessor three-year series. Thus, a lectionary developed for the sake of ecumenical unity is marked from the very start by diversity.

the Wisconsin Synod and the Evangelical Lutheran Synod. So it does still retain something of an ecumenical character. Yet, because there are differences, however minor, between the various redactions of the three-year series, we would still to some extent be doing "our own thing." At the same time, there are weaknesses inherent in any three-year series, many of them pointed out by those who defend the "historic" lectionary.

All of which suggests the possibility of another option: the opportunity to learn from both the past and the present, to build on the merits of the current lectionary options, while addressing their weaknesses in ways that are theologically sound. It is that approach which I now advocate.

But let me clarify something. Because I could not in good conscience endorse a "blank check" to do "our own thing" without having some particular content in mind, what I am advocating here is a quite specific lectionary proposal that I have developed on the basis of historical, theological, liturgical, and practical considerations. This is not to say that my proposal could not be improved, or that nothing else could ever be acceptable, only that I could not endorse doing "our own thing" with the lectionary without knowing what that "thing" might be.

One of the most important criteria that I have assumed is that we should do nothing completely new or "from scratch," but something in true continuity with the church catholic. This means that we must take seriously the practices of the church across the centuries and across the globe, from the early church to the present day; and that we make an effort to learn whatever we can from the best of those lectionaries that have found a place within the life of the church. "Historicity" and "catholicity" require more than a repristination of 16th-century Lutheran practices, just as true "ecumenism" requires something far more and quite different than compromise and "agreeing to disagree" with those who happen to live in the same century.

Here, then, is a thumb-nail sketch of what I am proposing.

Following the lead of the one-year series, I find a great benefit in the yearly repetition of the same reading(s) on the same Sunday, and this not only on the major feast days but throughout the festival seasons of the liturgical year. From a catechetical perspective, the consistency of such repetition is simply impossible to beat. In most cases, I therefore suggest that the Holy Gospel for Sundays from Advent through Easter remain fixed for all three years of the series, or else rotate through the synoptic parallels of the same narrative in the life of our Lord.

In considering the three-year series, I believe there is a recognizable benefit in the more extensive use of the full synoptic tradition (that is to say, Matthew, Mark, and Luke). Each of the Evangelists has his own distinctive perspective and emphasis on the single life of Christ. Thus, giving each of them his opportunity to speak to the church is undoubtedly appropriate. For this reason, I suggest that the Holy Gospel for the Sundays after Pentecost be taken from St. Matthew in Year A, from St. Mark in Year B, and from St. Luke in Year C. Likewise, acknowledging the step that was taken by the three-year series toward the most ancient practice of *lectio continua,* I also suggest that the Holy Gospel and the Epistle follow a semi-continuous course for those Sundays after Pentecost.

I have followed the lead of the *RCL* (and also that of the Episcopalians) by suggesting a rather different way of dealing with the variable length of the post-Pentecost season. In the first place, the variation is dealt with at the beginning of the season (immediately following the Feast of the Holy Trinity) instead of at the end. And in the second place, each Sunday in the post-Pentecost and Advent seasons is assigned to a particular seven-day period of the secular calendar so that the same Sunday falls within the same week each year.

I have also given attention to the Byzantine Lectionary (the truly historic one-year series) by taking into account and utilizing wherever possible its specific Gospel and Epistle pericopes. Thus, by way of some examples, I suggest the use of its pericopes from the Epistle to the Hebrews for the Sundays in Lent. I have also included in my proposal a good many of its (semi-continuous) pericopes from St. Matthew and St. Luke in the Sundays after Pentecost.

All told, approximately 75 percent of the pericopes in my lectionary proposal are taken directly from one or more of these other lectionaries. And the correspondence is even greater when one allows for the fact that most of the divergences are found in those periods of variable length, which would never all occur within the same year.

In spite of this high degree of correspondence (perhaps as high as 85 percent in any given year), it is nevertheless true that I am also making some "innovative" suggestions, with the goal in mind of strengthening the lectionary and the structure of the liturgical year.

The first and most obvious of these innovations is actually borrowed from the historic origins of the Advent season, namely, a seven-week "Advent," beginning with the Sunday closest to St. Martin's Day (11 November). Not only does this reflect the very early practice of the church, but I have also been given to understand that it has Lutheran precedence as well. In any case, I believe that a seven-week Advent offers a number of advantages. It accentuates the continuity between what are now the final Sundays of the liturgical year and Adventide, thereby underscoring the eschatological character of the season. It avoids a stuttering conclusion to one year and the immediate repetition of what has just been celebrated presumably as a climax. It also avoids the whole "Christ the King" observance with its origins in 19th-century Roman Catholic triumphalism. Instead, it allows the Sunday of All Saints to come into its own as a most fitting conclusion to the liturgical year, as well as an ideal turning point from one year to the next. Practically speaking, a seven-week observance might help to recapture Advent as a season in its own right, rather than the proleptic celebration of Christmas that it is typically reduced to. (I was encouraged in this suggestion by the example of the Anglican Joint Liturgical Commission, which successfully introduced a nine-week "Advent" several decades ago.)

The second major innovation in my proposal is found in my effort to give the season of Epiphany its proper due. For Rome and for the *RCL*, it is simply a little stretch of "ordinary time" without any particular character or definition. Then again, the historic lectionary is hardly any better in this respect, with its "gesimas" crowding out a lion's share of the Sundays after the Epiphany. Without the intrusion of these "gesima" Sundays, there are potentially seven Sundays between the Baptism of Our Lord and the Feast of the Transfiguration. The first of these is typically associated with the wedding at Cana—the first sign of our Lord's divine glory in the Gospel according to St. John. My suggestion is that the six other Sundays be assigned the six remaining signs of His glory recorded by St. John. Because all of these signs, properly understood, point forward to the hour of our Lord's divine glory on the cross, they also provide an ideal preparation for Lent (as well or better than the "gesimas").

This use of pericopes from St. John for the Holy Gospel throughout Epiphany reflects a rather full Johannine representation in my proposal in the festival half of the year. For the most part, the synoptics punctuate this period on the major feast days, while St. John is heard on the Sundays after Epiphany, the Sundays in Lent, the Sundays of Easter, and the Sundays that may (potentially) occur in my proposal between the Feast of the Holy Trinity and the Sunday of the Holy Apostles, Peter and Paul (at the end of June).

The Sundays that may follow the Feast of the Holy Trinity are another innovation, tied to my method of dealing with the post-Pentecost season. For the sake of giving greater definition to this long stretch of time, I have followed the fairly venerable practice of dividing the Sundays after Pentecost into "tides": Apostles' Tide, St. Laurence Tide, and St. Michael's Tide. In a similar fashion, I have designated the time prior to Apostles' Tide as the Tide of the Holy Trinity (which may include anywhere from zero to five Sundays—to which I have assigned Johannine pericopes that speak of the relations between the Father, Son, and Holy Spirit).

A final innovation in my lectionary proposal—and one that I regard as its particular genius (for good or for ill)—is the way in which the synoptic readings for each of the Sundays after Pentecost relate to each other from one year to the next. Although they are drawn from the Holy Gospels in a semi-continuous fashion, almost all of these Sundays have been assigned the same synoptic parallels over the course of the three-year series. That is to say, much like the major feast days, the same event in the life of our Lord is read from St. Matthew in Year A, from St. Mark in Year B, and from St. Luke in Year C on the same Sunday of the liturgical year. In those few cases where it was not possible to follow this approach (due to a lack of synoptic parallels), I have tried to identify Gospel pericopes for a given Sunday that clearly revolve around a strong central motif (such as forgiveness, or participation in the eschatological banquet of Christ).

These are the highlights of my lectionary proposal. I set it forth for the consideration of the church in the conviction that it stands in continuity with the historic practices of the church catholic, even at those points of innovation. I welcome the feedback and constructive critique of those who are likewise concerned about these matters.

Eucharistic Prayer

A Defense of Eucharistic Prayer

The Usage of Eucharistic Prayer: Concerns

Eucharistic Prayer: The Middle Ground

Worship Statement from the Lutheran Church of Australia

WHEN THE LUTHERAN CHURCH—MISSOURI SYNOD resolved not to adopt the *Lutheran Book of Worship* in 1979, one of the major concerns involved the issue of eucharistic prayers. While considerable discussion was generated at the time, little has been written since. The inclusion of a Prayer of Thanksgiving following the Sanctus in *Lutheran Worship*, and now more recently in *Hymnal Supplement 98*, suggests that the issue is not a simple matter of accepting or rejecting the concept of a eucharist prayer.

Not surprisingly, the three studies that follow are not as neatly distinguished as was the original assignment calling for presentations "pro," "con," and "middle ground." Each author recognizes the centrality of the Words of Institution and the need to give thanks. In discussions following the presentations, it was noted that further work needs to be done on the consecratory nature of the Words of Institution. In order to further this discussion, a position paper has been included from the Commission on Worship of the Lutheran Church of Australia that examines the implications of the words, "when He had given thanks."

A Defense of Eucharistic Prayer in the Evangelical Lutheran Liturgy
And a Concern That Now May Not Be the Time to Introduce One

BRUCE E. KESEMAN

Thanksgiving: Is God's Action Obscured by Our Action?

AMONG THE MANY WORTHY TOPICS FACING THE LCMS COMMISSION on Worship, not least is the question, "Does a eucharistic prayer have a place in an evangelical Lutheran liturgy?" While it may be argued that theologically responsible eucharistic prayers do have a place in evangelical Lutheran liturgies, it may not be pastorally or ecclesiastically wise to introduce such a prayer in the Synod at this time. (By eucharistic prayer is here meant a post-Sanctus Prayer of Thanksgiving that includes thanksgiving for God's saving acts, the *Verba* [Words of Institution], anamnesis, epiclesis, and doxology.) Please note from the beginning that the author does *not* share the theology that was predominant among those who defended the eucharistic prayers of the Inter-Lutheran Commission on Worship. Indeed, he shares a theology of the Lord's Supper with the majority of those who argued *against* the eucharistic prayers of the ILCW, but not their conclusion that Lutherans must reject all eucharistic prayers. The fact that some laws are bad does not mean that good laws should be discarded; by the same token, the fact that some eucharistic prayers are bad does not mean that good eucharistic prayers should be discarded.

> Our Lord speaks and we listen. His Word bestows what it says. Faith that is born from what is heard acknowledges the gifts received with eager thankfulness and praise. . . . His forgiveness is given us, and we, freed and forgiven,

acclaim him as our great and gracious God as we apply to ourselves the words he has used to make himself known to us.*

No better definition of worship has been written than these opening words from the Introduction to *LW*, and there is no better way to describe the proper purpose and use of a eucharistic prayer than those same words. While maintaining, first of all, that "our Lord speaks and we listen," and "His Word bestows what it says," a theologically sound eucharistic prayer gives voice to the "eager thankfulness and praise" with which faith receives God's gifts—in this case, the gifts of Christ's crucified and risen body for the forgiveness of sins. Freed and forgiven, we acclaim Him as our great and gracious God ("Blessed are you, O Lord . . .") as we apply to ourselves the words He has used to make Himself known to us (including the *Verba*). That is the proper function of an orthodox eucharistic prayer.

The most frequent criticism of eucharistic prayers is that they confuse human action with Christ's action. But sound eucharistic prayers can give voice to a sacrifice of thanksgiving without obscuring Christ's sacrifice of propitiation and without mingling the two together. Thanksgiving flows from His proclamation. To be sure, thanksgiving happens simultaneously with His proclamation when the *Verba* are included in a eucharistic prayer, but thanksgiving is in no way identical to His proclamation. Even if they happen simultaneously, thanksgiving remains secondary to, and resultant of, the proclamation of Christ. In order to make this distinction evident, musicians could provide a chant line that distinguishes the *Verba* from the rest of the eucharistic prayer (or, if the rest of the prayer is spoken, the *Verba* could be chanted). Further, the rubrics could direct a change in the posture of the celebrant to emphasize the words of Christ as *His* proclamation even when embodied in a prayer.

Is it possible to respond at the same time as God speaks? That is to ask whether it is possible to say "Thank you" at the same time a gift is being given. Not only is it possible, it is common. In fact, one can say "Thank you" even *before* the gift is received, if he knows the gift is com-

---

**LW*, 6.

A Defense of Eucharistic Prayer

ing. Thanks does not replace the words of promise or the gift itself as the primary event, nor does there need to be any confusion as to who is the giver and who the recipient. So also may a response be spoken at the same time as God is speaking and giving, without changing the sacramental gifts of God into a sacrifice, and without a confusion of God's work with the thanksgiving offered for it.

In fact, the sacramental elements of worship almost always require a resulting (*not* "causing") sacrificial response. For example, if the penitent Christian does not walk to the altar, if he does not open his mouth, if he does not swallow the gift, then Christ's body and blood will be of no benefit to him, no matter how true God's words and no matter how wonderful God's gift. Walking to the altar, opening the mouth, and swallowing—all of these are human actions. Certainly, they are done with Spirit-wrought faith at the prompting of God's Word. So should a eucharistic prayer be prayed with Spirit-wrought faith at the prompting of God's Word. The church does not assume that walking, gaping, or gulping replaces the action of God as that which makes the Supper a forgiving gift. Nor does she assume that human walking, gaping, or gulping is a *cause* for the gift of the Supper. Neither is a eucharistic prayer the essence of the Sacrament, or the cause behind God's gift of His Son's true body and blood. It is, rather, an expression of responding thanks.

Even if the *Verba* are voiced in the context of a prayer to God, they do not cease to be God's Word of proclamation to His church. Many psalms, many hymns, and even Solomon's prayer at the dedication of the temple (1 Kings 8:22 ff.) include proclamation in the midst of prayer, and prayer in the midst of proclamation. If a prayer from the pulpit is still a prayer, even though it occurs in the middle of the proclamation (Sermon), why should one assume that proclamation ceases to be proclamation when it occurs between "O heavenly Father" and "Amen"? In a proper eucharistic prayer, we say "back to him what he has said to us; we repeat what is most sure and true." Thus, the classic collect form includes a basis, or rationale, which is nothing else than proclamation—even in the context of a prayer and even being at the same time praise. For example, on the Feast of the Transfiguration, the church prays: "In the glorious Transfiguration of Your only-begotten Son You once confirmed the mysteries of the faith by the testimony of the ancient fathers, and in the voice that came from the bright cloud You wondrously foreshowed our adoption by grace." These words remain God's proclamation, even as they are addressed in praise to God. In much the same way, the Creed remains God's proclamation, even as it is confessed before God. And again, both the Proper Prefaces and the post-Sanctus Prayer of Thanksgiving remain God's word of proclamation, even when offered back to Him.

Let us take the argument further. In the liturgy of Divine Service II in *LW*, we pray, "Blessed are you, Lord of heaven and earth, for you have had mercy on us children of men and given your only-begotten Son that whoever believes in him should not perish but have eternal life." This is a prayer. But would anyone deny that the Holy Spirit uses these words to strengthen the faith of those who pray them? No, indeed, because they are words of Gospel. And if they are Gospel, then either they remain God's proclamation even when spoken in a prayer, or else prayer has become a means of grace that delivers the Gospel. But in short, God's Word does not cease to be His Word just because it is spoken back to Him.

Anamnesis and Epiclesis: What Is This "Remembering" and Where Is the Holy Spirit Going?

The bulk of this essay has argued that a eucharistic prayer need not confuse thanksgiving with divine gift-giving. We may not, however, ignore concerns over anamnesis (a prayer of remembrance) and epiclesis (an invocation of the Holy Spirit). Many reject the use of eucharistic prayers largely because of the anamnesis. This is right if and when such prayers imply that human remembrance is the main thing in the Supper, or that such remembrance causes God to give His gifts. Many of those who advocated the inclusion of a eucharistic prayer in *Lutheran Book of Worship* argued that when Jesus said, "Do this," He was speaking of the Jewish *berakoth* (prayers of thanksgiving), and for that reason they also argued that an anamnesis is essential to the Lord's Supper. However, the referent of "do this" is not the *berakoth*, but that which Jesus invites His people to do, namely, to eat His body and drink His blood. Prayers that echo the Jewish *berakoth* are neither commanded by Christ nor necessary to His Supper; still, they may be helpful in expressing thanks with echoes of that faith and liturgy handed down from the beginning.

A Defense of Eucharistic Prayer

One does not offer a eucharistic prayer (or any other prayer, for that matter) to make God aware of something He does not already know. One does not offer a eucharistic prayer (or any other prayer) to make demands upon God or force His hand. One prays, not because *God* needs prayer, but because the church needs prayer. So in the *Verba*, the church does not call God to remembrance; she does not even call herself to remembrance. The *Verba* are God's Word. And as "God's Word bestows what it says," the church remembers what He has done and what He is doing, and remembering, she rightly uses His name, that is, to pray, praise, and give thanks—in this case, by using the words of a eucharistic prayer. Even more, as "God's Word bestows what it says," the church remembers what God has done and what He is doing, and remembering, she seeks the gift of God, and she receives that gift with the very faith engendered by His Word and Spirit.

Space does not permit a thorough treatment of the epiclesis, but something must be said, lest anyone presume the arguments of those who have written in the past. Some epicleses pray that the Holy Spirit would change the elements of bread and wine into the body and blood of Christ. But the epiclesis does not consecrate; God's Word consecrates as the *Verba* are spoken. An appropriate epiclesis prays that God by His Holy Spirit would do what He has promised to do. The epiclesis in *Lutheran Book of Worship* prays for the Holy Spirit without specifying where the Spirit is to work—whether on the elements, on the people, or somewhere else. Much better are the words of *LW*, in which the Holy Spirit is asked to keep His promise by working in His people: "Send your Holy Spirit into our hearts that he may establish in us a living faith and prepare us joyfully to remember our Redeemer and receive him who comes to us in his body and blood." Note the active work of the Spirit and the receptive nature of faith reflected in this prayer.

Because we do not share the theology of all those who use eucharistic prayers, the LCMS must be very careful in the wording of any eucharistic prayer we may choose to use and very clear about its theology. Jesus teaches that His Supper is not our action, but His. It is His Supper; it is His gift. To be sure, as He gives the gift, His people respond with thanksgiving, but His action, not ours, remains the essence of the Supper. Furthermore, the

Lord's Supper is not a re-presentation of Christ's sacrifice nor a re-actualization of what happened in the first century, as though a transfer of past events into the present. The crucified and risen Jesus comes to us now in His body and blood, but His crucifixion and resurrection remain past events. It is the *benefits* of His crucifixion and resurrection that are now present in His Supper. The Lord's Supper is not a re-enactment of the Last Supper, nor is it essentially our taking, blessing, breaking, and sharing. Rather the Lord's Supper "is the true body and blood of our Lord Jesus Christ under the bread and wine, instituted by Christ himself for us Christians to eat and drink" (SC vi). Simply put, therefore, a eucharistic prayer is not essential to the Lord's Supper, but it may be helpful and appropriate within an evangelical Lutheran liturgy, as a means of giving thanks for the gifts of God.

A Concluding Concern: Is It the Right Time?

This essay has defended the use of a eucharistic prayer. But given that such a prayer is not essential to the Supper, it is questioned whether it would be pastorally and ecclesiastically wise in the LCMS at this time. Shall we add yet another issue to an already confused state of affairs, especially an issue that may well divide those who are otherwise agreed on the nature, theology, and practice of worship and liturgy? The current situation may prevent some from hearing the teaching that would need to accompany the introduction of a eucharistic prayer. And the use of a eucharistic prayer in the service book—however sound it might be—could provide further incentive for well-intentioned but underinformed people to create their own, theologically-weak, homemade products. So, again, should we open ourselves up to a battle—even a friendly battle—between those who share a common theology of worship but disagree over the permissibility of a eucharistic prayer within that theology? It seems far better to unite for now in establishing the Synod upon a shared biblical and confessional understanding of worship, and meanwhile allow a new hymnal (in general) and a eucharistic prayer (in particular) to wait until the crisis subsides. Then Jesus and His work in the means of grace will again be the heart and soul of worship in The Lutheran Church—Missouri Synod.

The Usage of a Eucharistic Prayer
Theological and Pastoral Concerns

WILLIAM E. THOMPSON

THE DISCUSSION AMONG LUTHERANS REGARDING THE SUITABILITY OF eucharistic prayers is relatively new. It seems quite instructive that the first sanctioned Lutheran hymnal in North America to include a eucharistic prayer was the *Service Book and Hymnal* of 1958. It appealed to "deepened scholarship"[1] and departed from the "consensus of pure Lutheran liturgies of the 16th century"[2] that had informed the Common Service of 1888. Prior to the publication of its successor, *Lutheran Book of Worship*, there was heated debate on the subject. Many of the articles written at that time, both pro and con, are now helpful to the present discussion.[3]

The departure of the *Service Book and Hymnal* from the historic Lutheran rites, which keep the *Verba* on their own, came about because of

---

[1] *Service Book and Hymnal* (Minneapolis: Augsburg Publishing House, and Philadelphia: Board of Publication, Lutheran Church in America, 1958), vii.

[2] Luther D. Reed, *The Lutheran Liturgy: A Study of the Common Liturgy of the Lutheran Church in America,* rev. ed. (Philadelphia: Muhlenberg Press, 1959), 184.

[3] Examples of articles "pro": Frank Senn, "Martin Luther's Revision of the Eucharistic Canon in the Formula Missae of 1523," *Concordia Theological Monthly* 44 (1973): 101–18; Eugene Brand, "Luther's Liturgical Surgery," in *Interpreting Luther's Legacy*, Fred W. Meuser and Stanley D. Schneider, eds. (Minneapolis: Augsburg Publishing House, 1969), 108–19; Robert Jensen, "A 'Great Thanksgiving' for Lutherans?" *Response* 15, nos. 2–3 (1975): 52–60. Examples of articles "con": Oliver K. Olson, "Contemporary Trends in Liturgy Viewed from the Perspective of Classical Lutheran Theology," *Lutheran Quarterly* 26 (1974): 110–57; Oliver K. Olson, "Liturgy as 'Action,'" *Dialog* 14 (1975): 108–13; Oliver K. Olson, "Luther's 'Catholic' Minimum," *Response* 11 (1970): 17–31; Paul Rorem, "Luther's Objections to a Eucharistic Prayer," *The Cresset* 38 (March 1975): 12–16; Gottfried G. Krodel, "The Great Thanksgiving of the Inter-Lutheran Commission on Worship: It Is the Christians' Supper and Not the Lord's Supper," *The Cresset*, Occasional Paper 1 (Valparaiso, Ind.: Valparaiso University Press, 1976).

a new approach to liturgics that has its roots in the 1926 work of Hans Lietzmann, *Mass and the Lord's Supper*.[4] He applied the notion (from the History of Religions School) that Christianity is simply one religious phenomenon among many. Most significant for our purposes, Lietzmann taught liturgical scholars to work backwards in history. So, for example, in the phenomenological views of Odo Casel[5] and the "Four Action Shape" of Gregory Dix,[6] one starts with liturgical material from a later period and projects it back onto the New Testament. Conversely, the standard approach to liturgical decisions among Lutherans, beginning with Luther's approach, is to proceed from the Biblical accounts (*sola scriptura*), particularly the Words of Institution, and to evaluate liturgical forms on the basis of Holy Scripture. Post-Reformation Lutherans evaluate liturgical forms by the criteria of the Holy Scriptures and their correct exposition in the Lutheran Confessions. A decision regarding the suitability of a eucharistic prayer will depend on which hermeneutic is employed.

In order to avoid any confusion in this discussion, we must be clear about what is meant by "eucharistic prayer." For the purposes of this essay, it refers to a liturgical text, regardless of its content, which incorporates the Words of Christ's last will and testament within a prayer—whether that is a prayer from the Middle Ages, the current canon of the mass, or one from the modern period (as in *LBW*). The content of the prayer is not the issue; that the Words of Institution are in the midst of a prayer is the issue. (Please note: this does not include the prayers prior to the Words of Institution, such as those that have been used in Lutheran hymnals since the 16th century.)

---

[4] Hans Lietzmann, *Mass and the Lord's Supper: A Study in the History of the Liturgy*, trans. Dorothea H.G. Reeve (London: E.J. Brill, 1979).

[5] Odo Casel, *The Mystery of Christian Worship, and Other Writings*, ed. Burkhard Neunheuser (Westminster, Md.: Newman Press, 1962).

[6] Most influential on Lutheran liturgical scholars was Gregory Dix, *The Shape of the Liturgy* (London: A & C Black, 1993). His "shape" was taken up in the Missouri Synod's *Worship Supplement*, 1969. For an excellent analysis of Dix, see Bryan D. Spinks, "Mis-Shapen: Gregory Dix and the Four Action Shape of the Liturgy," *Lutheran Quarterly* 4 (1990): 161–77.

A Summary of the Theological Implications of a Eucharistic Prayer

The most significant theological error of a eucharistic prayer is that a prayer—any prayer—is a sacrificial act of man toward God, not a sacramental act of God toward man. Such sacrifice in connection with the Lord's Supper is in perfect harmony with Roman Catholicism, but in precise opposition to Lutheranism. For Lutherans, the Lord's Supper is a *sacramental* action of God on behalf of His people. It is completely the Gospel action of God as He bestows the forgiveness of sins through the very body and blood of Christ. A eucharistic prayer strips the Supper of its distinct, Gospel character. It results in a false doctrine of justification. As Bryan Spinks has shown,[7] Luther had this in mind as he reformed the medieval mass. In explaining the *Formula Missae,* Luther says, "Let us, therefore, repudiate everything that smacks of sacrifice, together with the entire canon and retain that only which is pure and holy, and so order our mass."[8]

Second, the inclusion of the Words of Institution in a prayer violates the nature of those words. The Words of Institution are Christ's last will and testament. They are words that bestow gifts to heirs. They are words with inherent power to bestow the body and blood of Christ for the forgiveness of sins. The nature of a prayer, by contrast, is that of a request, a thanksgiving, or an offering of praise. In any case, prayer is an action of man in response to God. Thus, the words of Christ's testament cannot be part of a prayer. By their very nature, these words give gifts. Including them in a prayer changes the words. This change is no less significant than the Reformed change of "is" to "represents." The words of Christ must be honored as His διαθήκη, that is, His "testament." This is a crucial translation, for when the Sacrament is understood as a testament, then the appropriate liturgical form of the Words of Institution is that of a free-standing proclamation to the worshiper, not a prayer to God.

---

[7]See Spinks, *Luther's Liturgical Criteria and His Reform of the Canon of the Mass* (Bramcote: Grove Books, 1982). See also, Ronald R. Feuerhahn, "Luther's Mass: Origin, Content and Impact, 1521–1529" (M.Phil. Thesis, Cambridge University, 1980).

[8]Martin Luther, "The Misuse of the Mass," AE 36:186.

Third, the Sacrament is the *Lord's* Supper, not the Christian's supper. Luther put it well when he said, "We know, however, that it is the Lord's Supper, in name and in reality, not the supper of the Christians. For the Lord not only instituted it, but also prepares and gives it Himself, and is Himself, cook, butler, food, and drink." Contrast this description with the following from Zwingli: "The Eucharist is never bread or the body of Christ but the action of giving thanks."[9] The inclusion of the *Verba Christi* in a prayer changes the Sacrament to become the Christian's supper. This must be rejected.

Fourth, the use of a eucharistic prayer violates the *sola scriptura* hermeneutic. Those Lutherans who would use a eucharistic prayer are imposing later history upon the scriptural narratives. Scripture is then bent according to the witness of the early and later Christian tradition. In this approach, the criteria by which liturgical forms are evaluated has shifted from Scripture to Christian tradition. Lutherans, until recent times, have rejected such an approach. Luther, and all who followed him—until recent times—started with Holy Scripture and evaluated later liturgical developments on its basis and on the basis of its correct exposition in the Lutheran Confessions.

Fifth, the use of a eucharistic prayer opens the door for a false ecumenism. Many have said that the impetus for *LBW* was the desire to have one Lutheran hymnal used by all the major Lutheran church bodies. The logic is that if we worship from the same book, then we have one piece of the ecumenical puzzle in place for later union. Of course, such ecumenical efforts are not new. The interims of the 16th century and the Prussian Union of the 19th century sought to do the same thing. It now seems evident, given the recent ecumenical actions of the ELCA, that the desire for false union goes far beyond the hope of uniting all Lutherans. If there is no difference between Rome and the ELCA on justification, the door is open for further action toward union. This union will be facilitated by the fact that the ELCA has been using a eucharistic prayer; thus, the canon of the mass would be considered no great innovation.

---

[9]Quoted in Krodel, title page.

Practical Implications of a Eucharistic Prayer

First among the implications of using a eucharistic prayer would be some blurred catechetical distinctions. Many Lutheran pastors teach catechism from the hymnal and use the various liturgical rites of the church to show the unity of doctrine and practice. Specifically, with regards to the Sacrament of the Altar, one can demonstrate the correspondence between the Roman sacrifice of the mass and the canon of the mass, and the correspondence between the Reformed "real absence" and the rites found in various Reformed hymnals. (Interestingly, many Reformed hymnals use eucharistic prayers that are consistent with their emphasis on the Sacrament as a memorial meal.) Pastors have also been able to demonstrate the correspondence between the Lutheran confession that the Sacrament is the very body and blood of Christ and the way in which the Words of Institution stand on their own as pure Gospel. These distinctions enable parishioners to discern for themselves the truth or falsehood of a particular liturgical rite. The opportunity to teach with such clarity regarding the doctrine and practice of the Lord's Supper would be removed if a eucharistic prayer were included in the Service of Holy Communion.

The inclusion of a eucharistic prayer would also cause a great deal of confusion in parishes where there has been clear and thorough catechesis on the Sacrament of the Altar. For example, there would be concern and disagreement expressed by parishioners who have been catechized to discern the distinction between liturgical rites. In fact, it would produce significant opposition and difficulty. Because of this, well-catechized congregations would be hesitant to use such a hymnal.

Conclusion

A word must be said about the age in which we live. The church must always distinguish herself from the world. And following the lead of the 16th century, the church with a pure confession and practice of the Gospel must distinguish herself from heterodox churches. Liturgical rites have always contributed to such distinction. But accepting the use of a eucharistic prayer among Lutherans significantly blurs this distinction. In evaluating liturgical forms on the basis of Scripture and the Lutheran Confessions, we must be mindful that rejecting heterodox forms is a confessional *damnamus* ("we reject and condemn") against churches of a heterodox confession. In this pluralistic age of both the world and the church, we must confess the truth and reject falsehood in the clear manner of the Lutheran Confessions: "We believe, teach, and confess. . . . We reject and condemn."

Finally, in evaluating the use of a eucharistic prayer, we need to look no further than the clarity of Dr. Luther. We close with appropriate words from his "Treatise on the New Testament" and from the Smalcald Articles.

> To be brief and to the point, we must let the mass be a sacrament and testament. . . . Otherwise, we should lose Christ, the comfort [of the sacrament], and every grace of God. Therefore we must separate the mass clearly and distinctly from the prayers and ceremonies which have been added to it by the holy fathers. We must keep these two as far apart as heaven and earth, so that the mass remain nothing else than the testament and sacrament comprehended in the words of Christ.[10]

> The Mass in the papacy must be regarded as the greatest and most horrible abomination because it runs into direct and violent conflict with this fundamental article [of justification]. . . . The Mass is and can be nothing else than a human work, even a work of evil scoundrels (as the canon and all books on the subject declare), for by means of the Mass men try to reconcile themselves and others to God and obtain and merit grace and the forgiveness of sins. It is observed for this purpose when it is best observed. What other purpose could it have? Therefore, it should be condemned and must be abolished because it is a direct contradiction of the fundamental article. . . .[11]

---

[10] Martin Luther, "Treatise on the New Testament," AE 35:97.
[11] SA II, II, 1, 7. Tappert, 293–294. Emphasis added.

Eucharistic Prayer
The Middle Ground

WILLIAM C. WEEDON

IN CONSIDERING THE POSSIBILITY OF A EUCHARISTIC PRAYER, BY "MIDDLE ground" we mean the inclusion of the *Verba Christi* in a Prayer of Thanksgiving with Lutheran theological integrity. Such a middle-ground prayer would accent thanksgiving to the Father for the gift of His Son; it would highlight the *Verba* as consecratory of the elements; it would include a remembrance (anamnesis) of Christ and a prayer for the beneficial reception of His body and blood. Such a prayer would *not* include an epiclesis over the elements, nor the notion of the body and blood as a sacrifice to be offered, nor an excess verbosity that might obscure the words of Christ.

Clearing the Ground for the Middle Way

Before a middle ground prayer can be considered, it will be necessary to clear up some common, but quite inaccurate, notions about eucharistic prayers in Lutheran theology.

Myth 1: Including the *Verba Christi* in any sort of a prayer of thanksgiving is theologically inappropriate.

Oliver Olson,[1] Gottfried Krodel,[2] Theodore Knolle,[3] and even

---

[1]Oliver K. Olson, "Contemporary Trends in Liturgy Viewed from the Perspective of Classical Lutheran Theology," *Lutheran Quarterly*, o.s., 26 (1974): 110–157.

[2]Gottfried G. Krodel, "The Great Thanksgiving of the Inter-Lutheran Commission on Worship: It Is the Christian's Supper and Not the Lord's Supper," *The Cresset*, Occasional Paper 1 (Valparaiso, Ind.: Valparaiso University Press, 1976).

[3]Hermann Sasse, *We Confess the Sacraments*, trans. Norman Nagel (St. Louis: CPH, 1985), 130.

Hermann Sasse[4] held that the *Verba Christi* may not be included as part of a Prayer of Thanksgiving. Against this position must be urged the scriptural *lex orandi* of the Lutheran liturgy (and of all historic liturgies). The Preface confesses: "It is indeed meet, right, and salutary that we should *at all times* and *in all places* give thanks to Thee, O Lord, holy Father, Almighty, Everlasting God, through Jesus Christ our Lord." It is theological nonsense, therefore, to maintain that *any* time or place is inappropriate for giving thanks to the Father through Jesus Christ. His words remain His words, whether in a prayer or in proclamation. The preface to *LW* states the matter with simple elegance: "Faith that is born of what is heard acknowledges the gifts received with eager thankfulness and praise."

The Lutheran Church acknowledges the Lord's life-giving body and blood as a gracious gift from God. She also acknowledges the *Verba Christi* as His gift, a gift of words that consecrate and give the body and blood, "which words, besides the bodily eating and drinking, are the chief thing in the Sacrament (SC VI)" Such gifts may surely be received with thanksgiving and praise.

Myth 2: Luther opposed the inclusion of the *Verba Christi* in a Prayer of Thanksgiving.

Luther's theology and his reform of the mass have been urged as the primary reason for retaining only the V*erba Christi* apart from a eucharistic prayer in the Lutheran liturgy of the Holy Communion. Such objections must be heard and answered on their own terms. But one can have Luther as a champion opponent of eucharistic prayer only by ignoring or explaining away the contribution of his *Formula Missae*. If his *Deutsche Messe* were some liturgical and theological advance

---

[4]Ibid. Also in *Scripture and the Church: Selected Essays of Hermann Sasse*, ed. Jeffrey J. Kloha and Ronald R. Feuerhahn, (St. Louis: Concordia Seminary, 1995), 301–302: "They [the Words of Institution] could not remain part of a eucharistic prayer, venerable as such a prayer may be which goes back to the second century. To insert the most sacred words of our Lord which contain, or rather are, the Gospel itself as a relative clause ... in a man-made prayer would rob them of their unique character and make them a part of a human sacrifice, even if this would be understood as a thankoffering only."

Eucharistic Prayer: The Middle Ground

beyond the *Formula Missae*, then perhaps it would be true that Luther rejected the eucharistic prayer. But the facts speak differently.

In the *Formula Missae* (which is not really a self-standing liturgical order but a set of directions for the evangelical use of the missal), Luther indicates that one must draw a line straight through from the *Te igitur* all the way down to the words *Qui pridie*. He takes the middle part, the *Verba Christi*, and joins them directly to the end of the Preface:

> It is truly meet and right, just and salutary, for us to give thanks to Thee always and everywhere, Holy Lord, Father Almighty, Eternal God, through Jesus Christ our Lord . . . who on the day before He suffered, took bread, and when He had given thanks, brake it, and gave it to His disciples, saying, "Take, eat; this is My body which is given for you." After the same manner also the cup, when He had supped, saying, "This cup is the New Testament in My blood, which is shed for you and for many, for the remission of sins; this do, as often as ye do it, in remembrance of Me."

The choir then sang the Sanctus during the elevation of the Lord's body. But what do we have here, if not the *Verba Christi* precisely in a Prayer of Thanksgiving to the Father? Yes, even joined to the Preface by way of the dreaded "relative clause"![5] In fact, the *Verba Christi* have become the very cause for that thanksgiving which is offered always and everywhere. Though Luther does call for a brief silence prior to the *Verba Christi*, he suggests that these Words of Christ be intoned according to the same tone as the Lord's Prayer. Thus, by grammatical and musical construct, the *Verba* are part of the prayer.

Luther's *Deutsche Messe* is another story. In this case, the *Verba Christi* have been removed from a Prayer of Thanksgiving, and they are sung according to the tone of the Holy Gospel. Knolle, Sasse, Spinks, and others have explained this liturgical model as a genuine breakthrough in Luther's theology, as though he were getting it right for the first time here. Words of proclamation to the people: Gospel words. It is a wonderful idea. But to set the *Deutsche Messe* against the *Formula Missae* doesn't stand up to the facts.

In his preface to the *Deutsche Messe*, Luther writes: "Now there are three kinds of divine service or mass. The first one is the Latin, which we

---

[5]See previous note.

published earlier under the title *Formula Missae*. It is not now my intention to abrogate or to change this service. It shall not be affected in the form which we have followed so far; but we shall continue to use it when and where we are pleased and prompted to do so."[6] Clearly, Luther did not regard the *Deutsche Messe* as a replacement for the *Formula*, but as a supplement to it. Side-by-side the orders stood: in the one, the *Verba Christi* sung to the tone of the Lord's Prayer and attached to a Prayer of Thanksgiving by way of a relative clause; in the other, the *Verba Christi* sung to the tone of the Gospel apart from any prayer. Luther himself apparently saw no contradiction between them.

Furthermore, as Luther was preparing his *Deutsche Messe* for publication, Hausmann (impatient for a service in the vernacular) sent him copies of some current German masses, almost certainly Kanz and Münzer included. Luther looked them over and sent them back with the following note attached: "I am returning the masses and have no objection to their being sung in this manner. But I hate to see the Latin notes set over the German words."[7] The only modification of the text that Luther suggests is a replacement of the Preface with an exhortation that he provided with his note.[8]

Now the Kanz Mass (1522) has the following after the Sanctus: "O all-good Father, merciful, eternal God, help that this bread and the wine become for us and be the true body and the pure blood of your beloved Son, our Lord Jesus Christ, who on the day before his suffering took bread in his holy hands. . . ."[9] Surely, if Luther had objected to the inclusion of the *Verba* in a prayer, then he would have voiced his objection to this.

We do know that Luther also gave approval to Münzer's Mass, perhaps without realizing the source. It was adopted in a somewhat expanded form by the city of Erfurt and submitted to Luther for his approval. He wrote back at the end of October 1525 to say that the mass did indeed

---

[6] *AE* 53:62, 63 (*WA* 19:73, 74)

[7] *AE* 53:54 (*WA Br* 3, no. 812, 142).

[8] *AE* 53:104, 105 (*WA Br* 3, no. 847, 462–463). It is curious to note that this exhortation does not seem to have been used in any of the German church orders until Gerhard included it in the Casamiriana in 1626, one hundred years later.

[9] Julius Smend, *Die evangelischen deutschen Messen bis zu Luthers Deutscher Messe* (Göttingen: Vandenhoeck & Ruprecht, 1896), 75.

EUCHARISTIC PRAYER: THE MIDDLE GROUND

have his approval; also, that he was about to publish his own *German Mass*, and they could decide for themselves whether to remain with the mass they already had or replace it with his.[10] What follows is the pertinent portion of Münzer's Mass, which Luther approved as the *Deutsche Messe* was about to be published:

> On the day before Jesus would suffer, he took the bread in his holy hands and lifted his eyes toward heaven to you, God, his Almighty Father, gave it to his disciples, saying, ..."Take and eat of it. This is my body, which will be given for you." In the same manner, when he had eaten, he took the cup in his holy, precious hands, and thanked you and blessed it and gave it to his disciples, saying, "Take and drink you all from this. This cup is my blood of the new and eternal covenant, a mystery of faith that will be spilled for you and for many for the remission of sin. So often as you do this, do it to remember me by," and so let us all pray: Our Father. . . .[11]

Once again, if Luther had objected to the inclusion of the *Verba Christi* in a prayer, then he certainly would have expressed that opinion here; yet, all we find is his approval.

Finally, when Luther published his treatise on *The Abomination of the Secret Mass* in 1525, for all the fault that he finds with the Roman canon of the mass (and there is much fault to be found), he nowhere criticizes the canon for being a prayer. It is always and only the *doctrinal content* of the prayer that he faults, especially its constant emphasis on human giving and offering instead of that which Christ is here bestowing.[12] For example:

> As [the priest] began, so he concludes, always making an offering and praying that it may be pleasing. The good Christ is not pleasing to the Father unless the holy canon comes and makes him pleasing, in that the offering reconciles him with God. And so again Christ is dead and of no avail, since only the work is supposed to forgive sins and obtain favor with God so that he is gracious to Christ and to us.[13]

In light of the foregoing evidence, Luther cannot be held as the champion of those who regard as sinful or inappropriate any eucharistic prayer that embraces the *Verba Christi*.

---

[10] *WA Br* 3:591–592.
[11] Smend, 104, 118ff.
[12] *AE* 36:311–328.
[13] Ibid, 327.

Myth 3: Classic Lutheran liturgy does not include the *Verba* in a Prayer of Thanksgiving.

While it is true that the overwhelming majority of the *German* church orders did not follow the way of the *Formula Missae* in including the *Verba Christi* in a prayer, this does not mean that Lutheranism had settled on the *Deutsche Messe* form of the consecration as the one and only correct one. Indeed, against such a notion, there stands as a bulwark the liturgy of the Church of Sweden.

In 1531, Olavus Petri, disciple of Luther, published his order for the Swedish Mass. This order followed the pattern set in the *Formula Missae* but went further in its thanksgiving. Following the introductory dialog of the Preface, we have this:

> Verily it is meet, right, and blessed that we should in all places give thanks and praise to thee, holy Lord, almighty Father, everlasting God, for all thy benefits, and especially for that one that thou didst unto us, when we all by reason of sin were in so bad a case that nought but damnation and eternal death awaited us, and no creature in heaven or on earth could help us, then thou didst send forth thine only begotten son Jesus Christ, who was of the same divine nature as thyself, didst suffer him to undergo death instead of our all dying eternally, and even as he hath overcome death and risen again unto life, and now dieth nevermore, so likewise shall all they who put their trust therein overcome sins and death and through him attain to everlasting life, and for our admonition that we should bear in mind and never forget such his benefit, in the night that he was betrayed celebrated a supper, in which he took the bread in his holy hands, gave thanks to his heavenly father, blessed it, brake, and gave it to his disciples, and said . . .[14]

Here is a genuine Prayer of Thanksgiving and the words of the Testament are built right into it. Here there is no mention of any sacrifice of ours, but only rejoicing in the Father's gift of His Son. No one ever cried foul. (In fact, Martin Chemnitz appears to have made use of much of the material of this prayer in his third exhortation to communicants in the 1569 Brunswick Church Order.) No one said that the Swedes had

---

[14]Eric E. Yelverton, *The Mass in Sweden: Its Development from the Latin Rite from 1531 to 1917* (London: Harrison, 1930), 39.

forsaken the true faith in doing this—and this was almost uninterruptedly their eucharistic prayer from 1531 until the middle of this century.[15] Ironically, even Sasse, who agrees with Knolle in his critique of eucharistic prayer, affirms that in Sweden, the Lutheran Mass was preserved in perhaps its purest form.

Myth 4: Any Prayer of Thanksgiving including the *Verba* tends toward confusion of our action with God's action.
The notion that in the Eucharist the church offers a sacrifice to the Father is very ancient.[16] The heresy that the sacrifice we offer is Christ's body and blood is almost as ancient.[17] The fact that many eucharistic prayers from antiquity tended to accent the church's sacrifice and offering has led to the mistaken notion that all eucharistic prayers *of necessity* confuse our sacrifice and God's gift. The fact that it often has been so, however, does not mean that it always must be so. The Petri prayer cited above shows that for centuries in Lutheranism a Prayer of Thanksgiving was known which did not in the least confuse God's action with our own: a prayer in which our action is confessed to be absolutely helpless and we find ourselves in the posture of sheer grateful reception, nothing more.

The Desirability of a Eucharistic Prayer

If it is finally granted that there is no reason why Lutheran liturgies may not properly include the *Verba Christi* in a Prayer of Thanksgiving, the question of the desirability of such a procedure needs to be answered. The criterion for desirability should be: would it be fitting for the Divine Service? Would such a prayer assist in hearing the *Verba Christi* as Gospel and would it accord with the reverence that properly

---

[15]The story of King John's "Red Book" is a fascinating chapter in liturgical history, but its blatant Romanizing provoked an almost Puritan reaction. When the pendulum stopped swinging, the liturgy was simply restored to Petri's Mass once more. For more on this, see the book mentioned in the previous note.

[16]As Martin Chemnitz argues in his *Examination of the Council of Trent,* trans. Fred Kramer, 2 vols. (St. Louis: CPH, 1978), 2:443-45.

[17]It can even be found as early as *The Apostolic Tradition* of St. Hippolytus.

attends the solemn transactions between Christ and his beloved bride, his giving and our receiving?[18] The answer can only be "yes."

Sadly, the days when it was normative practice for the *Verba Christi* to be chanted by the celebrant seem to be over. Even though the words of the holy testament were not joined to a eucharistic prayer in the Saxon tradition, there was something distinctly reverent in their being chanted. If nothing else, the chanting slowed down the words and the melody wrote them on the people's hearts. Chanting them made clear that these words were important, vital; they needed to be heard. Now, especially in those parishes that have succumbed to church growthery (but certainly not limited to them), the words of Christ are read often at a quite horrendous clip, and then the Sacrament is distributed to the resounding music of "Just as I Am" or worse. The impression given is that time spent in praise and thanksgiving to the Father of our Lord Jesus Christ is so much wasted time; better to get on to the important stuff, the stuff that centers the attention where it belongs: on us!

Were a eucharistic prayer to be introduced into such an environment, might it not have the salutary effect of slowing everything down, of reminding the people and, above all, the celebrant that such thanksgiving is at the very heart of a biblical Christianity—that we live our lives only at the receiving end of God's giving? Might it not serve to call our attention precisely to the holy words of the testament as they are rejoiced in before the Father's throne and received from the Son as the very words by which we live? Might not the very wording of such a prayer rebuke the casual approach to worship that plagues the church in our day and that would make of God's holy house of prayer a theater for our entertainment? I believe it would, and I believe we should include such a prayer in our next hymnal.

---

[18]Chemnitz expresses this well when he speaks of "evangelical decorum" and praises the practice of holding the housling cloth under the elements as they are distributed because of the great reverence such a practice shows toward our Lord's body and blood. See his Church Order for Brunswick in Emil Sehling, ed., *Die Evangelischen Kirchenordnungen des 16.Jahrhunderts,* 15 vols. (Vols. I–V, Leipzig: O.R. Reisland, 1902–13; vols. VI–XII, Tübingen: J.C.B. Mohr, 1955–63), 6/1:149.

Eucharistic Prayer: The Middle Ground

Modern Examples of a Middle-Ground Prayer

Are there any modern examples of a Lutheran eucharistic prayer that do not slip into ambiguity or downright heresy? I believe that there are. Due to the limitations of time, we'll look at just two of them, though I will refer you also to a third.

The first is actually in our hymnal. Divine Service I contains a dismembered eucharistic prayer lifted from the *Agende für evangelisch-lutherische Kirchen und Gemeinden*.[19] The first two paragraphs of this eucharistic prayer are fairly faithfully reproduced, but then, instead of a transition to the Lord's Prayer as in *LW*, the original contained the *Verba Christi*. Then followed a prayer which, for some odd reason, ended up at the end of the Prayer of Church in *LW*. The original of this prayer included a specific reference to the Sacrament: "And as we all are one body in Christ through the communion of his body and blood, so gather together your whole church . . ." Put together, here is what the German *Agende* has:

> Lord of heaven and earth, we praise and thank you for having had mercy on those whom you created, sending your only-begotten Son into our flesh to bear our sin and be our Savior. With repentant joy we receive the salvation accomplished for us by the all-availing sacrifice of his body and his blood on the cross.
>
> Gathered in the name and the remembrance of Jesus, we beg you, O Lord, to forgive, renew and strengthen us with your Word and Spirit. Grant us faithfully to eat his body and drink his blood as he bids us do in his own testament.
>
> *[Verba Christi]*
>
> Therefore we remember, O Lord, heavenly Father, the sufferings and death of your dear Son, our Lord Jesus Christ, for our salvation. Praising his victorious resurrection from the dead, we draw strength from his ascension before you where he ever stands as our own high priest. And as we are one body in Christ through the communion of his body and blood, gather us together we pray from the ends of the earth to celebrate with all the faithful the marriage feast of the Lamb in his kingdom which has no end. Graciously receive our prayers, deliver and preserve us, for to you alone we give all glory, honor, and worship, Father, Son, and Holy Spirit, one God, now and forever.

---

[19] *Agende für evangelisch-lutherische Kirchen und Gemeinden* (Berlin: Lutherisches Verlagshaus, 1955), 1:70–74. Please note that *Lutheran Worship: History and Practice* inaccurately cites the origins of the prayers in Divine Service I and II by reversing them. Divine Service I is of German origin; Divine Service II is Swedish.

Here is a fine example of a "middle-ground" Lutheran eucharistic prayer, which is neither verbose nor contains any theologically objectionable material.

Yet another such example is to be found in the prayer offered in the *Worship Supplement* (CPH, 1969) as a translation of the eucharistic prayer in the Synod's Spanish hymnal, *Culto Cristiano*. This prayer was a simple revision of the prayer that appeared in the *SBH*. A careful examination of this prayer reveals it to be constructed of some happy phrases from the great eucharistic prayers of antiquity, with a little bit of the Small Catechism thrown in as well. The Synod's version eliminated a few ambiguous phrases, removed the epiclesis, and de-emphasized the notion of our sacrifice of praise. It reads as follows:

> Holy are you, O God, almighty and most merciful Lord, holy are you and great is the majesty of your glory. You did so love the world that you gave your only Son, that whoever believes in him should not perish but have eternal life, and you did send him into the world to fulfill for us your holy will and to accomplish our salvation. He,
>
> [*Verba Christi*]
>
> Remembering therefore his salutary precept, his life-giving passion and death, his glorious resurrection and ascension, and the promise of his coming again, we give thanks to you, O Lord God almighty, and we beseech you mercifully to accept our praise and thanksgiving, and to bless us, your children, so that all we who partake of Christ's holy body and of his precious blood may be filled with heavenly peace and joy; and also that we, in receiving the forgiveness of sins, together with the gifts of life and salvation, may be sanctified in body and soul and spirit and have our portion with your saints in light.
>
> To you, O God, Father, Son, and Holy Spirit, be all honor and glory in your holy Church forever and ever. Amen.

The third example is largely a reworking of the classic Swedish thanksgiving of Olavus Petri, which Lee Maxwell and I prepared a few years ago. The text can be found in Timothy J. Quill's book, *The Impact of the Liturgical Movement on American Lutheranism*.[20]

---

[20]Timothy J. Quill, *The Impact of the Liturgical Movement on American Lutheranism*, Drew Series in Liturgy, No. 3 (Lanham, Md. and London: The Scarecrow Press, Inc., 1997), 209–210.

Conclusion

I contend that a "middle-ground" eucharistic prayer would be of great benefit in the next hymnal. In a day and age when the liturgy is being pushed toward anthropocentrism, for the church to stop the hurrying which panders to the impatience of men and stand for a while before the Father, giving Him praise and thanks for what He has done for us in His Son, for what the Son gives us in the holy words of the testament, and asking for a blessed reception of the same would surely be a wholesome corrective—in every sense "meet, right, and salutary." For it is in thanksgiving that the church finds her true vocation. We live perpetually at the receiving end of God's giving, and so thanksgiving is our life's breath. We are, after all, a peculiar people, a people who "declare the praises of Him who called us out of darkness into His marvelous light" (1 Peter 2:9).

The Celebration of the Lord's Supper with Thanksgiving
Worship Statement No. 32 from the Lutheran Church of Australia*

1. Increasingly, the Lord's Supper is being celebrated without the traditional Preface and Thanksgiving or any form of thanksgiving.
   a. The Words of Institution are recited either after the Sermon, or after the Prayer of the Church, or after some didactic sentences about the significance of the Sacrament, or after an admonition about its proper reception.
   b. The Preface with the Thanksgiving, the Sanctus, the Lord's Prayer before or after the Words of Institution, and the Lamb of God are omitted from the celebration of the Sacrament.
   c. It is argued that, since the Words of Institution effect the real presence, all other parts of the traditional orders have the status of adiaphora.

2. Since the thanksgiving is commanded by Christ, it is not a matter of adiaphoron, but should be observed in the celebration of the Sacrament.
   a. The words and form of the thanksgiving are not specifically prescribed by our Lord. Nevertheless the evidence clearly indicates that Christ's command to "do this" in remembrance of Him (Luke 22:19; 1 Cor. 11:24, 25) includes the act of thanksgiving over the bread and the wine (Matt. 26:26–28; Mark 14:22–24; Luke 22:19–20; 1 Cor. 11:23–25).

---

*Used by permission of the Commission on Worship of the Lutheran Church of Australia.

The Celebration of the Lord's Supper with Thanksgiving

1. The Gospels indicate that the thanksgiving of Jesus at the Last Supper is similar to the prayers of blessing and thanksgiving said by Jesus in the meals where He acted as host with His disciples (Matt. 14:19; 15:36; Mark 6:41; Luke 9:16; 24:30; John 6:11; cf. Acts 27:35).
2. By doing this Jesus did not establish something completely new but acted according to the Jewish custom of acknowledging Yahweh as the source of every blessing before a meal and of giving thanks to Him for His blessings at the end of each meal.
3. These prayers were called "benedictions" or "eulogies" since they normally began with the formula: "Blessed are you, Adonai..." This is followed by relative clauses which listed the mighty acts of God in creating the world and providing food for humankind. They are therefore acts of praise addressed to God. This custom may be behind the use of the Greek verb for "blessing" with reference to the bread in Matt. 26:26 and Mark 14:22 (cf. 1 Cor. 10:16).
4. The variation in Matthew and Mark between the "blessing" with the bread and the "thanksgiving" with the wine probably reflects the different wording in the Jewish tradition for the benedictory grace with the bread at the beginning of the meal and the thanksgiving with the wine at the end of the meal.
5. The words of thanksgiving are the first in a sequence of acts to be performed in the celebration of the Lord's Supper.
    a. The four accounts given of the institution of the Sacrament all report the act of thanksgiving with a Greek aorist participle rather than an aorist indicative tense as in the case with most of the other acts.
    b. This may be taken in one of two ways.
        i. It may indicate that the customary words of thanksgiving were spoken before the rest of the rite was performed, i.e., it was the first in a series of acts.
        ii. It may indicate that the rite not only began with the words of thanksgiving but that the thanksgiving accompanied some or all of the subsequent acts,

including the words of Christ for the bread and the wine.

These two alternatives in the understanding of the extent of the thanksgiving are evident in the difference between the *Service with Communion* and *The Service—Alternative Form*. But either way, the thanksgiving, according to all New Testament accounts, is an essential part of the celebration.
  b. Just as Jesus addressed the thanksgiving to His Father, so the eucharistic thanksgiving is addressed to the first person of the Holy Trinity.
     1. Just as the Father is the source of everything we receive in worship, so all prayer is offered to Him in the Lord's Supper.
     2. In the eucharistic prayer Jesus leads us in our thanksgiving to the Father for His gifts in creation and redemption.

3. **The apostolic fathers testify unanimously to the celebration of the Lord's Supper with thanksgiving.**
   a. In his letter to the *Smyrneans* Ignatius refers to the Lord's Supper as the Eucharist (7:1; 8:1).
   b. The *Didache* calls it the "Eucharist" (9:2, 5), mentions the giving of thanks with the breaking of the bread (14:1), and gives prayers of thanksgiving for the cup and the bread (9:1–5) as well as a Post-Communion Prayer of Thanksgiving (10:1–6).
   c. Justin also calls it the Eucharist (1 Apol. 66), mentions the offering of praise and thanksgiving to the Father (65, 67), and refers to the consecrated elements as "eucharisted food" (66).

4. **Our Lutheran Confessions associate the Sacrament of the Altar with the performance of thanksgiving.**
   a. Since the preliminary act of thanksgiving was not a matter of contention at that time, the Formula of Concord did not discuss it but merely assumed that the Words of Institution would be accompanied by thanksgiving.

The Celebration of the Lord's Supper with Thanksgiving

  1. The Formula of Concord seems at times to limit the act of consecration to the mere recital of the Words of Institution (FC Ep VII, 9; FC SD VII, 82–83). It, however, thereby takes the essential part of the act to refer to the whole of it, for the Latin text speaks in 84 about the consecration of the elements with a "blessing" (*benedictione*).
  2. It also quotes the words of Justin with approval where he maintains that the food of the Sacrament has been consecrated (Latin) or blessed (German) by Christ through Word and *prayer* (FC SD VII, 39).
  3. Both the Latin and the German text regularly refer to the consecrated elements as the "blessed" bread and wine (FC SD VII, 44, 52, 56, 57, 63, 75, 83, 86, 126).
 b. The importance of thanksgiving is evident in the Apology to the Augsburg Confession which refers to the Sacrament as the "Eucharist" (Ap XXIV, 66–67, 76, 87; cf. AC XXII, 6; XXIV, 12), and teaches that it is our true sacrifice of thanksgiving and praise to God (Ap XXIV, 19, 30–33, 35, 74–77).

  Even though the Confessions hold that the Words of Institution constitute the real presence of Christ's body and blood, they still seem to envisage that they would be preceded by words of thanksgiving and prayer.

5. **Liturgically speaking, the thanksgiving functions as an important part of the whole sequence of acts in the liturgy from the Preface to the Lord's Prayer. These acts prepare for the Words of Institution and so contribute something significant to the right administration and celebration of the Sacrament.**
   a. The initial Salutation invokes and acknowledges the Lord Jesus as the host and celebrant of the Sacrament.
   b. The Thanksgiving not only fulfills Christ's command to celebrate the Sacrament with thanksgiving but also joins the congregation with Him in addressing His holy Father in the act of thanksgiving on behalf of the church and the world (cf. 1 Tim. 2:1). It also reveals the messianic significance of the Lord's Supper, for, as the faithful receive

the body and blood of the promised Messiah with thanksgiving, they also already now in this age celebrate the life of the age to come.

c. The Sanctus not only joins the eucharistic celebration of the congregation with the adoration of all the saints and angels before the very throne of God but also expresses the eschatological dimension of the Sacrament as a foretaste of eternal life with God.

d. The Benedictus acknowledges the advent and presence of the promised Messiah in the Sacrament. It comes from Ps. 118:26, the culmination of Psalms 113–118 which constitute the Egyptian Hallel sung by Jesus and His disciples at the Last Supper (Matt. 26:30; Mark 14:30).

e. The Lord's Prayer functions as the eucharistic prayer in the Lutheran liturgy. By it we join with Jesus in interceding for the church and the world in the celebration of the Sacrament. Since, according to Paul in 1 Tim. 4:5, all things are consecrated by the Word of God and prayer, it has been understood by some Lutherans as the prayer for the consecration of the elements.

f. All these acts, from the Salutation to the Lord's Prayer, therefore, join the people of God with Christ in the performance of the heavenly liturgy. He not only serves them sacramentally as the victim but also ministers sacrificially as their great high priest who leads them in their service of thanksgiving, adoration, praise and intercession.

g. While the wording of these acts may vary from time to time and place to place, the Words of Institution are recited in the context of Christ's own ecumenical, eschatological ministry of intercession and praise.

6. **Therefore some form of thanksgiving and praise to God the Father should normally be spoken or sung in connection with the Words of Institution in every public celebration of the Sacrament by pastors of the Lutheran Church of Australia.**

Adopted by the Department of Liturgics
October 13, 1994

The Future of Hymnals

Do Hymnals Have a Future?

Why a New Hymnal Now?

MANY PEOPLE ARE NATURALLY ASKING not only whether we need a new hymnal at this time, but whether the whole concept of a hymnal is out-of-date. The two essays in this section explore the issues from a number of perspectives. The first urges, among other things, that our hymnals be seen as prayer books for use in the home. The second essay builds on this perspective and also addresses issues like who should determine the confessional faithfulness of our hymnals, what makes a hymnal a success or failure, the intricacies of worship planning, and what in worship can be legitimately creative.

Do Hymnals Have a Future?

ROBERT M. ZAGORE

MY TOPIC HAS CALLED ME TO LOOK INTO THE FUTURE TO ANSWER THE questions: does or should the hymnal have a future? And, is it possible to resurrect the concept of the hymnal as a personal prayer book? Unlike the more scholarly topics discussed here, I have been asked to delve deeply into the realm of sanctified opinion, even prognostication. Since, as a Lutheran pastor, I'm not allowed to use a crystal ball and have, unfortunately, misplaced my Urim and Thummim, let me begin by telling you about the data I gathered to arrive at and bolster my conclusions.

I began by using the Internet—to research the trends in book sales and to determine whether these trends indicate a coming end of traditional publishing or if book publishing is entering a new era as a result of computers and the Internet. What I found was that book sales are strong, and industry analysts expect the trend to continue for the foreseeable future. New technologies seem to be enhancing rather than diminishing book sales. Some 1.028 billion books written for adults were sold in the U.S. in 1995. Of that number, over 7 million were classed as "religious" book sales.[1] For religious book sales alone, gross sales amounted to nearly $1.8 billion.[2] If children's books are added to the total, the number of books sold in 1995 was over $2.15 billion. In 1996 and 1997 those numbers were expected to grow two to three percent.[3] Although the nature of what is offered may change somewhat, we should not expect publishing or book use to pass away.

---

[1] *Book Industry Trends, 1996* (New York: Book Industry Study Group, 1996); data available from http://www.booknotes.org/stats3.htm; Internet; accessed 1/98.
[2] Data available from http://www.booknotes.org/stats2.htm; Internet; accessed 1/98.
[3] Data available from http://www.booknotes.org/stats1.htm; Internet; accessed 1/98.

Following the Internet search, I used electronic mail, the phone, and the opportunity provided by the West Michigan Pastors' Conference[4] to conduct an unscientific survey of brother LCMS pastors. I was careful especially to seek the opinions of those who do not regularly use the services in *LW* or *TLH*. Finally, I used electronic mail to survey a number of Lutheran laymen on a Lutheran layman's bulletin board concerning their use of the hymnal.

The goal of my surveys was not to get a statistical opinion concerning the state of our Synod. It was not to discover the reasons why a hymnal was important. I wanted to find out generally about the use and objections to use of the hymnal and the historic liturgy. A second object of the survey was to find out if people knew how to use the hymnal as a prayer book.

Before the survey, as a matter of pastoral practice and as a churchman, I had already determined that a hymnal of high quality, that is orthodox and theologically rich, is an irreplaceable gift for any church body and congregation. I freely admit that I had already answered the first question before the topic was assigned to me. There is a future for a hymnal because there must be a hymnal in our future. The reasons for this are manifold. But the chief reasons I am about to mention may also hold the key to reintroducing the hymnal as a personal prayer book.

A hymnal serves as a church body's most public summary and application of theology. This is also true of false religions, the cultists, the a-liturgical—in short, any group. Anyone who is more than a casual observer already knows how *lex orandi, lex credendi* plays out and demonstrates its truth within congregations of The Lutheran Church—Missouri Synod. Where the theology of a particular pastor and congregation is anthropocentric, their worship life centers on the expressed desires and perceived needs of the congregation. It focuses outwardly on seekers and evangelism. Its goal is to achieve numeric growth by providing a suitable, growth-oriented environment. Its inward focus is on personal development and enrichment.

---

[4]The Michigan District of The Lutheran Church—Missouri Synod, Grand Rapids, Mich., February 1997.

Do Hymnals Have a Future?

In this paradigm, God is the facilitator of man's dreams and goals, not the object to which man clings for salvation. Recent issues of *The Reporter*, especially those articles dealing with the Church Membership Initiative, demonstrate with great assertion that those who concentrate on man as the center of worship also seek to rid themselves of theocentric worship. A quick tour of the Synod's evangelism materials in the CPH catalog or on the Synod's web site will reveal a vast number of resources that teach congregations how "courageously" to rid themselves of the inhibiting trappings of the liturgical worship, overcome the objections of those who do not have "church growth eyes" or a "love for the lost." They will learn instead to make the church a place where evangelism prospects have their desires and dreams divinely fulfilled and then become "assimilated."[5] Programs are designed, and worship is focused on what will get people in the door and make God accessible. Since the desired outcome is to attract people by fulfilling their needs and making the church attractive to them, the natural course of such efforts is to make the church man-centered.

By contrast, theocentric worship in our Synod generally follows the contours of the historic liturgy. "Historic" does not mean, "locked in the past." It refers to that which is handed on as a faithful deposit from one generation to the next. The adjective, "historic," means that what is going on in this liturgy has happened over a long period in many places. God has given gifts to His people throughout the world, throughout the generations, by means of this liturgy. So it reasonably follows that those who desire to receive the Lord's gifts in worship would seek them where He has promised to give them and has historically given them.[6] To faith, history is also an incarnational matter. God works among His people. God has dealt with His people in sign and promise, Word and Sacrament, throughout time—continuously, predictably, assuredly. It goes with the

---

[5] I have intentionally avoided naming specific resources for two reasons. First, the length of the presentation does not allow for expansion of the topic. Second, the general content of these works is well known, and there is not enough time to address fairly the specific errors of these resources.

[6] The link between the history of God's salvation and the worship of God's people is seen most profoundly in the Psalms. With great regularity Israel's hymnbook retells

nature of the Gospel that the people of God are not left in doubt about where and how their Lord will give His gifts.

The adjective generally used to describe the alternative to the historic liturgy, "contemporary," speaks of something which has only been done by individuals and small groups. If no one else has ever received or confessed God's gifts like we're doing it, how can we be sure we're getting them at all? The answer to that question is usually, "search your feelings," or "has it changed the way you live?" No lasting confidence can be found in those answers. Any answer that forces a believer to find a positive change in feelings or accomplishment makes worship anthropocentric, subjective, and uncertain. The Gospel and an historic liturgy give certainty. An orthodox, catholic[7] hymnal is a witness to our standing within the orthodox, catholic, historically traceable, people of God.

This point leads to the next important purpose of an historic, catholic hymnal—namely, to avoid temptations to sectarianism. A church body is not a sect because it withdraws from others of its age. It has always been a valid and proper response of the church to sever worship ties and fellowship with errorists. The orthodox church is not found by counting adherents. It is marked where God's Word and Sacraments are joined to faithful public confession. In other words, ecumenism is not only (or even best) practiced through trying to forge unity with one's contemporaries. A sectarian group is sectarian because it severs ties with the historic, catholic and apostolic church that has existed in every age. This becomes most pronounced when worship and hymnody are considered. When St. Paul implores the Corinthians to adopt God-pleasing worship practices, he commends to them the use of the παράδοσις (1 Cor. 11:2, 23)—those worship practices which have been faithfully hand-

---

the story of the exodus, the giving of the Law, the promise to Abraham, etc. The songs of Moses, Deborah, Zechariah, Simeon, Mary, etc., are further examples of how the song and worship of the people of God set forward and preserve the meaning of the historic acts of God for the nurture and worship of successive generations. Rehearsing the Lord's past deeds as evidence of His present work is an essential element in the piety of the Old and New Testament church. But it also expresses the transgenerational nature of worship.

[7] I.e., universal. Unless otherwise specified, every use of the word "catholic" in this paper means universal, and is not a reference to the Roman Catholic Church.

ed down to them just as they have been received by the apostle. In rebuking contentious Corinthian factions in matters of worship, Paul makes the theological point that "we have no other practice, nor have the churches of God" (1 Cor. 11:16.) The wide use of an orthodox, catholic hymnal and liturgy is a public way of holding to the apostolic παράδοσις and maintaining the endowment of an orthodox, catholic worship life among us.

Being orthodox and catholic is a matter of public confession. It is never based on the privately held beliefs of individuals. Properly speaking, worship is characterized by "homology,"[8] that is, "confession." Homology literally means, "to say the same words." The people of God say back to God what He has first said to them. They speak the very words of the Holy Spirit as He has given them in Holy Scripture to the holy catholic church. Worshipers do not stand primarily before the world, the pastor, or even fellow believers. They stand *coram Deo*—in the presence and on the receiving end of God.

The worship life of the church is trinitarian. The Father and Son send the Holy Spirit. The Holy Spirit calls, gathers, and enlightens His church. Sanctified by His gifts and led by the indwelling Spirit, the people of God confess that the words of the Father and Son are true. The Spirit intercedes for us in the voice, liturgy, and song of the people. The Son intercedes for His church, which is so intimately connected with His life that it is called His body. Because His atonement has made us His brothers, He gives us His Father. The Father hears and responds to the prayers and praise of Son and Spirit and gives them what they ask. Through them, the Father bestows His gifts to all His children because we are in Christ and the Spirit is in us. In the working out of this divine economy, confession is made publicly: in the world; before the pastor, God's called representative; and in unity with fellow believers.

As a practical matter, to accomplish this it is necessary that the people of God have a joint, printed confession of faith. In spite of the often-leveled charge, such a liturgy does not stifle the work of the Holy Spirit.

---

[8] From the Greek word, ὁμολογεῖν, meaning literally, "to say the same thing back." See its usage in Philippians 2:11, 1 John 1:9, and elsewhere in the New Testament.

Rather, it affirms that what is confessed is genuinely God's Word, not our fantasies or feelings. The individual humbles himself and receives what God speaks, confessing the truth of His words. For example, in the Divine Service's opening Confession of Sins, the believer does not search his heart and give account of all he feels guilty about. Instead, the stark words of Scripture, by which God has described man's nature, are spoken. By confessing the Lord's words, the worshiper confesses that God's judgment is true. Such a confession is theocentric—what God has said. It prepares the way for Absolution, God's gracious response for Christ's sake. It is the opposite of a man-centered confession, which leads to a man-centered solution, e.g., "I'm sorry and I'll try harder." An orthodox, catholic hymnal stands believers *coram Deo*. Before God, the confession of His word is properly made whether individually, where two or three are gathered, or in the midst of a whole company of believers.

But the mere existence of worship or a hymnal is not a guarantee of orthodoxy. While ideally every Christian would be a skilled theologian with the ability rightly to discern truth and error, this is not the case. There is an implied trust between the worshiper, the congregation, and Christ's undershepherd. The congregation trusts, sometimes blindly, that their order of worship is orthodox. Congregations further rest on the assurance that the Synod constitutionally guarantees the orthodoxy and catholicity of its published worship materials. When a hymnal is published, it is a declaration of what is and, to some extent, what is not acceptable and theologically proper worship.

Of course, there are other very important reasons to have a hymnal and to produce one as a Synod. But these are the chief reasons why an orthodox, catholic hymnal should be a believer's personal prayer book. These further serve as the groundwork for the means by which the hymnal may be restored to such a place.

It may appear to some that hymnals are becoming the new "buggy whip" in church circles. The general feeling of many in the Synod is that hymnal use is declining and will continue to decline. An analysis of the situation shows that this is not the case. Even congregations that are abandoning Lutheran hymnals seem to be using other hymnals and supplements. In many cases, the choice not to use a synodical hymnal is a choice to be divergent in doctrine and practice. This is a problem no orthodox hymnal can solve. In fact, the time may be upon us when pastors who wish to worship like the Methodists or Baptists should be asked to join them rather than tearing down the church.

In some cases, however, the nonuse of hymnals is not a theological statement at all. The recent fad that causes entire services to be printed out in full is, in part, a symptom of an underlying problem that a new hymnal can solve. It is also something we can capitalize on for the sake of the church.

While the historic Lutheran liturgy is orthodox, meaningful, and inviting, hymnals often are not. The number of options available at each turn of the service, the incessant page flipping, etc., are confusing and frustrating even to those who love the liturgy. For example, in our Synod's latest hymnal, *Lutheran Worship,* the Order of Morning Prayer ends in three different places depending on the content of the service. This has left predecessors in my present congregation so confused that the congregation now sings every ending every time Morning Prayer is used. While it does make a nice illustration when teaching on the Revelation to St. John (which describes the end of the world three different times), it should be a goal of our service books to avoid such confusion.

A new hymnal needs to cut down on the array of options presented to the congregation within each service. Page confusion should be avoided at all costs. Some have suggested that the rubrics should be more descriptive or obvious. Unfortunately, I think adding more words to a page, even if they are in red, will just add to the confusion. Manifold options, optional endings, varied prayers, etc., can all be offered, but should be offered as a supplement—perhaps even on a computer disk, or in a "pastor's edition" of the hymnal. This will answer the desire for variety while cutting down on confusion. People who leave church confused (especially life-long Lutherans who get confused by the service options) become enemies of the liturgy because they simply cannot follow the hymnal. That is a tragedy.

The initial marketing of a new hymnal should stress its "user-friendly" character. When people are convinced that they can follow the hymnal, they will be more likely to use it, both in and out of church. This would benefit more than corporate worship. Making the hymnal less intimidating is the first step to reintroducing the hymnal as a personal prayer book.

The next step is perhaps less obvious. An intriguing outcome of the survey I conducted occurred in answer to the following questions, which were asked only of pastors:

1) Do you have an adequate personal prayer and devotional life?
2) Do you have an adequate family prayer and devotional life?
3) Do you teach church leaders how to conduct devotions?
4) Do you know how to teach someone to develop a plan for personal and family devotions?

Of the 71 respondents, the overwhelming majority (82%) answered "no" to each question. Only one of the 71 pastors answered "yes" to every question. The answers were often accompanied by admissions of guilt and shame. I understand that the questions themselves are Law, not Gospel. The Law always brings about guilt and shame, for no one measures up to the Law. However, I believe there is more to it than that. It has been my personal experience that neither pastors nor people are taught how to plan and conduct a prayer life. This is not simply a matter of falling short in their efforts. There seems to be a genuine void that faithful men and women long to have filled yet don't know where to turn. I honestly believe, as a result of this survey and follow-up conversations, that many who are turning to evangelical prayer guides, journals, etc., would turn to a Lutheran source if they knew and understood where and how to turn.

The most ideal plan for prayer and a devotional life would be to convince all the people of God to gather for Matins and Vespers daily. As said above, orthodox worship is homological and confessional by nature. While it may be impractical to try to institute a general observance of Matins and Vespers gathered at the church, there is no reason the people of God could not use these at home. Worship is *coram Deo*. Before God, the people of God who pray the church's prayer are joined together. An orthodox prayer life is rooted in the liturgy of the church. Ideally, the church should teach her members to pray her corporate prayer, even when alone. While prayer may draw a believer into his closet privately, he goes in with the church, the angels and archangels, and all the company of heaven.

Do Hymnals Have a Future?

As a simple matter of pastoral care, it is necessary that the church provide for her members orthodox, accessible devotional materials. If we do not do it, they will find it elsewhere. Anyone with ten minutes experience in the parish knows what people are likely to find.

The hymnal is the ideal means by which solid devotional material may be offered. But I also believe simplicity and ease of use will be the key to its success. While the compilers of our latest hymnal, *Lutheran Worship*, should be commended for helping this along by marking a simplified morning and evening prayer for devotional use, for including psalms for daily prayer, and even including an order of daily devotion, these sections have not received much publicity. In fact, 41 percent of the pastors I surveyed did not realize morning and evening prayer were thus marked. Consequently, it seems there is little chance their people are praying them daily.

The publication of a new hymnal would provide the opportunity for a much-needed education campaign which could teach pastors and people how to use the hymnal for private and family devotions. It would bring theological depth and meaning, draw people away from the emotional, man-centered, need-centered exercises that characterize so many devotional materials today. The hymnal could incorporate an easy-to-follow schedule of devotional readings based on hymns, return psalm- and hymn-singing to the family, and from the ground up, encourage an appreciation for the church's prayer.

Additionally, new technologies available could provide family altar CDs and CD-ROMs that coordinate with the hymnal. Stories about the source of hymns, materials about the hymn writers, lessons about the meaning of the liturgy and the theology of worship could enlighten and edify our people in a way never before possible. Further, these would allow for hymn singing and liturgical song at home even among the most musically inept. The use of CD-ROM, DVD, and other emerging technologies could afford an almost unlimited range of opportunities for education and a variety-filled devotional life that would be liturgical and orthodox. Homilies on DVD and CD-ROM, choral performances, or simply being able to find the melody line of a hymn could all add great substance to the personal and family altar. As key leaders in each congregation learn the meaning of the church's song and prayer and grow to understand the homological nature of worship, this would almost certainly be brought into the life of the congregation.

The educational effort could concentrate on teaching the theology of worship in a simple, understandable way, using the hymnal itself as the textbook. Thousands leave our services every Sunday singing and humming the hymns. This shows us that the battle is half won.

The hymn stanza,

> Eternal Spirit of the living Christ,
> I know not how to ask or what to say;
> I only know my need, as deep as life,
> And only you can teach me how to pray.[9]

is a great example of the theologically accessible, yet deeply meaningful material available in the hymnal itself to teach an orthodox prayer life. This has always been one of the goals of good hymnody. The hymn "Rock of Ages" was written as an outstanding response to the increasingly emotionalistic revival theology which was corrupting orthodox worship and teaching. While it was placed in a musical setting reminiscent of such emotion-based hymns, Toplady's words stand as a firm witness to God's monergistic action in salvation, and derivatively, in worship:

> Not the labors of my hands
> Can fulfill thy law's demands;
> Could my zeal no respite know,
> Could my tears forever flow,
> All for sin could not atone;
> Thou must save, and thou alone.[10]

While I'm aware of Toplady's other problems, his is a great example of the power of hymns to influence theology for the good. The power and influence of an orthodox hymnal and worship life could ripple throughout our Synod. As people stand before the Lord, saying His words, calling upon His name, and recalling how that name was placed upon them, our church will grow in every important way. In short, the material is already extant to teach an orthodox theology of worship and

---

[9]"Eternal Spirit of the Living Christ," *LW*, no. 432.
[10]"Rock of Ages, Cleft for Me," *LW*, no. 361.

to extend that to the family altar. What is missing is a means by which to teach pastors and people how to use it.

Finally, not everyone will embrace the hymnal as a personal prayer book. But technology and need have come together to provide the church an unprecedented opportunity to offer it to those who wish to be faithful. It is my firmly held belief that the church's hymnal can be a personal prayer book for many. While the production of a hymnal has economic ramifications, if it is rightly conceived and assembled, it can be a mission tool of enormous importance. It can be a catechetical tool of great theological richness. And it can transform our church's worship life by restoring homological, orthodox, catholic prayer to the homes of God's people.

Why a New Hymnal Now?
'And Everyone Did What Was Right in His Own Eyes'

Larry A. Peters

How did we get to this point?

At one point in the late 1960s and early 1970s, things were changing—even for a rather staid and conservative church like the LCMS. An invitation from the LCMS to the ALC and LCA led to the creation of the ILCW and the start of a common hymnal for most North American Lutherans. Mühlenberg's dream was on the verge of becoming reality—except that other factors at play would radically change the end product and affect the whole of Lutheranism forever. I speak not of internal events within the LCMS but the dawn of accessible, quality printing technology for the average parish. The advent of the copier, computer, and laser printer, combined with projection technology, has proven to be more of a force for shaping the way Lutherans worship than the official hymnals of any Lutheran group.

The Roman Catholic Church began this era with a profound shift from a Latin mass, with largely memorized responses, to a brand new vernacular liturgy, usually in missalette form, which required a level of congregational participation unknown to this church for centuries. Printed on newsprint and containing a host of new liturgical songs in the contemporary musical idiom of the 1970s, the era of the throw-away liturgy and the disposable hymn was born. The Episcopal Church joined this movement in a small way with the publication of its *Services for Trial Use* and hymnal supplements in preparation for a new prayer book and hymnal for this communion. Of all the liturgical churches, the Episcopal Church made the best transition to a permanent prayer book and hymnal, once finished with experimentation.

Why a New Hymnal Now?

Lutherans who were out to reinvent the way Lutherans worship sought approval all along the way with a whole series of temporary, trial-use booklets called the *Contemporary Worship* series (11 in all). From the lectionary to the mass to the occasional services to hymns, this series attempted to cushion the radical change about to come. Before this era of change, a typical congregation expected the service to remain pretty much the same from Sunday to Sunday. Now the idea of change created a situation where one Sunday's liturgy might be radically disjointed from the Sunday that preceded or followed it. A variety of musical settings and a variety of liturgical forms suggested a pattern of change that went well beyond the imagination of those early efforts at a common liturgy and hymnal for all Lutherans.

Even before these were published, the LCMS printed and distributed a portion of its progress toward a new hymnal in a softcover volume titled *Worship Supplement* (1969). It was seen as a temporary bridge between *The Lutheran Hymnal* and the eventual pan-Lutheran hymnal. The Commission on Worship saw this as a "modern experiment in applying timeless truths to timely needs . . . and . . . an attempt to give voice to the cries and joys of today's Christian by means of contemporary creations."[1]

With a copier and some cut-and-paste work, the new trial-use forms could be intermingled with the liturgical resources of *TLH* and *SBH*, but it did not stop there. The liturgical resources of Methodists, Episcopalians, Roman Catholics, and a host of other groups could now be mixed and mingled with the officially sanctioned worship materials and forms. Eventually, the introduction of the personal computer and laser printer would make it possible for every parish and every pastor to create a unique liturgy from any number of resources and duplicate it in a quality form week after week after week.

The most recent development in this rapid evolution has been the advent of the copyright license that allows congregations and pastors unlimited, facile, and legal access to songs and hymns from a myriad of sources. With a copyright license and a quality desktop publishing sys-

---

[1] *Worship Supplement* (St. Louis: CPH, 1969), 9.

tem, every congregation and every pastor has the ability to produce a quality product—every parish a miniature publishing house. The real question, however, is whether any serious theological review takes place—but we will turn to that question later. The availability of quality projection systems has offered the congregation the option of a paperless Sunday worship experience and suggested to many that the hymnal is obsolete.

As the LCMS prepares to issue a hymnal supplement and to begin work on a revision of *LW* and *TLH*, the first and foremost question in the minds of many is *why waste the resources of the church on something that does not seem to be necessary?* Even if the decision is made to publish, the marketplace will eventually determine whether any new hymnal is used or not.

It is the opinion of this author that a new hymnal is essential to the church, but it is also this author's belief that the church will have to be convinced of the need and value of such a new hymnal and that a great deal more effort will be required before any new hymnal has the same impact on the congregation and Christian family as *TLH* has had over its now 57-year life.

Why is a hymnal important to the church?

Before we can deal with the future of the hymnal we must define what a hymnal is and why it is important to the church. In other words, *is a hymnal part of the public doctrine of the church?* In a very practical sense, a hymnal is the church's chief publication of her public doctrine. We don't need to spend hours rehearsing the history of the phrase, *lex orandi, lex credendi,* to come to the conclusion that the hymnal is the foremost place where the church declares what she believes, teaches, and confesses.

The practical proof of this can be found in the constitutions of most LCMS congregations, where one of the articles requires that only worship books and hymnals that conform to the doctrinal standard outlined in a previous article may be used in that congregation. Here the obvious connection between what we say we believe and how we worship is prescribed in legal terms. Our synodical constitution lists as one of the very objectives of the LCMS the promotion of unity in church practices and the appreciation of responsible practices that are in harmony with our common profession of faith.[2] Implicit in this article are worship practices. One step further is the requirement for membership in Synod that binds both voting and advisory members to the exclusive use of doctrinally pure agendas, hymn books, and catechisms, and restricts them from taking part in services of churches with a mixed or heterodox confession.[3]

This is not an exhaustive review of the question but a mere summary to show that the agenda, hymnals, and other worship resources have always been included in the definition of public doctrine of the church. Lutherans are not the only ones to come to this conclusion. Presbyterian William Taylor observed that "a hymnal reflects the history of the church, embodies the doctrine of the church, expresses the devotional life of the church, and demonstrates the unity of the church."[4]

Walter E. Buszin noted that the Missouri Synod has always concerned itself with purity of doctrine. "This insistence has contributed both to the fame and to the ridicule the LCMS has received in the past, but it remains that this concern applies in both hymnody and liturgy."[5] Paul Bunjes is even more forceful in his challenge that "if the Lutheran church professes a distinct and significant doctrinal stance, it should marshal the courage to confess the same in its worship resources."[6] Paul H.D. Lang writes similarly that "the liturgy does not merely express what we feel, but it first teaches us what we are to feel."[7] E. Theodore

---

[2]Art. III, 7, as found in *Handbook of The Lutheran Church—Missouri Synod, 1995 Edition* (St. Louis: The Lutheran Church—Missouri Synod, 1995), 10.

[3]Art. VI, 4, in *Handbook*, 11.

[4]Quoted by Fred Precht, *LWHP*, 131.

[5]Walter E. Buszin, "Tradition and Meaning in Our Worship Today," in *Liturgical Reconnaissance: Papers Presented at the Inter-Lutheran Consultation on Worship*, February 10–11, 1966, Chicago, Illinois, ed. Edgar S. Brown, Jr. (Philadelphia: Fortress Press, 1968), 85.

[6]Paul G. Bunjes, "Progress Reports: Synodical Conference," in *Liturgical Reconnaissance*, 117.

[7]Paul H.D. Lang, *Liturgy, Theology, and Music in the Lutheran Church*, ed. Mandus A. Egge (Minneapolis: S.P.A., Inc. for International Choral Union, 1959), 8.

Bachmann agrees that the hymnal and liturgy are part of the public doctrine of the church: "The liturgy reflects the theology of the church; liturgy is prayed dogma and the reception of divine salvation."[8]

If these statements are not explicit in the Lutheran Confessions, they are most certainly assumed. The most care given to Luther's introduction of change is reserved for what takes place in the liturgy and hymnody of the church. For Luther, the liturgy of the church is theological; it speaks to man about God so that man may speak back to God.

Paul H.D. Lang uses careful language to express the fact that corporate worship is always formal—that is, it formally confesses to the world what it is that God has revealed to us, and that it follows certain prescribed rites and ceremonies. There is an essential distinction between the *informal* of the individual and the *formal* worship of the community. "Informally, individually, Jesus has these words about prayer. 'When you (singular) pray, go into your closet and speak to your Father who sees in secret . . . but when you (plural) pray, pray thus, "Our Father, who art in heaven . . ."'"[9]

Arthur Just speaks to this issue when he writes that "the liturgy and hymnody of the church *shapes* the faith of the people more than anything else. In addition, a church's beliefs are more accurately determined from her liturgy, hymns, preaching, and catechesis than [from her] official resolutions."[10] Clearly, the published hymnal and agenda of the church puts into writing, as the building puts into stone, the particular theological understanding of church and worship.

Confession and liturgy belong inseparably together if the church is to be healthy. Liturgy is prayed dogma. Dogma is the content of the liturgy. In his encyclical, *Mediator Dei*, Pius XII insisted that the public doctrine of the church determine what the liturgy shall be. *Dogma should be the norm for the liturgy.* A right understanding of the Gospel as the primary criterion for determining the content of the liturgy should

---

[8]E. Theodore Bachmann, in *Liturgy, Theology, and Music*, 25.

[9]Lang, *Liturgy, Theology, and Music*, 8.

[10]Arthur Just, *Structure, Culture, and Theology in Lutheran Liturgy* (paper presented at the Symposium on the Lutheran Confessions and the Liturgy, Concordia Theological Seminary, Fort Wayne, Ind., January 1992). Typed doc. Emphasis added.

be no less important to the Lutheran Church than it is to Rome. This is not to say that any liturgy is prescribed by the Word of God. The church is free to order her ceremonies to preserve the liturgical heritage of Christendom, to maintain liturgical texts, forms, and ceremonies consistent with the Gospel, and to expect that a certain level of uniformity will issue forth in worship just as it does in the confession of faith. The hymnal is not merely a book of worship resources but a book of doctrine and faith.

I readily admit that there are those within the Synod who do not see either the wisdom or urgency of this connection and who wish a public debate to revisit these issues. But I would suggest that it is precisely because there are many who reject this conclusion that the church must expend the resources necessary to publish agendas, hymnals, and other worship resources that are consistent with the confessional standard of the church.

Who is capable of or desires the responsibility of judgment required to insure that all worship materials are consistent with the confessional standard of the church?

If pastors and parishes were both capable of exercising this standard of judgment and were desirous of the responsibility incurred in exercising such oversight, it would be theoretically possible to provide only the briefest outline of materials on the synodical level and allow those on a local level to publish resources faithful to the church's confessional standard, applicable to the local situation, and appropriate to the individual congregation. However, it is that very capability and acceptance of the responsibility for judgment that is in question.

What level of training is necessary for those who must exercise such judgment? Is the one required seminary-level course in worship enough preparation for the responsibility of theological, liturgical, musical, and aesthetic review? I would suggest that the vast majority of parish pastors and musicians are neither capable nor desirous of this responsibility on a weekly basis. Judging from the number of typographical errors that regularly appear in the average parish newsletter and worship bulletin, it seems that we are expecting a level of knowledge and expertise that congregations and their pastors are either not capable of giving or are unwilling to commit the time to do so.

What does this responsibility of judgment entail? First, it requires an understanding of what worship is and is not. It is not the purpose of this paper to offer an extensive definition of worship other than to recount the fine words of the Introduction to *LW:*

> Our Lord speaks and we listen. His Word bestows what it says. Faith that is born from what is heard acknowledges the gifts received with eager thankfulness and praise. Music is drawn into this thankfulness and praise, enlarging and elevating the adoration of our gracious giver God. Saying back to him what he has said to us, we repeat what is most true and sure.[11]

Worship is not a program of the church nor is it an educational activity. Worship is not one of many things the church does, but the very core and center of the church's life and reason for existence. Worship shapes everything else in the life of the church, from the people worshiping to the vision of ministry within the congregation to the myriad of programs and events within the congregation.

Second, the responsibility of judgment requires a deep familiarity with the liturgical forms that today's church has inherited from the church that went before. This means using the framework of the liturgy as part of the personal devotional life of the pastor, a thorough knowledge of the forms and rubrics within the published hymnals of the church, and an awareness of the resources that both explain and direct the use of those hymnals. *(Lutheran Worship: History and Practice* is but one important example.) Implied in this is an awareness of the rich liturgical heritage and treasure trove of hymnody that has been passed down to us, to which our own generation has added forms and examples that are both theologically faithful and liturgically appropriate.

Third, the responsibility of judgment requires a willingness to expend the time necessary to understand, review, and choose the liturgical options and hymns that faithfully support the theme and witness

---

[11]*LW*, 6. These oft-quoted words seem more profound with each reading.

of the pericopes and connect Sunday worship to the church year. Implied in this is a willingness also to expend the financial resources to build a library of volumes that can assist the pastor and parish musician in the formal planning of the liturgy and hymns for each Sunday of the church year. It is a scandal to the church that so little of the average congregation's resources are designated for the most central activity of the church—worship. Included in this scandal are the shameful wages and treatment given to parish musicians (both professional and volunteer). The sad truth is that parish musicians often have a better sense of what is appropriate and faithful in worship than do the pastors who are given the responsibility of oversight by their office.

Abundant examples exist to prove that while some pastors and parishes delight in presenting something new and different each week, there are very few who are expending the time and wise judgment necessary week after week to ensure that such liturgies are theologically, liturgically, and musically excellent. Hymns are often chosen at the last minute. Sermons are written on Saturday night. If pastors find it hard to prepare a few days ahead now, how will they bear the full weight and responsibility for writing, editing, reviewing, and evaluating the faithfulness, effectiveness, and integrity of a new liturgy week after week? Until pastors begin to take their role as presider seriously enough to give the time necessary to prepare adequately for the liturgy as well as the Sermon, they will continue to purchase packages from outside sources or follow the book without change—neither of which is an adequate response to the responsibilities of pastor, preacher, and presider.

As examples of the problems in our liturgical practice, I point to the practice of adding the *Verba* to Matins or Vespers to create a communion service, or the frequent misunderstanding about what constitutes an adequate hymn substitute for the Hymn of Praise. What about the indiscriminate cutting up of the liturgy solely to shave a few moments off the length of the service? I have served as organist for services at pastoral conferences and other larger church events where hymn stanzas were cut that completely destroyed the theological and poetic structure of a hymn, or where a mix of things was added to the service either in the guise of offering a little something to please everyone or in the name of something festive. Sadly, it often seems that the worst examples in the church often happen when pastors gather together by themselves for circuit or pastoral conferences and other meetings.

What we have learned is that the vast majority of pastors and parishes are not looking for this kind of serious study and leadership but for a quick and easy pathway to variety and freshness in the weekly liturgical rhythm of Word and Sacrament. What they seek are reliable, faithful, and usable resources they can adapt to the particular parish situation they serve—a situation that may vary greatly in terms of history, musical ability, human resources, etc. In other words, what they seek is a hymnal, complete with a fair representation of hymns, liturgies, and liturgical options to provide a varied yet faithful worship life consistent with the church's faith, appropriate to the season or Sunday of the church year, and with a ceremonial as elaborate or simple as is appropriate to the congregation and its resources.

This does not mean that worship is best left only to the "experts." Rather, it means that it is precisely the function of the larger church to provide on behalf of every congregation the agenda, hymnal, and other resources for worship that are consistent with the church's confession of faith and that maintain an essential standard of uniformity necessary to that common confession.

Ultimately, it is to the benefit of both pastor and people that the church provide a hymnal and worship resources faithful to the Scriptures and consistent with the doctrinal standards of the church. Without such hymnals and liturgical resources, the vacuum will not last long. It will be filled either by resources that do not conform to the doctrinal standards of the church or by the whims and fancy of a pastor, parish musician, or worship committee. It is for the protection of the pastor and people from the tyranny of the banal, novel, and trite that the church been given both the responsibility and the authority to publish such resources. It is to safeguard the Gospel and to ensure that this Gospel is accessible weekly to the people through the liturgy that the church has expended the time, energy, and resources to publish a hymnal and its related volumes every generation or so.

We need to remember that there is intense pressure on the pastor and parish musician to dumb-down the liturgy and to use only those hymns and spiritual songs that are old favorites or easy to sing. This pressure and the doctrinal indifference of too many have led to what Walter Buszin describes as the intrusion of sentimental and fundamentalist hymns into Lutheran practice (and this was written nearly 40 years ago!).[12]

The kind of study, discussion, and debate necessary when the church publishes liturgical texts, forms, or hymnody can seldom be fit into the busy life of the average parish pastor. Yet this is exactly what is required if the responsibility for determining the theological and musical integrity of the hymns, texts, and liturgy falls to the average parish pastor. Study, discussion, and debate must ensue regarding each and every hymn, text, and liturgical form—all on a weekly basis if a service is constructed almost from scratch Sunday after Sunday.

Why does an individual Christian or family need a hymnal?

Historically, a church's hymnal also has functioned as a personal prayer book and family devotional resource in the home. Part of the very reason many LCMS people were reluctant to accept *LW* when it was introduced is that *TLH* had been so much a part of the personal piety and family devotional life of the people for generations. It was not just Sunday morning that changed but their individual and family devotional life. In thousands and thousands of homes across our Synod, the hymnal stands on the music rack of the family piano. It is both a symbol of their participation in the life of the church and the place they go to find a Christmas carol, the words to pray, or a word of encouragement to face life's challenges.

While part of the reason that *LW* has found such opposition is due to the circumstances within the Synod at the time it was prepared, another reason is that *LW* failed to replace *TLH* on that family piano or on the nightstand by the bed. Nevertheless, the people deeply desire and need a common book that focuses their unity as Lutheran Christian people and that can serve to teach them to pray as individuals and as a family. The hottest market in religious books lies in devotional literature. The weak link in all of this is that the church has done a poor job

---

[12]Buszin, *Liturgical Reconnaissance*, 86.

convincing the people that the hymnal is a worthy companion to their Bible and catechism. Clearly, this will be the challenge that faces any future hymnal.

Fred Precht was absolutely right when he writes that, through the centuries, "popular religion was molded [more] by the thoughts expressed in hymns" than by any other single factor.[13] Religious songs sink into the memory, color the thoughts, and fashion the theology of the individual even more than the church's deliberate instruction in the faith. What Lorenz Blankenbuehler wrote on the eve of the introduction of *TLH* continues to be true today: "No book is so universally used in the church as the hymnal. . . . There is perhaps no spiritual tool so valuable as the hymnal for the furtherance of God's kingdom here on earth and for the heightening of spirituality. . . ."[14] And Rabbi Abraham Joshua Heschel has noted: "We do not know what to pray for. It is the liturgy that teaches us what to pray for. It is through the words of the liturgy that we discover what moves us unawares, what is urgent in our lives."[15]

Why does the congregation need a hymnal?

The congregation needs a hymnal to embody its confession of faith, to teach it to pray, to serve as its tie to the past, and to provide a foundation for the future. In addition, the hymnal serves as a focal point for the congregation's unity and the means of expressing its unity and connection with other congregations with whom it is in fellowship. M. Francis Mannion observed that the unity the Christian, Roman, Byzantine, and barbarians found following the fall of the Roman Empire was in large

---

[13]Precht, *LWHP*, 137.

[14]Lorenz Blankenbuehler, "The Christian Hymn: A Glorious Treasure," in *Proceedings of the Third Convention of the Iowa District West of the Evangelical Lutheran Synod of Missouri, Ohio, and Other States,* Sioux City, Iowa, Aug. 26–30, 1940 (Ogden, Iowa: Ogden Reporter Print, 1940), 3.

[15]Abraham Joshua Heschel, *Man's Quest For God* (New York: Charles Scribners & Sons, 1954), 32–33.

measure the result of the church's liturgy.[16] The power of a common liturgy and hymnal to promote and even sustain unity at a time when diversity pulls at every fiber of the church's life should not be minimized.

Consider the common situation today where one building houses several congregations throughout a weekend and weekday. What is it that gives to those different assemblies a sense of their unity and common life together except a common liturgy and hymnal?

The sad truth is that in far too many of these situations, there is no unity. Where each service time uses a different liturgy, a different core of hymnody and spiritual songs, and is structured to appeal to different groups and tastes, different congregations are created that neither want nor are able to worship together. They choose a service to fit their personal taste and have neither the desire nor the ability to worship together since they do not know the hymns and liturgy used by the other congregations that share their same facilities.

While a smorgasbord may be a good idea for Ponderosa Steakhouse, it is the poorest choice for a Christian community of believers where unity and harmony are both a given and the goal of that church. A common hymnal and liturgy is the most powerful expression of the unity within a congregation that worships at multiple times on a given weekend and within a Synod that contains congregations from one geographical coast to the other and a variety of cultural backgrounds.

Indeed, the growing practice of providing vastly different choices to the prospective worshiper segregates the people of any given congregation according to the worst possible criterion—*personal taste.* Everyone would agree that there are legitimate reasons for providing a certain level of difference to the various services offered weekly in any one congregation, but the rationale for those differences must meet a greater standard than mere personal preference. The liturgy must be appropriate to the particular circumstances of the assembled congregation, and this may mean that the liturgy is spoken rather than sung or that the music of the

---

[16]M. Francis Mannion, "Liturgy and the Present Crisis of Culture," *Worship* 62 (1988): 98–99, referencing Christopher Dawson, *Religion and the Rise of Western Culture* (New York: Doubleday, 1991).

liturgy and hymns be familiar or easily accessible to the congregation in the absence of well-trained musicians. The level of ceremonial and the number of assisting roles within the liturgy may vary from service time to service time. Even certain considerations of time are appropriate to the conversation when worship planning begins. However, the practice of segregating a congregation by personal taste and preference is unscriptural, sub-Lutheran, and sub-Christian. It is antithetical to the very nature of the Gospel that what God has brought together in Christ be divided by the individualistic desires to do whatever we want on Sunday morning.

Hymnal-use surveys of our Synod have revealed how important a hymnal is to the worship life of the congregation. Should the church stop preparing hymnals that are theologically and liturgically faithful, congregations would shop in other places for their hymnals and create a diversity that would both threaten the unity of the Synod and undermine the church's confession of faith. A survey completed only last year[17] shows that as important as a hymnal is to the congregation, our Synod remains divided over which hymnal commands its loyalty and acceptance. For all practical purposes we have two official hymnals and one semi-official hymnal within the Synod. Various events in the life of our Synod have turned the choice of which official hymnal to use into a debate over how orthodox one is. For some, choosing *TLH* or *LW* says something well beyond a simple decision to purchase an officially sanctioned hymnal for the congregation. In addition, there are others who have chosen *LBW* or *The Other Song Book* precisely to reject either the past or current direction of the LCMS.

Some 61–63 percent have *LW* available for use in the pew and regularly use it in the worship life of the congregation. In addition, some 46–49 percent of the congregations either use or have *TLH* available in the pew. Some congregations continue to have both hymnals available or use a liturgy from *TLH* while retaining *LW* as their primary hymnal resource. A significant minority has available and uses *All God's People Sing*, the chil-

---

[17] 1996 survey. Information on the surveys conducted by CPH is available from the Music Department of CPH or the Commission on Worship.

WHY A NEW HYMNAL NOW?

dren's hymnal published by CPH (12–15%). About the same number of congregations use and have *LBW* and *The Other Song Book* available in the pew (8–12%). While there has not been a great deal of change since a previous survey was taken in 1995, clearly the trend continues to favor a diversity of resource books in addition to the primary hymnal as those resource books become more and more available. Generally speaking, the larger the congregation, the greater the chance that congregation uses other worship resources in addition to an officially-sanctioned hymnal.

What should that new hymnal look like?

Do we need a hymnal and agenda? Yes, but what should be included? There are two extremes that must be avoided. On the one hand, the church must avoid the temptation to include everything, thus creating a hymnal of unmanageable size that is cumbersome to use. On the other hand, the church should avoid a hymnal that is so basic that every group will require supplemental hymnody and worship resources.

We have learned from *LW* that the extensive space given to the propers is probably too much. More than 10 percent of its 1,005 pages consist of the texts and tones of the Introits, Graduals, Collects, Verses, Offertories, and propers for each Sunday and festival day of the church calendar. Many congregations already duplicate this material in the service folder, and many others purchase one of the publishing houses' inserts that include this material.

CPH reports that almost 25 percent of the congregations in the LCMS subscribe to their service which provides the propers in an insert form. In addition, many feel that page turns often lose the worshiper who is new to a Lutheran service. One of the most common complaints is that neither *LW* nor *LBW* include all the Psalms. Clearly the next hymnal will need to include more. The Divine Services encompass some 60 pages, occasional services and morning/evening services some 75 pages, and with its 520 hymns, all combine to make up *LW*.

While it is often desirable to have a variety of musical settings and to include the setting of the liturgy from the hymnal that preceded it, it will be impossible in the future to retain all of the old services and settings and still have room for anything new. In addition, complaints about the size of the type suggest that the next hymnal will face the daunting task of providing a readable yet complete collection of hymns and liturgical settings for the church.

What format will the next hymnal use? Already Augsburg Fortress and Northwestern provide their hymnals or a portion of them on CD-ROM. CPH will catch up this summer [1998] with its own version. In the future, the definitive edition of the hymnal will most likely be in an electronic media form. This will provide the average parish and pastor, using ordinary desktop-publishing software, with the resources to utilize a full range of hymnody and liturgical resources not possible in printed form in the pew. There remains the issue of copyright protection and the potential of abuse of copyrighted texts and tunes to be resolved, but this will have to be resolved no matter what.

In conjunction with an electronic media format, the hymnal will need to be in a form that encourages its wide use in the congregation and in the home. This would suggest that a melody-only edition of the liturgy and hymns would not be as useful as one including the complete musical setting of the liturgy and hymns.

It should be noted that the size and weight of *LW* (and a poor quality binding) has considerably shortened its useful life in the pew. After only ten years of use, many parishes are finding that their copies of *LW* require either rebinding or replacing. Since this is a considerable expense that congregations are chary to undertake, practical consideration must be given to a binding and format that will extend the useful life of the book as long as possible.

The size of a book indicates that about 600 hymns are the most that can be reasonably included. Which 600 of the thousands of hymns available? One possibility is to weigh the hymn section according to copyright—including those currently under copyright and not including those in public domain. The only real problem with this is that beloved hymns may well be omitted from a new hymnal, thus depriving the people of these important resources and of their ties to the past.

There is also the more important question as to how many hymn tunes a congregation can learn and use successfully. There is no one answer to this question. The ability of a congregation to welcome and learn new hymn tunes (or musical settings of the liturgy) is often depen-

Why a New Hymnal Now?

dent upon a variety of factors.

Chief among them is the quality of musical leadership of the parish musicians and of the organ (and other instruments available) to lead the congregational singing. In a parish with an adequate organ and a talented parish musician, the congregation may find new hymn tunes and musical settings of the liturgy an easy task. In other congregations, which lack a good musical instrument and a trained and talented parish musician, the number of new tunes it can learn will be greatly reduced. The architectural setting and the acoustical atmosphere of the worship space can also play a crucial role. Facilities with low ceilings, acoustical tile, heavily-padded pews, and thick carpeting can make singing even the most familiar hymn tune a difficult task.

My own experience is that one to two newer hymns among the five or so normally used on a Sunday morning is not a problem for the congregation I serve. In part this is due to a committed, talented, and experienced organist who makes even difficult music easy to sing. Likewise, the presence of a cantor whose strong voice gives foundation to the rest of the singers and is often used to introduce the first stanza of a new or less familiar hymn tune is also a valuable asset. The congregation knows and uses regularly two settings of the Divine Service from *LW*, the liturgy from *TLH*, page 15, as well as most of Matins, Morning Prayer, Vespers, and Evening Prayer from *LW*. In my previous congregation we introduced a new hymn tune only once or twice monthly and rehearsed the hymn prior to the start of the liturgy. The congregation did learn both settings of the Divine Service even before the arrival of a talented organist who made a world a difference for the singing.

How many texts may be introduced is a far different question. There is probably no limit to the number of new texts that can be used with existing, familiar tunes. Care must be given, however, to make sure that text and tune complement each other. Even text and tune with the same meter may not be a good match for singing. Historically, the church has wedded many texts to the same tune, especially when hymnals normally printed text only. This is both a blessing and a problem for the church. The blessing is that it is possible to use a host of texts that more carefully fit the theme of the propers without placing a heavy burden upon the ability of the congregation to learn new music. The problem is that it is easy to rely upon a small repertoire of hymn tunes, increasing the possibility of boredom with the music and thus depriving the congregation of the joy of singing.

In any discussion concerning which hymns should or should not be included in a new hymnal, a better means of determining which to include would be the applicability of those hymns to the lectionary so that the propers of the church year are fully reflected in the hymn corpus available to the pastor and parish. If it is understood that the goal of liturgical planning is to use the resources of the liturgy and hymns to support the theme(s) of the lectionary, then this should be the criterion used to select hymns for inclusion in the hymnal.

Supplemental volumes could be prepared for a variety of needs, from ethnic congregations to congregations that desire more modern hymns to a collection of old favorites that are beloved by many but that do not necessarily fit within the church year or the lectionary.

What about the printing out of the liturgy and hymns?

Clearly the trend toward printing out the liturgy and all or some of the hymns every Sunday is not likely to decline anytime soon. The wise and careful layout of the options within the framework of the liturgy may minimize the need for such duplication, but we must accept the fact that this current practice is not going to change. Therefore the church will need to provide the access and resources that will allow such duplication and encourage a level of liturgical integrity beyond what we have known today. Contrary to what some might believe, printing out the liturgy on a weekly basis is not limited to those congregations that compose a new service week after week. In fact, many congregations that are among the most committed to the use of the historic liturgy print out the service in order to include options or musical settings not currently available in any one hymnal.[18]

Not every congregation desires great variety even within the options provided for in the liturgy. Not every congregation has the musical lead-

---

[18]Redeemer, Ft. Wayne, and Zion, Detroit, to name but two.

ership or musical instruments to introduce effectively new hymn tunes or settings of the liturgy. But some will continue to expect a full array of options within the framework of the liturgy as well as new hymnody. How else can the church provide for such diversity of taste and circumstance unless the full use of electronic media are provided? By providing doctrinally pure and musically accessible resources for the options within the liturgy and new hymns, the church can help the local congregation maintain a high level of theological and musical integrity. In addition, the local congregation can be encouraged to use a common form and the common texts that will ensure that there is a high degree of uniformity and unity in the worship practices of the church while at the same time allowing for a broad diversity.

Printing out the hymns is less justified. By printing out all hymns, the congregation soon forgets the hymnal entirely, and its role within the devotional life of the people is discouraged. Also, because of copyright issues, it may be more difficult legally to print out hymn tunes and texts along with the liturgy (which is usually covered under one copyright by the church-owned publishing house and held in trust for the entire Synod).

CPH reports that its subscription service to *Creative Worship for the Lutheran Parish* averages between 1,800–2,100 per quarter and that nearly 95 percent of those subscribing are LCMS congregations. This would seem to indicate that there is a great desire on the part of pastors (and parishes?) for a resource that uses a fairly consistent liturgical form but provides a variety of options that are not included in any one hymnal at the present moment. Regardless of what one might think about *Creative Worship* as a resource, the church would do well to consider the desire of these subscribers when preparing a new hymnal and when determining the format of that hymnal and its accompanying resources.

CPH appears to have had uneven success with *Creative Worship*. Some of it is both creative and faithful, and other parts of it are merely novel. If this resource is not as faithful or effective as it could be, part of the reason is that it was developed and marketed outside of the LCMS Commission on Worship. In order to reclaim and improve this resource, all that is required is that CPH and the Commission on Worship work more closely to produce it. I wonder if such complaints would continue if those who complain would give their good gifts to prepare some of the resources for publication? With nearly one-third of the congregations of the Synod using *Creative Worship*, the church will need to provide faithful resources that coordinate with any future hymnal, or those congregations may turn elsewhere and end up using less-faithful resources produced by others.

Clearly there continues to be a confusion among us concerning what constitutes *creativity* and what is simply *novelty*. Martin Franzmann enjoined the church to caution when he wrote that the church that marries the spirit of this age will become a widow in the next generation.[19] Yet this is exactly what happens in far too many parishes of our Synod. Sunday after Sunday, the service is planned without consideration of the liturgical heritage of the church, the practice of the church year, or something of lasting value and a sense of integrity. Instead, novelty is what has too often guided the pastor, parish musician, or worship committee in their pursuit of something relevant and timely that will *really speak to the people.*

Novelty, however, is often the domain of the trite, the shallow, and the temporary, so bound to a particular time or place as to be unusable in any other context. Novelty turns the Gospel itself into something trite and temporary and erodes the very foundation of the faith of the baptized. This is not merely a worship problem but a theological and confessional issue. When the various liturgical texts, forms, and music of the church are replaced with mere novelties, it is the very faith itself which is at risk. Buszin noted this long ago when he wrote that "the integrity of Christian worship will not improve until the intimate relationship between theology and church music has been reestablished and until each student of theology is required to study church music [and the liturgy] before he becomes a pastor." Again:

> Liturgical worship attains its goal best when its music expresses the spirit of the liturgy ... [Too much of] what is heard in the services today is an irrelevant intrusion [into the liturgy]. And, do we think of music [in service to the Word of God] as an agency of the Holy Spirit . . . or do we link song only with purely human pleasure and enjoyment.[20]

---

[19]Quoting Dean William R. Inge in Paul Waitman Hoon, *The Integrity of Worship* (Nashville: Abingdon, 1971), 31.

[20]Walter E. Buszin, "Music in the Life of the Church." Typed doc. N.d.

Why a New Hymnal Now?

Is it creative or is it novel when the Confession and Absolution are moved to a different point in the service? Is it creative or is it novel when homemade ditties are substituted for the great ecumenical creeds of the church? Is it creative or is it novel when the congregation is turned into an assembly of spectators and the primary work of worship is done either by professionals or by volunteers? Is it creative or is it novel when the congregation is kept guessing from week to week as to what will happen when they are gathered together in the Lord's house on the Lord's Day?

Creativity is a powerful word that can and should be used to describe that use of the liturgy and hymns which connects the service together under the theme established by the pericopes and fully uses the options inherent in the liturgy and the musical resources available to the congregation. "Creative" is not an antonym for "traditional." In fact, the traditional liturgy cries out for the wise and faithful planning of the service so that texts, tunes, liturgy, and hymns may work together to support the theme of the lectionary. Just as the Collect does not stand alone but connects the themes of the Lessons together in prayer form, so each part of the liturgy is connected and functions to support the Word of the Lord for that particular Sunday, within the context of that festival or season of the church year.

Genuinely creative worship begins with a commitment on the part of the pastor and the congregation to expend some serious resources in both dollars and energy for the worship life of the parish. This means providing educational resources and teaching that will give understanding to the liturgical heritage of the church and the dollars to provide for competent musicians and musical instruments for worship. Creative worship means a willingness to expend serious time planning in advance for Sunday—the liturgy, the Sermon, and the hymns which come together under the guidance of the propers for the day and its place within the church year. This means setting aside planning days for pastor, parish musician, and, perhaps, worship committee to work together in study and preparation for Sunday morning. Creative worship means knowing the flow of the church year and the weekly rhythm of the Lessons so that each Sunday connects to the previous and future Sundays while at the same time representing a particular and cohesive setting for the Word and the Supper of the Lord on that day. This means a serious program of education for the people in the pew as well as the worship leaders so that the worshipers may appreciate if not understand the full background and meaning of the weekly rhythm of the liturgy as it flows through the church year.

Such creative worship also begins with a much more thorough preparation in the seminary and a deliberate and ongoing process of review and study following the seminary than we have currently enjoyed. It will equip the pastor in his pivotal roles as presider, worship leader, preacher, and teacher—not to author a new service week after week, but to apply carefully and wisely the full resources of the church's liturgical heritage to the present day congregational setting in a manner that is both faithful to the church's confessional standard and effective in the use of its worship options and resources new and old.

Will the Lutheran Church continue to offer the Divine Service in a manner that bears witness to its Confessions? It cannot be a matter of repristinating an unrepeatable past but only of understanding anew the teaching of the Scriptures, the witness of the Confessions, the catholic heritage of the liturgy, and the kind of music that best expresses the spirit of the liturgy and communicates the church's faith. A generation ago, Lutherans were happy to note the recovery of the liturgy among their Protestant brothers and sisters: "The revival of liturgical interest and the imposition of form on near-chaotic worship procedures in some churches is a significant and welcome accent in modern American church life."[21] Now it is our own household that cries out for such renewal and revival. We can do no less.

Several years ago, I walked into K-Mart wearing my clerical collar when a youth approached me. "Are you feeling better," he asked. I had been ill and, although I did not know this young man, I was most appreciative of his concern. "Yes, I am," I responded. "Was it a bad accident?" he asked. "What accident?" I replied. "Well, I assumed you were in a car accident since you are wearing a neck brace," he said. I explained to him that it was not a neck brace but a clerical collar worn by a pastor of the church. After

---

[21]C.E. Huber, *The Lutheran Witness* 81, no. 3 (Feb. 6, 1962): 7.

a few moments of studying the collar, he asked me if it was uncomfortable. "Yes," I replied, "it is a bit uncomfortable." "Then why do you wear it?" he asked. It was time for *me* to think a few moments. I finally answered, "It's the kind of uncomfortable feeling that I'm supposed to feel to remind me that I'm a pastor and that this is how people like you see me."

The liturgy is kind of uncomfortable too, especially in light of our modern day infatuation with the new and different. Yet is it the kind of uncomfortable feeling that we need to feel. Worship is not about us; worship is about God. He invites us into His presence. He attaches Himself to Word and Sacrament in order to be accessible to us. He gives us the rich gifts of His grace which come at the cost of Jesus' suffering and death on the cross. Yes, we do need to feel a bit uncomfortable in His presence. Worship is no casual experience.

However you might feel about Luther's liturgical legacy, it is the careful legacy of a reformer who was both conscious of the great treasures of the past as well as the pastoral need of the present. He was a conservative reformer who was vehement in his condemnation of the accretions to the liturgy that had obscured the Gospel, as well as the liturgical chaos unleashed when pastors and parishes decided to go their own way in liturgical reform. As much as we are reminded of Luther's bold words, "we must dare something in the name of Christ,"[22] we must be careful that what is dared is faithful to Christ and to the church which has proclaimed Him from the first days of Christianity to the present. We carry with us the weight of history, and the church of the future will be shaped either by our callous indifference to our liturgical heritage and its wealth of hymnody or by our slavish devotion to texts and forms to which nothing may be added from the present day. This is the tension in which we live, and it is a creative tension—if not given by God, then allowed by God so that His church will worship Him in spirit and in truth, today and for eternity.

---

[22]Martin Luther, *Formula Missae*, 1523. AE 53:19.

Liturgy, Music and Culture

Holy Ground and Counter-Cultural Music

The People's Song

Liturgy and Culture

THE FIRST ESSAY IN THIS SECTION explores the relationship between theology and music, arguing that the primary function of music in worship is theological proclamation that is shaped by the church year and lectionary. It suggests that the church needs to draw on music from its own creative culture rather than from the secular entertainment industry.

The second essay examines the different types of congregational song. Exactly what is the difference between a hymn and a liturgical song? When is repetition in a melody helpful and when is it not?

The third essay considers some of the missiological issues concerning liturgy and culture. It examines the church's response to an anti-sacramental culture, the task of proclaiming the Gospel to the growing ethnic populations in the United States, and the use of the liturgy and catechesis in mission fields throughout the world.

Holy Ground and Countercultural Music
Or, Save the Polkas for Saturday Night

Daniel A. Zager

THIS ESSAY APPROACHES THE TOPIC OF MUSIC IN WORSHIP WITH THE following questions: "Are there certain styles of music that do not serve the text?" "Are there any criteria that can aid us in determining what is appropriate?" The first of these questions may be asked in slightly more specific terms: "Are there certain styles of music that cannot participate effectively in the theological function of proclaiming the Word of God?" Posing the question in this way reveals an overarching precondition for the discussion of music in the context of Christian worship, namely, that music has the specific function of participating in the proclamation of the Word of God. Robin Leaver conceptualizes this role of music in worship with the following words:

> Its function is to proclaim the word of God to the people of God. Sometimes this is done through the single voice of the cantor or minister, sometimes through the combined voice of choir and instruments, and sometimes through instrumental music alone. And then there is that unique proclamation of the whole people of God when they join their voices in one, in psalmody and hymnody, as they proclaim their response of faith to God and give witness of that faith to each other. All the Church's great composers have understood the proclamatory nature of their art, that through it the eternal sound of God's grace focused in Jesus Christ is made known and shared with his redeemed people.[1]

---

[1] Robin A. Leaver, *The Theological Character of Music in Worship*, Church Music Pamphlet Series, ed. Carl Schalk (St. Louis: CPH, 1989), 11. This essay was first published in *Duty and Delight: Routley Remembered* (Carol Stream, Ill.: Hope Publishing Co., 1985).

The primary function of music in worship is not to entertain those who have gathered or to establish a mood. Rather, proceeding from the dual contexts of church year and lectionary, music takes on the specific function of theological proclamation.

To say that questions of musical style within worship constitute one of the most vexatious areas of current church life would be a colossal understatement. Indeed, much of the current discussion of (one might say fixation on) "church growth" focuses on areas of worship, but devolves finally to considerations of music, where the ensuing discussion is usually framed in terms of "traditional," "contemporary," and "blended." That issues of musical style, framed in such simplistic and ill-defined terms, are at the heart of the church growth industry is a significant indictment of that movement, which is so little concerned with matters theological. "Change your musical style," church growth consultants tell us, "and your attendance will increase."

The Lutheran Church—Missouri Synod is hardly exempt from such matters. To cite only two examples:

The church where this author is currently serving as organist lost two of its three pastors in a period of six months, one by way of retirement and the other by way of a call elsewhere. This circumstance, together with declining attendance, prompted the hiring of a church growth consultant to assist in discussions of staffing and the church's future. The primary reading given the church's leaders during this process was Kennon Callahan's *Twelve Keys to an Effective Church,* from which the following passage was soon quoted by some of the lay leaders:

> If the preaching tends to be complex, comprehensive, and intellectual, then it becomes important that the music be simple, profound and emotional so that a wider range of the spectrum is covered during the course of the worship service.[2]

According to this point of view, the music of worship operates on a vaguely psychological level to complete a spectrum of emotions: intellectual and objective preaching being complemented, in Callahan's view, by simple and more subjective musical expressions. Obviously, this is a

---

[2]Kennon Callahan, *Twelve Keys to an Effective Church* (San Francisco: Harper and Row, 1983), 27.

very different role for music than that of the premise with which we began: that music works on a theological level to complement the proclamation of the Word, determined specifically by the context of the church year and lectionary.

A second example of the situation within The Lutheran Church—Missouri Synod comes from the author's hometown in Wisconsin. A November 1997 newspaper clipping states:

> Immanuel Lutheran Church will have a polka service [on] Sunday. Traditional church hymns will be sung to polka music, and the liturgy will be done to the polka beat. In the past, this service has proven to be a favorite with the many people of German origin in [this] area.

Common to both of these examples is a conscious and calculated use of diverse musical styles that is relatively new to the church's musical life. The first example is illustrative of the church growth phenomenon's impact on the way a church may be led to think about music. If music has only a balancing effect within the service, it stands to reason that virtually any musical style may potentially be useful. If music is to be simple and emotional, as Callahan would have it, popular styles may be preferable, lest the entire service require an active engagement with what is being taught. The second example illustrates that an LCMS congregation has been able to accept the occasional use of an ethnic dance style as the basis for its congregational song, largely because it has proven to be a favorite of a specific ethnic group.

But such a notion, that any musical style may be used in the church, is relatively recent. The generation coming of age in the 1940s had a great love for big band music, exemplified by Glenn Miller, Tommy Dorsey, and others. Yet, it never occurred to Lutherans of that generation to demand such a musical style as a basis for Sunday morning worship. Indeed, they likely would have been scandalized had such a scenario transpired during the 1950s. They would enjoy Lawrence Welk on Saturday night television, but they expected that on Sunday morning they would encounter liturgy and hymnody from the *The Lutheran Hymnal* (1941) the source of the church's song at that point in their history.

One is reminded at this point of a passage from Dietrich Bonhoeffer's *Life Together:*

> It is the voice of the church that is heard in singing together. It is not I who sing, but the church. However, as a member of the church I may share its song. Thus all true singing together must serve to widen our spiritual horizon. It must enable us to recognize our small community as a member of the great Christian church on earth and must help us willingly and joyfully to take our place in the song of the church with our singing, be it feeble or good.[3]

Bonhoeffer's thought resonates at this point, because it suggests that the previous generation had it right. By not demanding or expecting the popular styles of their time in worship, they said, implicitly, it is not we who sing, but the church; we will not demand our own song, because we want to share in the church's song. The situation is vastly different today.

The style-consciousness endemic to the church today derives in large part from the church growth and megachurch movements, which base their evangelism programs around very consciously-chosen styles of worship and music. Such evangelism programs are referred to in different ways: Walt Kallestad refers to "entertainment evangelism," Timothy Wright to "visitor-oriented" or "outreach-oriented" worship, and Sally Morgenthaler to "worship evangelism."[4] While these approaches to worship and music have very quickly made an impact on a broad cross section of American Christianity, their proponents fail to distinguish between worship and evangelism as two important but different activities within the church. They also fail to realize that "pre–Christians," "the unchurched," and "the irreligious" (terms used by Kallestad and Wright to describe their target audiences) cannot worship a God they do not yet know. Some churches are very clear that opportunities for evangelism in a worship-like scenario are not times of worship for believers; the so-called "believer's services" are often relegated to a midweek evening. Thus do we have the ironic situation described by Frank Senn, in which "the

---

[3] Dietrich Bonhoeffer, *Life Together; Prayerbook of the Bible,* Works, vol. 5, ed. Geffrey B. Kelly, trans. Daniel W. Bloesch and James H. Burtness (Minneapolis: Fortress Press, 1996), 68.

[4] Walt Kallestad, *Entertainment Evangelism: Taking the Church Public* (Nashville: Abingdon Press, 1996); Timothy Wright, *A Community of Joy: How to Create Contemporary Worship,* Effective Church Series (Nashville: Abingdon Press, 1994); Sally Morgenthaler, *Worship Evangelism: Inviting Unbelievers into the Presence of God* (Grand Rapids: Zondervan Publishing House, 1995).

Lord's Day is given over to those who do not yet confess themselves to be a part of the Lord's people."[5] The attempt to bring such people into the church through worship (or worship-like activities) apart from catechesis is a matter of enormous confusion, which lies at the heart of the current misuse of music in Christian worship.

What role does music play in such evangelism programs? It is much less a matter of theological proclamation than it is a matter of enticement to an evangelistic event. Wright, a pastor at the Community Church of Joy in Phoenix, believes that music is enormously influential in church growth:

> Contemporary music—pop, rock, country/western, rap—continues to be the heart music of today's generations. As people shop for a church, they look for congregations that value them by valuing their music. In designing worship services attractive to today's generations, no factor has greater impact than the choice of music.[6]

In discussing what he calls "liturgical worship," Wright identifies "several barriers or obstacles to reaching non-churched people, people who are totally unfamiliar with any style of worship"[7] (a premise that might suggest to Wright that perhaps worship is not the appropriate means to reach the unchurched). One of the barriers he articulates is classical music:

> Liturgical worship uses classically oriented music.... However, classical music accounts for only 2 percent of all music sold in the United States. A very small segment of the population listens to it. . . . The generations born after 1946 have forever changed the course of music. By far, their number-one music preference is adult contemporary—the heart language of today's generations. They will not develop a craving for classical music as they age, nor will they mature into it. They will rock and roll to their graves.[8]

These quotations illustrate the style-consciousness of the church growth movement, but they also show how poorly defined is such style-consciousness. Initially, Wright defines contemporary music as pop,

---

[5]Frank C. Senn, *The Witness of the Worshipping Community: Liturgy and the Practice of Evangelism* (New York: Paulist Press, 1993), 3.
[6]Wright, 22.
[7]Ibid., 30.
[8]Ibid., 33.

rock, country/western, and rap. Later, he speaks simply of adult contemporary. Kallestad describes the five weekend services at the Community Church of Joy in terms of their musical style: contemporary country/western, spirited traditional, contemporary blend, new contemporary, and modern contemporary.

Except for explicitly identifying country/western as a separate style, Kallestad couches his discussion in the now familiar terms of "traditional," "contemporary," and "blended." Thus, from the multiplicity of musical styles that members of a congregation may enjoy on their own—Western art music (sometimes referred to as "classical"), jazz, blues, folk, rock, pop, country/western, rap, new age, and various ethnic musics—the church has essentially been given two poorly-labeled choices, dubbed "traditional" and "contemporary" ("blended" presumably occupying a middle ground between the two). In this sense, when discussing the appropriateness of various musical styles for worship, one need not deal with each individual style or type of music in Western culture. But more importantly, to interrogate classical, jazz, blues, folk, rock, pop, country/western, rap, new age, and ethnic musics individually for their potential appropriateness to Christian worship is to begin from the wrong vantage point. The point of departure must rather be theology, not musical style. One should ask, in other words, what does theology require of music, instead of asking what a particular style of music might have to offer.

What criteria can help to determine what is appropriate? First, music must find its meaning in theology, especially as defined for any given Sunday by the church year and the lectionary. Leaver comments:

> We need to speak about the reciprocal relation between theology and music. It is when the two are divorced that problems arise. Cut off from its theological roots music in worship takes on the nature of music to entertain the congregation, mood music to create the right atmosphere.[9]

Second, music rooted in theology, like theology itself, must be countercultural; and it must assist the church in perceiving that she stands on holy ground. As Pastor Harold Senkbeil remarks:

---

[9]Leaver, 9.

Holy Ground and Countercultural Music

> Liturgical worship is the historic way the church has chosen to acknowledge the profound mystery of God's presence in its midst. These forms of worship may indeed seem unnatural to some, but this is the way the church removes its shoes; the place on which it stands is holy ground (Exodus 3:5).[10]

As we "acknowledge the profound mystery of God's presence in our midst"—in Word and Sacrament—we do so in ways that differ from other moments in our lives, including times of work or recreation. Music may also play a part in such other moments: the sheer pleasure of hearing a creative and virtuosic jazz improvisation at a concert, the marching band music that may accompany an athletic event, or the music heard privately through the headphones of a Walkman (which may help to make repetitive work or a long airline trip pass somewhat more quickly). Almost everyone listens to a variety of music, for various purposes, in widely differing contexts. The notion that virtually any music from any of these contexts can also function in Christian worship is asserted widely within the church today. Kallestad, for example, states that he chooses music for worship that is "similar to the kinds of music people listen to all week long,"[11] a point of view that fails to recognize that the people of a congregation listen to all kinds of different music throughout the week. Kallestad greatly underestimates the diversity of musical tastes and interests inherent in any group of people, including Christian congregations. More to the point, however, he fails to realize that, as people encounter "the profound mystery of God's presence in their midst," they need something other than "the kinds of music they listen to all week long." They need to realize that in worship they are on holy ground; and just as Moses was told to remove his sandals, so they do well to divest themselves of "the music they listen to all week long," whether that music is country/western, rock, or Beethoven string quartets. Instead, Christians open themselves up to the church's music— music that finds its meaning in the dual contexts of the church year and

---

[10]Harold L. Senkbeil, *Sanctification: Christ in Action, Evangelical Challenge and Lutheran Response* (Milwaukee: Northwestern Publishing House, 1989), 179. See also his more recent *Dying to Live: The Power of Forgiveness* (St. Louis: CPH, 1994), 128–29.

[11]Kallestad, 64.

lectionary; music that is bequeathed from the past, as well as music recently created by the church's best composers; music that inevitably speaks various stylistic languages, because it comes from the church's own diverse cultures; music that is finally countercultural with respect to those musics encountered "all week long."

Christian theology, when proclaimed faithfully on the basis of the inspired writings of the Old and New Testaments, runs very much counter to late 20th-century ways of thinking. Modern culture values "achievers" (even "overachievers") who are well-educated, highly motivated, and hard working. Citizens of this culture strive for and may find success in their work and, consequently, perhaps, in their personal financial rewards. But the countercultural message of the church says that 1) successes come only from the hand of a gracious God, who provides education, jobs, and money; and 2) none of these successes will result in eternal life. While the church hardly disparages education, hard work, or financial success, it points to eternal realities and reveals that "successes" stand for nothing in that context. In Christ, however, is a love so compelling that, as O.P. Kretzmann once wrote, "He preferred to die rather than be without us."[12] But that is not the stuff of late 20th-century American culture.

In a recent article, "Lutheranism as Countercultural? The Doctrine of Justification and Consumer Capitalism," Robert A. Kelly poses this central issue: "How to live a 'doctrine of justification' way of life in the midst of a culture that opposes such a way." He goes on to write:

> The number one item of discussion should not revolve around "church growth," "spirituality," or "the public square," but around the question of what our way of life would look like if we really believed with all our hearts and minds that God has spoken an unconditional promise to us in Christ. This promise does not just make pursuing success North American style pointless, but reveals the ideology that supports such a quest as demonic.[13]

---

[12] O.P. Kretzmann, in *Festschrift Theodore Hoelty-Nickel, A Collection of Essays on Church Music*, ed. Newman W. Powell (Valparaiso, Ind.: Valparaiso University, 1967), v. [Cited in Leaver.]

[13] Robert A. Kelly, "Lutheranism as a Counterculture? The Doctrine of Justification and Consumer Capitalism," *Currents in Theology and Mission*, 24 (December 1997): 497.

Holy Ground and Countercultural Music

It is impossible to believe that the proclamation of a countercultural theology may be complemented by music that is "similar to the kinds of music people listen to all week long." This very similarity makes it all the more difficult to detach the people from the predominant culture and introduce them to "the 'doctrine of justification' way of life."

Specifically, with respect to music, the notion of countercultural theology is not a thinly-veiled attempt (as critics might have it) to maintain a sort of status quo tradition, perhaps devoted to the 17th- and 18th-century music of northern Europe. Nor is it an attempt to define a single style of music for use in the church. The church has through the ages embraced an astonishing diversity of musical styles for its song: chant, the German chorale, metrical psalmody, the enormous repertory of English hymns, American folk hymnody, black spirituals, Taizé hymns, Gelineau psalmody—to name only a few. For the church to use countercultural music is simply to rely upon the full multiplicity of the church's traditions, and to draw on the music created by the church's finest living composers. To call on the church to use countercultural music is to state emphatically that the church's music is not to be rooted in the music of adult contemporary or soft rock radio stations, but that it is to be rooted in the church's own vital and varied traditions, of both the distant and the very recent past. To call on the church to use countercultural music is to require the church to draw widely on various traditions; Lutherans will seek out the best of Roman Catholic psalmody, of hymnody by Marty Haugen, David Haas, Michael Joncas, and others. Catholics (and other denominations as well) will look to Lutherans for the hymnody of Jaroslav Vajda and Carl Schalk, just as Lutheran chorales have long since become a staple in most Christian hymnals. Drawing on the full spectrum of the church's varied musical traditions, both historic and current, is very different from offering the people of our parishes country/western services, polka services, or adult contemporary/easy listening/soft rock-influenced styles. The latter is particularly in favor these days, and is perhaps particularly misguided, for it fails to engender that sense of holy ground. Indeed, it seeks to do just the opposite—to bring the predominant musical culture into the sanctuary, where, instead of encountering "the profound mystery of God's presence in our midst," as Senkbeil terms it, the music points us back only to ourselves, to our favorites from an entertainment, "feel good" culture.

To summarize: all too frequently of late, the church is engaging in a misguided attempt to draw "the irreligious" and "the unchurched" into her sanctuaries by providing an informal worship style filled with music that is "similar to the kinds of music people listen to all week long." This proposition fails in its expectation that the unchurched can either actively worship a God they do not yet know or passively encounter that God through entertainment. This proposition fails, as well, in its expectation that "the irreligious" should come to us, that they should fill our sanctuaries. Instead, we must realize that we need to go out to them. There are no fish to be caught on the shore; we must go out into the deep waters where the fish are to be found, as a Gospel appointed for the Fifth Sunday after the Epiphany (Luke 5:1–11) reminds us. The church must assert that there is a difference between evangelism and worship. Evangelism reaches out to all those who, in the beautiful words of the Bidding Prayer from the Christmas service of Nine Lessons and Carols, "know not the Lord Jesus, or love Him not. . . ." Worship is different than evangelism; it is the one activity to which Christians are privileged both here and in the world to come. Finally, the church must be reminded that unbelievers are brought to faith not through worship as much as they are brought into contact with the Word of God in an active program of catechesis. The best outreach will look to catechesis rather than to music.

With Phillip Pfatteicher we must renew our understanding of the liturgy as the school of the church.[14] In our liturgical worship we need to foster musical expressions that are rooted in the church year and lectionary, thus taking on specific meaning and participating in the proclamation of theology. We must privilege meaning rather than style when considering music for the sanctuary. We must cease the current fixation on musical styles.

We must seek musical expressions that come from the church's most talented poets and composers, insisting on texts of great theological

---

[14]Phillip H. Pfatteicher, *The School of the Church: Worship and Christian Formation* (Valley Forge, Pa.: Trinity Press International, 1995).

Holy Ground and Countercultural Music

integrity, clothed in music that is always well-crafted. Instead of seeking music rooted in an adult contemporary or soft-rock idiom, we must seek music having its origins in the church's own creative cultures, music that does not find an analog on today's radio airwaves. In this sense, we walk a narrow line, guided by the church's best musicians. We look forward to singing the hymns and liturgies of Marty Haugen, while realizing that the music of Amy Grant is best reserved for entertainment—whether in the form of private listening or in the public concert arena. We must not be afraid to make such distinctions. We need to complement a countercultural theology with countercultural music. After all, worship—complemented by its music—occurs on holy ground; and we come, not to be entertained, but to be separated from the commonplace and to encounter the divine presence of God.

The People's Song
What Distinguishes a Hymn from a Liturgical Song?

Kent A. Tibben

To speak of the "people's song" is to speak of that song which is sung by the baptized, by those who have been given to drink of the one Spirit and who, by the power of that Spirit, confess one faith and one Lord (1 Cor. 12:13; Eph. 4:4–6).

When the baptized are assembled in the presence of their Lord to receive and extol His gifts, there is singing. As Luther says, "God has made our hearts and spirits happy through His dear Son. . . . He who believes this sincerely and earnestly cannot help but be happy; he must cheerfully sing."[1]

This song of the people of God may belong to one of three different categories: hymnody, liturgical song, and liturgical chant. This essay discusses the differences between hymns and liturgical songs, beginning with a rather summary definition of each.[2]

A "hymn" is a song of praise to God. The text of a hymn consists of one or more stanzas of sacred poetry, usually employing meter and rhyme. Each stanza is sung to the same tune. A hymn may be sung in the context of the liturgy, but the hymn itself is not a standard part of the historic liturgy.

A "liturgical song" carries the standard prose texts of the historic liturgy. It may or may not employ a musical meter, but a liturgical song always does have a consistent beat to organize its rhythmic flow.

---

[1] Cited by Carl Schalk, *Music in Lutheran Worship*, Church Music Pamphlet Series, Carl Schalk, ed. (St. Louis: CPH, 1983), 6; cf. AE 53:333.

[2] Dr. Paul Bunjes discusses the various types of congregational song in *LWHP*, 536ff.

So, what are the differences between a hymn and a liturgical song, and what significance do these differences have in planning for a new hymnal? The most notable difference is found by comparing the overall form of each song type. Vocal music may be composed in strophic form, in which the same melody is repeated for each stanza of text; in a modified strophic form, in which the melody is repeated for each stanza but with slight modifications; or in a through-composed form, in which the melody is not repeated but is different throughout the setting of the text.[3]

The vast majority of hymns (though not quite all) are composed in strophic form: the same tune is repeated for each stanza of text. By contrast, the liturgical songs in Divine Service II, in both settings, are all through-composed (with the exception of "This is the Feast"); thus, the melody is not repeated but different throughout each of these songs.

To what end these observations? One difference between a hymn and a liturgical song is the amount of repetition occurring in each. And repetition, it has been said, is the mother of learning. In a hymn there is much repetition, and of different kinds. The fact that most hymns have a number of stanzas sung to the same tune means that a congregation will most likely become familiar with a hymn tune more quickly. For in the singing of any given hymn, the people of God have repeated opportunities to master the tune. In addition, many hymn tunes repeat certain musical phrases or motifs within each stanza, and both the repetition and the ease of learning are thereby increased.[4] The repetition of text is likewise significant. So, for example, many hymns make use of textual refrains that either frame the hymn or follow each verse.[5]

---

[3]Willi Apel, *Harvard Dictionary of Music*, 2nd ed. (Cambridge: The Belknap Press of Harvard University Press, 1969), s.v. "Through-composed."

[4]*LW*, no. 72, "The Only Son from Heaven" and no. 141 "Come You Faithful Raise the Strain" are excellent examples of hymns that repeat entire musical phrases. *LW*, no. 214, "Isaiah, Mighty Seer, in Spirit Soared" and no. 107, "The Death of Jesus Christ, Our Lord" have an identical rhythmic pattern for each phrase of the hymn even though the pitches of each phrase of the melody are different.

[5]Examples of hymns with refrains include *LW*, no. 40, "Oh, Rejoice, All Christians Loudly," no. 140, "This Joyful Eastertide," and no. 55, "Angels We Have Heard on High."

The liturgical song, on the other hand, does not have the same amount or kinds of repetition. As already indicated, the liturgical songs in the two settings of Divine Service II (except "This is the Feast") are through-composed. That is to say, the text is not set into stanzas, and the tune is not repeated but is new for each phrase of the text. Furthermore, there is (generally) very little repetition of musical phrases and motifs within the melody of a liturgical song.[6]

However, liturgical song does enjoy a repetition that is not afforded most hymnody: the repetition of weekly use throughout the church year. Most hymns are typically sung only a few times each year (with the possible exception of Lord's Supper hymns). But liturgical songs are sung throughout the year, the frequency depending on the number of liturgical orders being used by a congregation.

What does this mean for us in the planning of a new hymnal, especially with regard to the people's song? We must be mindful that learning liturgical song takes longer because it is through-composed and lacks internal repetition. It is not so quickly or easily learned as a hymn. This may account for the almost immediate popularity of "This is the Feast," a liturgical song that is far more hymn-like in its form (strophic, with a refrain) and, therefore, more easily learned and more popular.[7]

We must remember that congregations are largely comprised of amateur singers. If they find the learning of new hymns difficult, in spite of their great repetition, one can well imagine the challenge they face when presented with a new liturgical song. Frustration levels grow quickly in a congregation when new liturgical orders are thrust upon them, especially when those orders are not introduced and taught with great patience, explanation, and modeling.

Perhaps the composers of liturgical song could employ more internal repetition, patterns of melody and rhythm that might assist the learning and retention of these songs by congregations. But that is not

---

[6] The Agnus Dei from Divine Service II/1 repeats the first phrase musically as well as textually. The Gloria in Excelsis from Divine Service II/2 has instances where two or three measures are repeated musically.

[7] Several recent Protestant hymnals include "This is the Feast" in their hymn sections.

to suggest the use of repetition solely for its own sake. The repetition of something that lacks musical quality and integrity soon becomes tiresome and annoying (as anyone subjected to the endless repetition of the "Macarena" knows).

We should also be sensitive to the frequency with which any given liturgy might realistically be used. There are some that simply don't (and won't) enjoy the repetition of weekly use throughout the year. For example, most congregations probably use the various liturgies of evening prayer only rarely, perhaps during Advent and Lent (if even then). Consequently, due to the sheer lack of repetition, it is more difficult to learn the liturgical songs of those orders. The same problem might also occur with some of the morning liturgies. For example, one of the potential casualties of weekly Communion might be the congregational singing of Matins and Morning Prayer.

What should prevent us from discontinuing the use of liturgical song altogether and casting the people's song entirely in the form of hymns? The answer is the text. Composers, both sacred and secular, have used a through-composed form to serve the text that they are setting. And that, after all, is the point of sacred music: to serve the text. The composer of strophic hymn tunes is able, at best, only to match the general spirit of the entire hymn. But the composer of a through-composed liturgical song is able to develop the music of each phrase, even individual words, setting the text it in a way that best serves the proclamation of each particular Word of God.[8]

Furthermore, if liturgical song were restricted to a strophic form, the historic texts of the liturgy—many of which have been lifted verbatim from the Holy Scriptures—would have to be paraphrased. They would have to be changed in various ways to fit the straight jacket of a textual meter. Of course, there are many fine paraphrases of the ordinary

---

[8]The Agnus Dei from Divine Service II/2 is an excellent example of how the through-composed form is used in service to the text. Each successive plea to the Lamb of God is taken to a higher pitch level and thus gives the distinct impression of a cry for mercy that increases in its fervency and intensity. Likewise, in the Gloria in Excelsis from Divine Service II/1, the music ascends, appropriately, on the words "You are seated at the right hand. . . ." and "You alone are the Most High. . . ."

of the mass, the Psalms, and the major canticles. And no one questions the intention of those who craft these paraphrases to preserve the integrity of the scriptural and/or liturgical texts and the truth proclaimed in them. But it would still be a great loss, if—having just received the body and blood of Jesus—the church were nevermore allowed to join with Simeon in singing the very words of the Nunc Dimittis that he sang to the Lord as he cradled the Savior in his arms. And it would be a loss, if the children never learned to sing the actual Magnificat of Mary but only a metrical paraphrase of it. And if one of the benefits of the liturgy is the etching of God's Word upon the hearts and minds of His people, then the preservation of His texts (as He has given them) becomes an important consideration. Liturgical song allows those texts to be preserved and sung in their original form.

There is indeed a place for paraphrase, as well. So, for example, our present hymnals include many paraphrases of liturgical texts penned by Luther himself (those written for his *German Mass*). And our present hymnals include, as well, various paraphrases of the Psalms and canticles. But none of these have replaced the original Psalms, canticles, or the ancient liturgical texts.

Which raises one final question. Is there a need for uniformity in translation? Are we not placing obstacles in the way of learning when we have more than one translation of the Nunc Dimittis, the Te Deum Laudamus, and the Gloria in Excelsis within the same hymnal? Here Luther's advice in his preface to the Small Catechism applies. To paraphrase Luther: "Find one translation and stick to it."

Selecting the specific items to be included in the repertoire of song for the people of God is a daunting task, especially in our day. Let us pray for God's blessing on those who undertake that task, in order that we may continue to "raise to Christ a mighty song, and shout His name, His glories tell" (*LW* 83:4).

Liturgy and Culture
Can the Liturgy Be Made to Reflect a Particular Culture?

Naomichi Masaki

Missiological Issues in Liturgy and Culture

THE TOPIC "LITURGY AND CULTURE" IS A BROAD, AND YET VERY IMPORTANT topic. Both liturgy and culture comprise an organic whole so that they cannot be so easily separated. "Liturgy" has a "culture"—that is, a heavenly culture. On the other hand, human culture involves both worship and liturgy.

Since my beloved professors at the seminaries, whom I respect and regard as my catechists and teachers, have already spoken and written much on this topic, and I assume that an audience such as this has already read and heard them, I am not going to repeat what they have already said.[1] Likewise, cultural diagnosis and the problems with so-called post-modernism, as well as the very important study of ritual behaviors,[2] also will not be included in my short paper. Nor will I speak

---

[1] Among numerous resources, see Kurt E. Marquart, *Liturgy and Culture* (Fort Wayne, Ind.: Divine Service Institute, St. Paul Lutheran Church, 1996), audiocassette; Dean O. Wenthe, "Entrance into the Biblical World: The First and Crucial Cross-Cultural Move," *Logia* 4, no. 2 (1995): 19–24; John W. Kleinig, *The Function of Hymnody in its Cultural Context* (Fort Wayne, Ind.: Concordia Theological Seminary, 1998), audiocassette; and David S. Yeago, "Messiah's People: The Culture of the Church in the Midst of the Nations," *Pro Ecclesia* 4 (Spring 1997): 146–171. See also *Liturgy Digest* 3, no. 2 (1996), which devotes its entire issue to liturgy and culture; this is a publication of the Notre Dame Center for Pastoral Liturgy.

[2] John W. Kleinig, "Witting or Unwitting Ritualists," *Lutheran Theological Journal* 22 (May 1988): 13–22, makes an important point regarding Lutheran worship and rituals on

from the standpoint of linguistic theory or cultural anthropology. Rather, I would like to speak concerning a few concrete, missiological issues relating to our topic of liturgy and culture.

The missiological aspect of liturgy and culture is very important to the future formation of a hymnal because, as Wilhelm Loehe said, the church is always in motion.³ Scriptures testify that there is a movement from the Father to the Son to the apostles to the office of the holy ministry and to all people. This is the motif of "sending" (ἀπόστολος/שָׁלִיחַ), wherein the Holy Spirit delivers the forgiveness of sins achieved by Christ. When the sequence is disrupted at one point or another, the motion stops and the Holy Spirit is rejected. Thus, missiology and liturgiology are never unrelated to each other. Rather, in the final analysis, both point to the same goal of bringing people to baptism, then to

---

p. 19: "The Augsburg Confession defines the Church ritually. It maintains that, since faith is created through the ministry of the Gospel in Word and sacrament, the unity of the church is constituted by their proper administration. The Word and sacraments are the ritual means by which God's Spirit works in us and all Christians. These holy things make and keep us holy. With this emphasis on the means of grace with their interplay between word and action, the Lutheran Church can therefore never minimize or avoid ritual. It has generally avoided the anti-ritualist temptation to base the church on something subjective, such as the experience of conversion, or on some charismatic manifestation. Rather, it has traditionally defined membership in the church ritually, by speaking of baptized and communicant membership. Pastorally speaking, it has always regarded participation in the Lord's Supper as the best human measure of spiritual health."

³Wilhelm Loehe, *Three Books about the Church* (Philadelphia: Fortress Press, 1969), 59. To quote more fully, Loehe says: "For mission is nothing but the one church of God in motion, the actualization of the one universal, catholic church.... Mission is the life of the catholic church. Where it stops, blood and breath stop; where it dies, the love which unites heaven and earth also dies. The catholic church and mission—these two no one can separate without killing both, and that is impossible." Werner Elert, *Structure of Lutheranism* (St. Louis: CPH, 1962), 390, concurs, affirming that this statement of Loehe was "exactly what Luther thought." In fact, Elert says that the church *is* motion. William C. Weinrich, "Evangelism in the Early Church," *Concordia Theological Quarterly* 45 (Jan.–April 1981): 61–62, further notes: "To reflect upon 'mission' or upon 'evangelism' is to reflect upon the Church itself, for the act of mission or evangelism is not accidental or coincidental to the Church ... but the act of mission belongs to the very 'core' of what it means to be the Church.... The Church evangelized because it could not do otherwise...."

"heaven on earth" (the Lord's Supper) where they can receive the gift from the crucified and risen Jesus Himself.

There are at least three specific missiological issues to be included in our discussion of liturgy and culture. The first is the question as to how the church's liturgy should relate to an increasingly pagan culture here in the United States. There are a number of scholars who suggest that we need to learn from the history of pre-Constantinian Christianity. They suggest that this present culture of ours shares more in common with the cultural and social environment of the second and third centuries than that of the 16th century onward. I believe that Americans themselves would be better equipped to assess this notion than a stranger from Japan like I am—except to add that Japan has always experienced a situation similar to the cultural and religious condition of the early centuries of Christianity.

The second important issue to consider is the great variety of missionary situations in this country. We know that in America the populations of African-, Hispanic-, and Asian-Americans are increasing much faster than those of white, English-speaking origins. The LCMS serves in these "mission fields" of North America among such diverse peoples as Native Americans, Chinese, Koreans, Hmong, African immigrants, Muslims, Jews, and, yes, even the Japanese. Many congregations have Divine Services in more than one language. How should the church respond to this diverse situation when it comes to producing a hymnal for the future? Should we leave everything in the hands of the various mission departments? What should the liturgy of these North American mission fields look like?

The third critical issue regarding liturgy and culture is that of overseas missionary work. The question is: how should the new people of God in different cultures worship?[4]

---

[4]One attempt at discussing this issue appears in Todd E. Roeske, "Christian Worship in a Cross-Cultural Setting," *Missio Apostolica* 5 (May 1997): 19–33. See also John T. Pless, "Six Theses on Liturgy and Evangelism," *Concordia Theological Quarterly* 52 (January 1988): 41–52; and Kurt E. Marquart, *"Church Growth" as Mission Paradigm: A Lutheran Assessment*, A Luther Academy Monograph (Houston, Tex.: Our Savior Lutheran Church, 1994), 107–108, notes: "When a missionary plants a church in a culture in which

Through the Church the Song Goes On

Some Japanese corporations are doing very well throughout the world—Sony, Toyota, and Honda to name a few. Young Japanese executives in northern New Jersey have told me that these companies design their products according to the findings of their careful and thorough marketing research. For example, when Sony designs a "Walkman," they make rather simple and inexpensive models to sell here in this country because people in America like to use their Walkmans while they jog or work out. A Walkman in Japan, on the other hand, is a much more sophisticated piece of equipment. In Japan, companies gain respect from customers by demonstrating their ability to produce an ever tinier Walkman. In Japan, the Honda Accord is a completely different model in size and design than in North America or, for that matter, in Europe. While the Accord in Japan is narrower and more "high-tech oriented," the American Accord is longer, wider, and smoother.

Should the church imitate these corporations in order to be "successful" and to satisfy more of the people? Of course not! What, then, should the liturgy in our foreign mission fields look like? Do we really want to leave it to the discernment of the new Christians there? Are we to be satisfied when only small Bible study groups are started here and there?[5] Should conversion and baptism conclude our missionary activi-

---

there has not been a church before, he also brings the liturgy, above all the Service of Word and Sacrament. He cannot start from scratch, or leave it to chance or local whim, while perhaps thinking that he must devote himself to more urgent tasks, such as evangelism and catechesis. The church is not planted until there is a regular assembly around the Word and Sacrament of Christ, and that requires the liturgy. Since the liturgy is the confession of the church in the form of worship, it will require the same care as catechesis. The missionary will therefore normally implant in the new church, at least in embryo, the liturgy of the church which sent him."

[5] Justo L. Gonzalez, *The Story of Christianity: The Early Church to the Dawn of the Reformation* (New York: HarperCollins Publishers, 1984), 1:11, notes concerning the Judaism of the first century that the best-equipped group to survive after the destruction of the Temple was the Pharisees. It is interesting to observe the relationship between the loss of the Temple (God's dwelling place) and their legalistic beliefs. One may consequently observe that when a church loses the Lord's Supper together with the preaching of the pure Gospel, it is in grave danger of falling into a life governed by the Law. Without receiving the Lord's gifts from the outside, the Gospel does not have space to flow into the life of the baptized.

ties?⁶ Or do we want to teach the historic liturgy with its reverence, beauty, and theological depth and to proclaim the Gospel through it?

These issues and questions are very critical because liturgy is the bridge between Christology and ecclesiology. Ecclesiology is not simply the result of Christology but rather is shaped through the liturgy. If the ecclesiology of a given mission field does not look liturgical, then the Christology of its churches, and most likely of the sending church, will not be liturgical either.⁷ Vilmos Vajta left us some commonplace but rather profound words: "A person's picture of God determines his idea of worship."⁸ The LCMS, as a sending church, has an enormous responsibility in terms of its theology of worship and mission.

God in Human Flesh: The Body of Christ

Is there a common cultural threat to the liturgy in these three situations: multicultural congregations, churches in the mission fields of North America, and the church in foreign lands? If so, what is it? The answer, I would submit, is this: an anti-sacramental culture.

Let me begin to explain by considering Ignatius of Antioch, Martin Luther, and an example from Japan. I am interested, first of all, in Ignatius because he was an early bishop of Antioch where Christians first entered into a completely new culture—that is, a Hellenistic world.

---

⁶The so-called "Great Commission" text of Matthew 28:16–20 describes the office of the holy ministry (v. 16) in connection with baptism and catechesis. But the text and its context likewise point to Jesus' presence in the eucharistic assembly (v. 20). Arthur A. Just, *Luke,* Concordia Commentary, 2 vols. (St. Louis: CPH, 1996), 1:4–10, observes that evangelism contains as its goal the enrollment into the process of initiation, which begins with catechesis and culminates in Baptism and the Lord's Supper. This is the sequence found in all four Gospels. Missionary activities should not cease before the Eucharist is celebrated regularly with reverence and profound joy. Missionaries are there as catechists to teach the people and to deliver to them the riches of the Sacrament.

⁷The mission field churches tend to be shaped by the sending church's theology and practice. The point of importance is the central place of the means of grace in the life of the church. One does not confess the church out of one's confession of Christ. Rather, one's confession of the church results from one's confession of the means of grace, as will be demonstrated below.

⁸Vilmos Vajta, *Luther on Worship: An Interpretation,* trans. U.S. Leupold (Philadelphia: Muhlenberg Press, 1958), 3.

Ignatius understood the church to be very concrete, having locatedness and visibility. To paraphrase Ignatius' words in his letter to the Smyrnaeans: if one wants to find where the church is, he will find it where the bishop is. If one wishes to find the bishop, he will find him where the Eucharist is going on (Smyr. 8:2). Ignatius knew that even after the resurrection, Jesus lived in the flesh (Smyr. 3:1). But the flesh of Jesus is the Eucharist (Smyr. 7:1). Therefore, as one receives the body and blood of Christ, he becomes one with Him. In other words, Ignatius conceived of the church as the Body of Christ.[9] By receiving the very flesh of Jesus, the church participates in His passion and resurrection and becomes one body with Him. The Eucharist is life itself—"the medicine of immortality, and the antidote that wards off death but yields continuous life in union with Jesus Christ" (Ign. to Eph. 20:2). And since the bishop is the Lord's instrument as a "sent one," that is, the one who is put into the office of the holy ministry, the church recognizes him as the Lord Himself (Ign. to Eph. 6:1; Mag. 3:1, 6:1, Smyr. 8:2).[10]

---

[9] Hermann Sasse, *We Confess the Sacraments* (St. Louis: CPH, 1985), 143–144, observes that Paul first learned the idea of the church as the body of Christ by frequent participation in the Lord's Supper at Antioch. J.N.D. Kelly, *Early Christian Doctrines*, rev. ed. (New York: HarperCollins Publishers, 1978), 189, 401–406, notes that after Ignatius, the early church fathers constantly used this phrase.

[10] The accent is not on the right and privilege of the bishop as ruler or "boss" in the church. Rather, the opposite is the point. Hermann Sasse, *We Confess the Church* (St. Louis: CPH, 1986), 25, urges one to seek the Holy Spirit where He is found: "As God outside of Christ always remains the hidden God, so His Holy Spirit remains hidden from us unless we find Him in the Word and in the Sacraments. And just as the revelation of God in Christ is at the same time God's hiding in the human nature of Christ, so the Holy Spirit of God is deeply hidden in the means of grace. He is always an object of faith, not of sight." Sasse's point is that the Holy Spirit is located in His delivering of the forgiveness through the mouth of His servants. The office of the holy ministry exists even before a specific person is put into it—e.g., the Apostle Matthias in Acts 1:20 whose ἐπισκοπή existed prior to his election as an apostle. Just as the Holy Spirit reveals Christ while remaining Himself unrevealed, so the bishop (pastor), who is put into office at his ordination, points to Christ and delivers the benefit of His cross while remaining himself unrecognized. The importance of the office of the holy ministry is for the baptized to receive Christ with certainty. The minister remains anonymous as the Lord's official servant and "sent-one."

Where did Ignatius learn this theology? It did not originate with himself, but, as Norman Nagel demonstrates, he learned it from the liturgy of the church at Antioch (cf., Mag. 1:2).[11] The liturgy that Ignatius knew goes back to the liturgy in which Paul participated, which in turn reaches back to the Church of Jerusalem (Acts 11:19–26, 13:2–4; 1 Cor. 11:23 ff., 15:3 ff.). Jerome Crowe suggests that only when the disciples of Jesus came to a Hellenistic city—Antioch, for instance—did they became distinguishable from the Jews of the day.[12] The new people of God worshiped not only one God, but Jesus. People noticed this when they realized that the Christians worshiped Jesus by way of the Eucharist. For this reason, disciples were called "Christians" for the first time in history (Acts 11:26). For Ignatius and those who followed his theology, the church was the body of Christ—that is, the eucharistic assembly.

Turning to Luther and the Lutheran Confessions, we find the same expression in many places.[13] Ian D. Kingston Siggins observes that Luther is "less comfortable (and less clear) when he moves from the concrete to the abstract, from the historical to the ideal, from the practical to the theoretical."[14] Luther saw the church very concretely. Likewise, when the Augsburg Confession defines the church as "the assembly of all believers," the stress is not on man's act of gathering but on the liturgy where the Lord gives His gifts: "among whom the Gospel is preached in its purity and the holy Sacraments are administered according to the Gospel."[15]

---

[11]See Norman E. Nagel, "Medicine of Immortality and Antidote against Death," *Logia* 4 (Reformation/October 1995): 32. Werner Elert, *Eucharist and Church Fellowship in the First Four Centuries*, trans. N.E. Nagel (St. Louis: CPH, 1966), 40, also maintains that the liturgy was constructed not according to theological insights, but rather theological insights grew out of the liturgy.

[12]Jerome Crowe, *From Jerusalem to Antioch: The Gospel Across Cultures* (Collegeville, Minn.: The Liturgical Press, 1997), 126–127.

[13]For example, see Martin Luther, "Confession Concerning Christ's Supper, 1528," AE 37:367. See also Ap VII/VIII, 5, 12; Ap X, 3.

[14]Ian D. Kingston Siggins, *Martin Luther's Doctrine of Christ*, (New Haven: Yale University Press, 1970), 1–2.

[15]For Luther, Matt. 18:20, "where two or three are gathered together in My name, there am I in the midst of them," means the same thing as AC VII. The emphasis is on the specific locatedness of the Lord at work in the liturgy (see Martin Luther, "Lectures on Genesis," AE 5:247). Rather than conceiving the church "from below" (subjective), Luther and the Lutheran Confessions understand the church "from above" (objective).

While Ignatius and Irenaeus gave only one mark of the church, that is, Christ or the Spirit respectively,[16] Luther provides seven in his "On the Councils and the Church": the preaching of the Gospel, Holy Baptism, the Sacrament of the Altar, the Keys, the office of the holy ministry, the liturgy, and the cross (Christian suffering).[17] This is not because he was such a poor systematician, but because Luther could not leave out anything through which Christ comes and gives His gifts to the church. He knew that Christ gives His gifts "without measure" (John 3:34). One of the common characteristics in all seven of Luther's "marks" is the emphasis on the recipient, not the officiant. For example, Luther writes that the Sacrament "belongs to him who receives it, not to him who administers it, unless he also receives it." The office of the holy ministry is given "not to him who has the office, but to him who is to receive it through this office, except that he can receive it together with you if he so desires."[18] By these seven marks of the church, Luther humbly confessed that he and the church are only on the receiving end of the Lord's gifts.

Both Ignatius and Luther understood the church Christologically—that is, incarnationally. Their Christology guided their ecclesiology by means of the liturgy. Just as the liturgy of Ignatius goes back to Jerusalem through Paul and John and other New Testament writings, Luther's liturgical theology and practice go back to the same. They all knew that only in the flesh of Christ are heaven and earth joined togeth-

---

[16]There is an interesting contrast between Ignatius and Irenaeus. While for Ignatius the church is found where Christ is, and Christ is found where the bishop presides at the Eucharist, for Irenaeus the church is where the Spirit is (*Against Heresies*, 3, 24, 1). Irenaeus did not, however, abandon the incarnational aspect. The full phrase goes as follows: "'For in the Church,' it is said, 'God hath set apostles, prophets, teachers,' and all the other means through which the Spirit works. . . . For where the Church is, there is the Spirit of God; and where the Spirit of God is, there is the Church, and every kind of grace; but the Spirit is truth. Those, therefore, who do not partake of Him, are neither nourished into life from the mother's beasts, nor do they enjoy that most limpid fountain which issues from the body of Christ." As translated in Alexander Roberts and James Donaldson, eds., *The Ante-Nicene Fathers*, American Reprint of the Edinburgh Edition (Grand Rapids, Mich.: Wm. B. Eerdmans Publishing Company, 1996), 1:458.

[17]AE 41:3–178.

[18]Ibid., 152, 156.

er. Because of His flesh, Christ and the church are united with all the company of heaven at the table of the Lord.

Ignatius recognized the threat of Gnosticism, and Luther encountered the dangers of Enthusiasm. But what about us today? Satan does his best to diminish Christ's incarnation in the church because he knows so well that the flesh of Jesus is life itself, and that through the ever-fresh baptismal waters, the living voice of Jesus, and the reception of His very body and blood at the Eucharist, life itself is given out to the faithful with forgiveness and salvation.

Satan's tactics are the same today. We observe a manifestation of the practice of non-incarnational theology among us with such slogans as "everyone a minister" and "every Christian a missionary,"[19] not to mention church growth theory and church-marketing strategies. The single greatest threat against the church today (and always) is the temptation to forsake His flesh and the enfleshed life—the body of Christ at the Lord's Supper enlivening the body of Christ, the church.

The Flesh of Christ and Japanese Religiosity

An example from Japan may further illustrate the constant efforts of Satan to lead people away from the flesh of Christ. The children of Israel grumbled constantly in the wilderness because they had lost a sense of the presence of God. "Come, make us gods that shall go before us," they said as they gathered together with Aaron while Moses was away on the mountain (Ex. 32:1). They tested the Lord and said, "Is the Lord among us or not?" (Ex. 17:7) People need the presence of God in Christ. When they are unable to find Him, they will fashion their own gods to fill the gap. For the Japanese people, ancestors have traditionally filled that gap.

In Shintoism,[20] ancestors are a very important part of its belief system, but followers do not visit their ancestors daily, nor are their ances-

---

[19] See Naomichi Masaki, "Confessing Christ: Office and Vocation," *Logia* 7, no. 3 (Holy Trinity 1998): 5–11.

[20] Shintoism has taught for centuries that Japan was created by the gods, and that the people of Japan are children of those gods. The best way to please the gods is to continue to do what the gods began to do—namely, to create a good community. The most

tors willing to help them. Japanese Buddhism[21] teaches a Christ-like, speculative figure called Amida, but since there is no concept of sin, Amida never deals with man according to his deepest needs. Thus, neither Shintoism nor Buddhism provide a real basis for the Japanese prac-

---

appropriate attitude is to live with thankful hearts to the gods, which is expressed through various feasts. The worst thing to do is to harm the life of the community.

In this religious system, human nature by birth is seen as morally neutral; when one harms the community, one becomes a sinner. The object of sinning, however, is not against God but against the community. Since various feasts are the occasions to express one's highest thankfulness, insulting these feasts is the worst thing one can do. For Shintoism, corporate life is crucial.

Of all the festivals in Japan, the New Year's Day celebration is the most important. Every Japanese person celebrates it every year, yet very few know why they observe it. The reason for this celebration is to welcome the gods of the New Year into one's home. With this in mind, the customs related to this celebration begin to make sense. For example, December 13th is called "The Beginning" (Koto Hajime) and is a time to encourage all Japanese to begin preparing for New Year's Day. Thus, instead of the American custom of spring cleaning, people clean their houses very thoroughly toward the end of the year. This is to prepare thoroughly and give highest honor in welcoming the gods.

The climax of this celebration is in the meal. Only the best foods must be prepared. All the family members and relatives gather together to eat. Since the gods of the New Year are the gods of the family and their ancestors, the absence of any members of the family signifies a dishonoring of the gods who are present. Likewise, the gods of the New Year also join with the people to eat and celebrate. Thus, Japanese people use special pairs of chopsticks on this day. Not only the usual end for eating is made narrow and thin, but the other end of the chopsticks as well. This means that as a person eats, the gods can also eat from the other end!

In contrast to the Lord's Supper, the "gods" who come to Japanese feasts are merely guests; they must be entertained. The people must do all that they can to please the gods and make them feel comfortable. The gods are believed to eat together, yet give nothing in return. People do offer sacrifices. But this is only to show their gratitude to the gods, not for the purpose of atonement.

[21]Buddhism tries to offer a way to be rescued from the realities of suffering in this world. This inherited worldview from ancient India is a very pessimistic one; everything is regarded as suffering. Thus, after man dies, he is transferred into one of six worlds: the world of heaven, of human beings, of angry dragons, of animals, of hunger, or of hell. Such reincarnation has no end; man must suffer for billions of years. The only one who can escape from the cycle of reincarnation is called a "Buddha." However, there are two problems. First, the time required to become a Buddha is $(10^{64})^3$ hours, which means that one can never become a Buddha in one lifetime. Secondly, there is no definitive way of salvation for Buddhism.

tice of ancestor worship. The concepts of ancestors and Amida may be found there, but their existence is not "incarnational."[22]

It is Confucianism that supplies a viable foundation for the practice of ancestor worship in Japan. Contrary to popular belief, the teaching of Confucianism centers on a doctrine concerning life after death, not on moral or social orders. Confucianists believe that the world is an enjoyable place to be. Even after death, man wants to come back to this world.

In Buddhism, the way of salvation runs along the lines of its two major sects: "Theravada," which means "small vehicle," and "Mahayana," which means "large vehicle." The original teaching of Gautama is that of Theravada—that is, that one must first become a monk by retiring from the world to live in seclusion; then by training and doing good works as a monk, one is expected to reach a point where he no longer feels any attachment to earthly desires. Salvation depends on one's continual effort day and night. This type of Buddhism is predominantly in southeastern Asia.

Mahayana Buddhism is the variety that came to Japan. According to this view, Buddha is no longer a human being but rather a creator-like figure. In addition to Buddha, a speculative character called "Amida" was also created. Amida is not yet a Buddha, although he is very close to becoming a Buddha. If one is transferred into the world of Amida, then one is guaranteed eventually to become a Buddha himself. Thus, in Mahayana Buddhism, the object is not so much to become a Buddha as it is to get transferred into the world of Amida. At first, the way of being born in the world of Amida was through meditation. However, this method of salvation was later changed to a process involving the chanting of the name of Amida, then believing in Amida, and then of eventually recognizing that divinity (or Amidanity?) has been in one's own heart since birth.

Even though Amida is a figure similar to Christ, in Buddhism there is no teaching of an angry God. Likewise, because Amida is a mother-like figure who never accuses anyone, there is no doctrine of the forgiveness of sins or justification. Sin is regarded only as a burden in life, not sinfulness before God. In the Buddhist culture of Japan, people pretend to be self-sufficient, but in reality they are looking for something else. Neither Shintoism nor Buddhism can reach the human soul at the deepest level, where our true need lies.

[22]Consider the following also. People in Japan take great care of their ancestors' tombs and memorial tablets. If one believes in Shintoism, it is useless to take care of them because once man is deceased, he will lose his identity. He is even regarded as unclean, and nobody wants to have anything to do with him. On the other hand, if one believes in Buddhism, the deceased person is transferred into one of the other five worlds after the judging period of forty-nine days is over. Then he loses his own identity too, so there is no reason to build a tomb, either. In fact, in India, where Buddhism was born, the highest honor used to be to have someone throw one's bones into the sacred river of the Ganges after his body had been burned.

Confucianism knows of no other world apart from this one. When man dies, he is divided into body and soul. The body goes to a tomb; the soul departs from the body to float in the sky, just like the clouds. Man may return to this world after death if someone prays for him. Here comes the importance of training one's oldest son.[23] When one's son or other family members prays for the deceased parents before a memorial tablet, the dead bones in the tomb and the departed soul in the air are united once again. What was dead is made alive. Ancestors are present before the one who prays for them so that they may talk with each other.

Interestingly, the memorial tablet, which is of Confucian origins, is placed in a lowly position at the Buddhist family altar. Unaware of the distinction between the sacred statue of Buddha and the memorial tablet of the deceased, the ordinary Japanese person every morning brings his firstfruits (usually hot, steamed rice) to the altar and prays for the deceased members of his family. There, he talks to them as if they were still alive. Especially in times of trouble and decision-making, he may return frequently to the altar to speak to them. This practice gives him strength, comfort, and peace of mind. Ancestor worship gives Japanese people a sense of security, belonging, and community.

This religiosity of the Japanese people testifies to the fact that Satan has been successfully driving them away from the flesh of Christ through these religions and others. And yet, we cannot pass over another truth unnoticed: the Japanese people long for the incarnational God. Unsatisfied with Shintoism and Buddhism because these religions do not provide the bodily presence of their ancestors, Confucianism, under the guise of Buddhism, is needed to supply this kind of "real presence."

Of course, these "ancestors" are absent at the family altar no matter what people may believe. Prayers at the family altar are empty, and con-

---

Most Japanese believe that one becomes a Buddha immediately after he dies, even though this popular belief is not really found in Buddhism. As mentioned above, actual Buddhism teaches that without exception man must first be transferred into another world of suffering. Then, to become an actual Buddha takes an unthinkably long period of time and is accomplished by unreasonably hard training.

[23]This is also the origin of the Confucian teaching of respecting one's elders and being faithful to authority.

versations with them are really just monologues. But when the Japanese people are converted, baptized, and carefully and patiently catechized toward the goal of the Eucharist, they become exceptionally happy. Kneeling at the table with the Lord, they no longer need to pretend to have something important at the family altar every morning. Their joy now reaches beyond what any words can express as they realize that partaking of the body and blood of the Lord and receiving the blessings of the atonement create true communion and community.[24] They also begin to understand that as the Father and the Son are one, so they also are united with the Son, and "with angels and archangels and all the company of heaven."[25]

The flesh of Christ is, indeed, attacked and obscured by Satan through Japanese religions. At the same time, however, the very practice of ancestor worship points to the fact that people have a strong desire for a concrete, personal, and incarnate God.

I do not know much about other cultures, but I suspect that the flesh of Jesus Christ is both the target of Satan and the source of perpetual joy for people elsewhere as well. Part of the task of a missionary is to discover where and how the flesh of Christ is both obscured and longed

---

[24]David P. Scaer, "Matthew as Catechist," (unpublished manuscript, 1995), 130, says: "It [the Eucharist] provides the cultic structure for community to hold it together, but more importantly unites the community by making them participants in the atonement. Their status as 'community' (Paul would say 'the body of Christ') is derived from their partaking the body of Jesus. Catechumens understand what the life and death of Jesus is all about. Though the catechumen repents and enters the community as an individual through baptism, he benefits from the eucharist not as an individual but within the community."

[25]For example, one Japanese convert in New Jersey spoke to the congregation just prior to her baptism: "From my very young age, I had been looking for a solution to my guilt. Through the catechism classes, I came to know that what I had always believed [Japanese religions] really had no solid ground. It took me a long time, but when the Gospel message finally reached my heart, I said to myself, 'This is what I have always been looking for.' Christ is the answer to my life's question. He came to die for me. I am now here to seek baptism. I would like to become a child of God through it. I am now away from my home, my family and my friends in Japan. But I am extraordinarily happy because through baptism I will get my family also—the family of God, and the blood relationship through Christ. This is where I belong. I am so happy to have a family, even in this country."

for. Each missionary needs to engage in a serious study of that particular culture and its religion(s) in order to find out how this is being done. We need not invent new methodologies for missionary work. The starting point always remains the Lord's mandate and institution of the means of grace and the office of the holy ministry. Since the "how" of making disciples is already given (that is, by baptizing and by teaching), the interest of the missionary ought to be how he can best apply these divine means to a particular situation.

The goal of missionary work is not to make small Bible study groups and train lay leaders, but rather Baptism, the establishment of Lutheran altars, and ordination. The confessional, incarnational, baptismal, eucharistic, liturgical, and eschatological church bears these glorious marks. As Eastern Orthodox missiologist James J. Stamoolis wonders: "What else would one expect from a church in which the liturgy plays so central a role? What would be strange and out of character would be no mention of worship in the mission of the church."[26] The missionary work of such a sending church is not complete until the liturgy in the eucharistic assembly plays a pivotal role in its mission fields as well. Such a sending church will pay close attention to this crucial matter, for Lutheran missiology must constantly reflect the theology of the means of grace.

Some Practical Considerations

To conclude, let me suggest some practical considerations. The first is the importance of teaching the liturgy—that is, "liturgical catechesis" in our mission fields. In his *Lectures on Genesis,* Luther describes Noah not only as a minister but also as a missionary. Noah is said to have traveled over the entire world and preached everywhere. What did he preach? Luther answers: "Everywhere, [he was] giving instructions concerning the true worship of God." For Luther, the task of a missionary is to teach true worship. Since for Luther there is no true worship of God other than the God-given form of worship, which is the Sacrament together with

---

[26]James J. Stamoolis, *Eastern Orthodox Mission Theology Today* (Minneapolis: Light and Life Publishing Company, 1986), 87.

preaching, what Noah the missionary was doing was to guide people to sacramental worship so that they could receive the Lord God.[27]

In his article, "A Missionary in Fellowship with the Church," Jonathan F. Grothe demonstrates that Paul's letter to the Romans was written in order to prove that Paul had the same confession of faith that the Church of Rome had also received. On the basis of that common confession, Paul urged them to support him in his missionary journey further west.[28] Our church has enormous responsibilities when this is kept in mind.[29] As the church enters a new mission field, missionaries who are put into office carry with them not only the Holy Scriptures but also the liturgy and the catechism—whether it be to multicultural situations within a congregation, to North American mission fields, or to various missionary locations overseas.

This brings us to the second practical consideration, namely, the issue of translation. While we rightly have a strong interest in the translation of the Bible, why are we not equally as enthusiastic about translating the liturgy of the mother church? Walther brought with him not only the Scriptures and Baier's *Compendium,* but also the liturgy from his fatherland. Why do we not bring with us the liturgy of the sending church? Why do we not seriously consider how best the church might introduce the liturgy in its various mission fields? Should not missionaries acquaint the

---

[27]Martin Luther, *Lectures on Genesis,* AE 2:57. In this way, for Luther, liturgical theology and missiology come together.

[28]Jonathan F. Grothe, "A Missionary in Fellowship with the Church," *Lutheran Theological Review* 2 (Spring/Summer 1990): 7–14.

[29]Kurt E. Marquart, "Law/Gospel and 'Church Growth,'" in *The Beauty and the Bands: Papers Presented at Congress on the Lutheran Confessions, Itasca, Illinois, April 20–22, 1995,* ed. John R. Fehrmann, Daniel Preus, Bruce Lukas (Crestwood, Mo.: Luther Academy; Minneapolis: Association of Confessional Lutherans, 1995), 187, further explains that the new church in a new culture is to become theologically mature so that her "leadership can at least a) work with Holy Scripture in the original languages, b) understand and confess the *Book of Concord* in conscious contradistinction to other confessions and theologies, and c) take an informed confessional stand globally/ecumenically, for example, in opposition to the 'Lutheran' World Federation . . . Genuine confessional maturity obviously will not happen overnight. But it will not happen at all unless it is seriously and prayerfully desired and pursued!"

people with the liturgy before the work of catechesis begins?[30] The importance of translating the liturgy can be demonstrated by the fact that the sacramental theology of some Lutheran congregations in Japan has become Reformed partly because LCMS missionaries never brought with them to Japan the liturgy of their own mother church.[31]

At a minimum, the text of the liturgy should be consistent wherever LCMS missionaries go. I almost envy our sister church in Germany (SELK) where the official liturgy of the church is binding and normative for every pastor and congregation in order to express unity in the church and to prevent false doctrine from creeping in through unapproved formulas.[32]

---

[30]David P. Scaer, "*Cum Patre et Filio Adoratur*: The Holy Spirit Understood Christologically," *Concordia Theological Quarterly* 61 (Jan.–April 1997): 98–99, remarks: "Luther's Large and Small Catechisms are nothing else than explanations of the liturgy of the church—*lex orandi lex credendi*. His catechisms are liturgical hermeneutics, interpreting the teachings (doctrines) of the church first confessed in the liturgy and then explained by the pastor or the head of the household. The Creed, the Lord's Prayer, Baptism, and the Lord's Supper are things that people hear, say, or do in the church (the liturgy). . . . The liturgy does not originate in individual piety (as Pietism and Schleiermacher argued), but the Word and Sacraments give birth to the church. . . . Unless the Creed, the Lord's Prayer, and Holy Communion belong to the regular life of the church (the liturgy), there is little purpose in asking Luther's question, 'What does this mean?'" If a missionary teaches faith according to the Small Catechism, then what the catechumens are taught will be experienced in the liturgy. But ideally, the liturgy will be there before the catechism is taught.

[31]There have been three versions of the eucharistic text published in Japan (1952, 1964, 1983). Those texts were modeled after the eucharistic texts of *The Lutheran Hymnal*, *Service Book and Hymnal*, and *Lutheran Book of Worship*. In the liturgies of 1964 and 1983, a prayer following the Words of Institution uses the language of "bread and wine" instead of "body and blood." Likewise, in all three liturgical texts, in place of the Absolution, a prayer for forgiveness is said by the pastor as he faces the altar. Confession is made, but no forgiveness delivered.

A recent brochure from a Lutheran congregation in Japan reads: "Holy Communion is a ritual in which we remember the Last Supper which Christ spent with His disciples the night before He was crucified. In Holy Communion, the bread, which represents Christ's body, and the wine, which represents the sacrificial blood, are distributed."

Thus, a profound theological shift can take place when the liturgy is adopted or changed uncritically.

[32]Jobst Schöne, *The Christological Character of the Office of the Ministry and the Royal Priesthood* (Cresbard, S. Dak.: Logia Books, 1996), 1.

Liturgy and Culture

It is true that when a Japanese Lutheran attempts to socialize with LCMS members in a congregation, he or she does not feel at home simply because the ways of doing things and exchanging friendships are different. This is natural; it happens all the time in various social situations. And we should be thankful for the specific cultural heritage that the Lord has given us as a gift. It is indeed a wonderful thing to acknowledge each other's differences. However, at least while we attend the liturgy, should we not be one (Eph. 4:1–6)? To put it more precisely, in receiving the one body of Christ, the very flesh of Christ unites us first with Christ Himself, and then secondarily with the fellow-baptized through participation in the holy things. The liturgy has a unique culture—that is, a heavenly and other-worldly culture. The liturgy is not a place to express earthly culture, but an incomprehensively wonderful place to receive together God's heavenly culture, united with the one Lord. The liturgy is where Jesus comes; and with Jesus, comes heaven itself. Thus, the liturgy is "heaven on earth."

When I translated our Lutheran liturgical texts into Japanese, I consciously attempted to use even the same music as much as possible because my mission field was located in this country. I felt it wise to have an almost identical liturgy—not only so that when we had bilingual services, we could sing together in our own different languages, but also so that when our children grow older and begin to use English as their primary language, they can then easily attend the Divine Service of American congregations. When it comes to our overseas mission fields, the story may be different, but at least a fixed text of the liturgy should be established to serve the people well.

When the church is serious about handing on the faith to her mission fields for generations to come, the importance of translating the whole hymnal—including lectionary, propers, and agenda—ought not be ignored. This is another big topic. But for now, I would like to emphasize the importance of taking missionary situations everywhere into consideration right from the very beginning as our church begins work toward a new hymnal.

Variety in Worship

Responding to the Call for Variety

Psalmody

LIVING AS WE DO IN AN AGE THAT DEMANDS INCESSANT VARIETY, the following essays are a helpful reminder that the church's worship was never intended to be unchanging and rigid, a matter of merely doing "the same old thing" week after week. It might be argued, in fact, that some of the current debate over how to worship is the result of a failure to tap into the rich variety that is inherent in the church's liturgy.

The following essays are a mere glimpse into some of the treasures at the church's disposal. They are a reminder that planning for worship is never as simple a task as choosing the requisite three or four hymns for the day. Careful preparation by both pastor and musician is essential. They must constantly be expanding their horizons, becoming acquainted with the treasures of the past as well as with the best of what is new. Though the liturgy remains constant, the final form it takes from week to week will be as varied as the number of congregations at worship, for it is the responsibility of those who plan worship to do so considering the needs and situation of a particular people at a particular time and place.

Responding to the Call for Variety in the Church's Liturgy

Kevin J. Hildebrand

Perhaps no one in the church hears more calls for variety in the church's liturgy than pastors and musicians. They often find themselves caught between the cries of "nothing is the same around here anymore" and the groans of "it's always the same old thing" in regards to the parish worship life. How do pastors and musicians respond to the call for variety within the liturgy? It is not enough to address the call for variety without closely examining exactly what kind of variety is being considered and, perhaps more importantly, the motivation or reasons for desiring and implementing such proposed variety.

First of all, one needs to address the kinds of variety that are being proposed and why they are (or are not) desired. If the reasons are to broaden our sense of receiving God's gifts in *Gottesdienst*—to include, introduce, or even re-introduce a salutary way of sustaining and nurturing the faith or to move us to "a more profound alleluia" (*LW* 449:1)— then the alterations called for can certainly be cheered.

If, however, our motivation for desiring more variety in the liturgy is to "liven things up," to make worship more "effective" (whatever that means), or to avoid and disdain the gifts of the church's heritage, then perhaps we should not move so hastily toward such "variety."

God is a God of stability and strength. He is steadfast and immovable. "The Word of our God stands forever" (Is. 40:8). But neither is God a static, stagnant Deity. He is a God of variety. The variety of spiritual gifts He bestows on His people, the myriad creation He has given, the catholicity of the church across all times, places, and nations speak to the "variety" of God.

But variety, strictly speaking, can be both bane and blessing. When we address the worship of God and the activity we call Divine Service, the call for variety must be considered very carefully and in the light of Scripture and the Lutheran Confessions. Indeed, variety can be very beneficial. However, the call for variety must always be contemplated and answered within the context of what the church already has as the "norm"—that is, the church's historic liturgy.

Variety or Novelty?

The point must be made that what we are discussing is variety within the Divine Service and not novelty. One must be very careful with altering God's gift of liturgy which has developed over the centuries. Henry Letterman writes, "Worship materials have a profound influence on the life and faith that the church professes . . . [and in them] one finds the living embodiment of the creeds and confessions of the church. . . . Therefore one 'tampers' with the forms of worship with great fear and trembling."[1]

The Lutheran Confessions speak to this point as well, including the statement that in worship, "all frivolity and offenses are to be avoided" (FC Ep x, 3). The Reformers also made it clear that the catholicity of the church's worship continued with the Reformation, saying, "no novelty has been introduced which did not exist in the church from ancient times" (AC xxiv, 40). Indeed, avoiding frivolity leads to preserving good order (AC xxvi, 40) so that "particularly the weak in faith are to be spared" (FC Ep x, 3).

One may wonder if a true picture of the church, the Bride of Christ, is being presented to those aforementioned "weak in faith" when their worship life has been varied to such a degree that it is actually entertainment masquerading as Divine Service. Instead of our spiritual newborns being fed "pure spiritual milk" (1 Peter 2:2), many are subsisting on the equivalent of cheap Kool-Aid, which might taste good but has little nourishing value. C. Welton Gaddy summarizes these thoughts: "Quests for meaning in worship are best served by discovering how to

---

[1] Henry L. Lettermann, "Make It New: *Lutheran Worship* 1982," *Lutheran Education* 117 (Jan.–Feb. 1982): 158–159.

worship with integrity. Determining the nature of true worship is much more important than exploring the ways humans can bring novelty to worship."[2] Change and new "variety" is a natural part of the growth of the church. However, frivolity and novelty cheapen the divine worship of our Creator.

On the pragmatic side, we can analyze the abundance of "alternative" worship materials and forms in the market today, either supplied from a church publisher, church growth guru, or from the local parish word processor. There is a danger with a lack of consistency in some parish worship practices when every week there is something different or "creative" about the worship format, the so-called "liturgy." One danger is that the historic liturgy of the church becomes a matter of subjective taste and perceived time constraints and can be truncated, cut apart, rearranged, and "improved." Lack of consistency in the forms a church uses relegates a parish's worship life to something like a box of chocolates—the worshiper never knows what he's going to get!

A primary consideration in the role of consistency and ritual in worship life is the children of the congregation. When there is little routine for children, there can be little learning. Lack of consistency hinders memorization—for both children and adults. Martin Luther made reference to this in his preface to the Small Catechism in giving pedagogical theories for teaching the faith. He advocated, "adopt one form, adhere to it. . . . Young and inexperienced people must be instructed on the basis of a uniform, fixed text and form."[3] The church's aim in using consistent liturgies is not to bore people, but to make the liturgical life of the church also a natural part of the Christian's life.

The Variety That Is Already Out There

This does not mean or imply that the same setting of the liturgy must be used each week or that variations are never applicable. Where and what, then, is the role of variety within the liturgy? It all functions as part of the whole of the rites and ceremonies that nurture and sustain

---

[2] C. Welton Gaddy, *The Gift of Worship* (Nashville: Broadman Press, 1992), 200.
[3] SC Preface, 7; Tappert, 349.

the Christian life from Baptism to burial. As the church continues to grow and each age places its own mark on the ever-increasing heritage of the church's worship, let us not discount, neglect, or forget the variety that is already present in the church's liturgy. The first place to answer the call for variety within the liturgy is with what is already within the liturgy itself, perhaps unused or unconsidered as "variety." What follows is by no means an exhaustive list but consists of some major factors in considering how the role of variety already functions within the liturgy and how the church may use these already-present gifts.

1. The church year. The church has recognized the importance of celebrating variety by the use of the church year. The shape and scope of each season and festival give tremendous variety visually, aurally, and musically. The colors of the paraments and vestments provide visual variety. Aural variety is included, for instance, with omission of most organ and instrumental music on Good Friday, and perhaps throughout Holy Week and Lent. The omission of "alleluias" in Lent also provides an unspoken message of variety. Some parishes highlight the change of the seasons by consistently using a particular setting of Divine Service, a particular canticle, gradual, or other proper texts throughout a season. Again, visual and aural reminders and teachers of the faith are especially beneficial to the children of the congregation.

2. It's not "always the same." The notion that "every week it's the same old thing" is a myth that needs to be dispelled. Even if the same musical setting for the Divine Service is used, the church has never celebrated the same identical service two Sundays in a row because of the variety inherent in the propers. Every Lord's Day, festival, and commemoration has its own unique theme flavored by the variety in the propers (speaking here primarily of the appointed Scripture Readings). Although the Christological focus of the prescribed Readings remains constant, the specific circumstances and examples vary with the pericopes from week to week.

Furthermore, we should be thankful for the unchanging nature of Divine Service in which God freely and richly dispenses His gifts to His people. Week after week the Christian community has gathered to hear God's Word and feast at His table. The blessings of forgiveness, life, and salvation never vary but are always bestowed by our gracious God.

Responding to the Call for Variety

3. The variety provided by the choir. There is a vast wealth of variety within the propers assigned to the choir. For too many congregations, this resource remains untapped, with the choir functioning strictly as an "anthem presenter." How many parishes have their choirs singing the appointed verses and offertories? How many choirs regularly lead the psalmody of the congregation or present or respond to the Holy Gospel with a gospel motet? These short musical offerings put numerous Scripture texts into the mouths and hearts of the singers and hearers. This writer continues to marvel at settings of the proper verses and the limitless ways the Christian can sing "alleluia." Thanks be to God that especially with the advent of newer Lutheran worship books in the past twenty years, the historic liturgical role of the choir is being restored in many parishes. But there is much work to be done. Although commercialism should not be a factor, the day has not yet arrived when a publisher announces that a set of verses and offertories has become a "best seller."

4. The variety in hymnody. The church has an established variety in the appointed Hymns of the Day (*de tempore* hymns), in which an assigned hymn is chosen for every week of the church year. This is an excellent resource for congregations to introduce more "variety" into their core repertoire of hymns by implementing more of the prescribed hymns of the day. Numerous concertati on these hymns bring the choir into a more prominent role as leader of the people's song and provide variety for organists and instrumentalists in leading the hymn.

Of course, new hymn texts and tunes continue to be written. One of the most exciting and quickly-expanding areas of variety within the church's liturgy is the explosion of hymn writing and hymnal publishing in the last twenty years. Gifted poets and composers continue to give a new song to the church, including a wealth of legitimate hymns and responses from various ethnic groups. New hymnal supplements such as the LCMS's *Hymnal Supplement 1998* and the ELCA's *With One Voice* contribute to the expanding body of the church's song.

5. Composers. The so-called renaissance of church music in the 20th century has led to a wealth of composers writing a variety of works in a variety of styles and levels of difficulty for use within the liturgy. Within

American Lutheranism, the liturgical settings by Hillert, Nelson, Bunjes, and Moldenhauer, among others, have added variety for millions of worshipers in the past several decades. There remains a vast area of opportunities for composers of today and the future to add more variety to the church's song.

6. The hymnal. The treasures of the hymnal itself are often uncultivated. It is a rare congregation indeed, that has learned and regularly uses all Divine Service settings, Morning Prayer, Matins, Evening Prayer, Vespers, Compline, the Litany, Responsive Prayer settings, Corporate (and Individual) Confession, not to mention the varied rites and ceremonies located in the *Agenda,* including the Easter Vigil. This does not mean that every parish must learn every hymn, canticle, and liturgical setting from cover to cover (although not a bad idea), but points to the great amount of variety in our hymnals that often goes unused.

7. Extra-hymnal resources. The church has responded to calls for variety through church-wide availability of resources such as Concordia's *Creative Worship for the Lutheran Parish* and *Proclaim,* plus Augsburg Fortress's *Sundays and Seasons.* Although these extra-hymnal resources must also be carefully analyzed, in choosing useful material from these volumes, it is important to note again that they are designed to be used within the context and structure of the liturgy and do not replace the church's historic order. The introduction to *Creative Worship* states that "it is not intended to supplant or replace the liturgy." It also draws attention to the importance of the church's liturgical structure, advocating that "a greater understanding of the Preparation, the Liturgy of the Word, and the Liturgy of the Sacrament is engendered." It also bears restating that the strength of consistency and the power and role of ritual in worship needs prime consideration when using extra-hymnal resources.

Where Do We Go From Here?

The church's liturgy is, and has been, filled with variety for the Christian community for centuries. That variety continues to grow. Also continuing to grow is the need for understanding, teaching, and implementing the variety that is often right under our noses.

Responding to the Call for Variety

There is a desire and need for much more extensive education in the theology of worship in the church at large, and within the Missouri Synod in particular. The past few years have seen some important developments, including the "Real Life Worship" conference series, publication of President Barry's essay, "The Unchanging Feast," as well as the periodical issues of "Worship: A Lutheran Perspective" and the Commission on Worship supplement in *The Reporter*. These latter publications have included good information which has provided ideas for implementing variety already within the liturgy, such as the celebration of saints' days, as well as new hymnody. More publications and conferences such as these are necessary. With pastors and musicians searching for information on worship theology and practice, our own church body must provide scripturally and confessionally sound resources.

Worship and theology education must continue to be improved within our synodical colleges and seminaries, especially among church-work-professional students. Perhaps the time has come also for the theology of worship to be included within the religion curriculum materials provided for our Lutheran high schools and junior high schools, as well as lessons on how to use hymnals.

The decline of the synodically-trained teacher/Kantor in parishes has led, unfortunately, to a lack of theological education and awareness of many church musicians. The Synod must continue to ensure the finest in education for its church-work-professional students specializing in music, worship, and education, as well as providing outlets for the training and education of good and faithful servants who do not have the advantage or privilege of receiving a musical and theological education at our church colleges.

Finally, composers of the church have a marvelous opportunity to continue to bring new songs to God's people. New settings of verses, offertories, graduals, Gospel motets, psalmody, and other Scripture texts that need musical settings for today's choirs remain to be written. Hymn concertati and organ and instrumental chorale preludes still await composition for tunes that are existing or still unwritten. *Hymnal Supplement 1998* includes new settings of the liturgy. Future worship books will call for new, varied settings for the Christian community to learn and use. The hymn writer once penned those familiar words: "through the Church the song goes on" (*LW* 171:3). Composers of today and the future will help to ensure just that.

In conclusion, the Christian church is a church of both order and variety, especially within her worship life. Perhaps our goal is to ensure that these are not mutually exclusive terms, and that the variety inherent in the liturgy is orderly. As we approach the 21st century and continue to add to the expanding heritage of the church, let us also continue to make the treasures of the past new again and cultivate and celebrate the varied elements of the church's liturgy.

Psalmody

William M. Ickstadt

G*IVEN PREMISE: THE REVIVAL OF PSALM-SINGING AS PROMOTED BY* LW *and* LBW *has reached a plateau. What are some other ways of singing the Psalms that will encourage more congregations to explore the riches of the Psalter?*

Has psalm-singing as promoted by the *LW* and *LBW* reached a plateau? The answer is, "I don't know," but probably, "Yes." As a church musician responsible for the music of a single congregation, this author is not in a position to evaluate the broader practice of the church at large. But the answer is probably, "Yes," if a congregation has been using exclusively the tones in *LW* (which contains ten single tones, each assigned to specific psalms) and *LBW* (which contains five single and five double tones). These resources have been valuable, however, because they were such an improvement over the predecessor hymnals, namely, *The Lutheran Hymnal* (1941) and the *Service Book and Hymnal* (1958), neither of which provided many resources for the singing of the Psalms.

A more basic question may be, whether we should be concerned with *singing* the Psalms? One pastor may feel that worshipers should speak the Psalms in order to receive the meaning of the text, while another pastor may prefer that the congregation sing the Psalms, precisely in order to receive the meaning of the text. Which view is correct? In some respects, each is correct; however, the second opinion acknowledges the strong (often nondiscursive) function of the music supporting the text. The first opinion acknowledges that music may present a distraction for some. A type of musical encumbrance can occur at times, but if music is used judiciously, it will serve the text.

Another more basic question for hymnal planners might be: "Should we use the Psalms in worship?" It would seem that most congregations are currently using the Psalms. Some congregations most often speak the Psalms, while others may use a variety of methods for singing them. Either way, the Psalms are instruments of prayer. Both the believer's prayer to God and God's response are included in the Psalms. But how edifying is Psalm 137:9 as an instrument of prayer? It reads, "Happy shall he be who takes your little ones [babies of Babylon] and dashes them [i.e., "beats their brains out"] against the rock!" This seems less than Christian. Christopher Hill, the Bishop of Stafford and the Canon Residentiary and Precentor of St. Paul's Cathedral, London, explains in the preface to the *New St. Paul's Cathedral Psalter*, that "C.S. Lewis' solution was that we see the Psalms in their historical roots and primitive setting but that the feelings of revenge are also found in our hearts and that it is best when the whole of us is brought to God, not only in praise but even in frustration, anger and penitence."[1] However, in a social climate in which people often request (or church leaders think that people request) that worship be immediately and easily relevant to daily life experiences, and with the infusion of post-modern pragmatism, psalm-singing may be jeopardized.

Some psalms, for example, refer to enemies: "Sit at my right hand, until I make your enemies your footstool," and "The Lord will send the scepter of Your power out of Zion, saying, 'Rule over Your enemies round about You'" (Ps. 110:1, 2). Can people relate to "enemies round about you" in a country whose greatest threat is Iraq on the opposite side of the world? Again: "God spoke from His holy place and said, 'I will exult and parcel out Shechem; I will divide the valley of Succoth. Gilead is Mine and Manasseh is Mine; Ephraim is My helmet and Judah My scepter'" (Ps. 108:7, 8). Can people relate to a "holy place," when living room comfort and pleasure are a premium? And where are these foreign countries, anyway? Again: "Hallelujah! Happy are they who fear the Lord and have great delight in His commandments" (Ps. 112:1). "Fearing the Lord" and taking "delight in His commandments" may be more of a confrontation with the divine than most people can take, when "getting something out

---

[1]John Scott, ed., *The New St. Paul's Cathedral Psalter* (Norwich: Canterbury Press, 1997), v.

of the service" (one that is pleasurable and feels good) is looked upon as the primary goal. The Psalms emphasize the transcendent power of God as ruler over all natural occurrences. This is foreign for us in a time when we often see God primarily as our neighbor and friend.

The Psalms were used by our Lord and His apostles, since the Psalms were used in the temple and the synagogue. Gregory Dix explains in his classic book, *The Shape of the Liturgy*, that "between the lessons came the singing of psalms or other canticles from scripture (a chant known in later times as the 'gradual' because it was sung by soloists from the 'steps' of the raised lectern while the whole congregation joined in chorus in a simple refrain), a custom which must have been familiar to our Lord and His apostles."[2] In addition, a system of propers was used in the synagogue during our Lord's time, incorporating readings and psalms for the Sabbaths arranged in a three-year cycle.[3] Christopher Hill observes that Jesus and the disciples sang a hymn following the Last Supper (Mark 14:26):

> This would have been the Hallel, Psalms 113–118 sung as a whole at the great Jewish festivals, but particularly appropriate to the Passover because of Psalm 114, "When Israel came out of Egypt." The Psalms were also part of their personal vocabulary of prayer. Jesus echoes Psalms 22 and 31 in his words from the cross: "My God, my God, why hast thou forsaken me" and "Into thy hands I commend my spirit."[4]

In using the Psalter, the church united with those who have been worshiping God for the past 3,000 years. Also, "we are one with Jesus Christ," as Christopher Hill explains, for whom the Jewish Psalter was "a vehicle of prayer at the deepest moments of suffering."[5]

In our worship, the Psalms and our techniques for singing them allow for variety in worship. This does not imply variety simply for the sake of variety, but a variety that reinforces the rhythm of the church year and the central focus of the Readings appointed for a particular Sunday. Within the Hebrew poetic techniques is a large variety of expression, and the Psalter includes such varied categories as Israelite

---

[2]Gregory Dix, *The Shape of the Liturgy* (London: A & C Black, 1993), 39.
[3]Ibid., 360.
[4]Scott, *New St. Paul*, v.
[5]Ibid.

poems, royal psalms, hymns, thanksgiving songs, laments, and pedagogic psalms. Different methods of singing the Psalms can serve this variety and so also help to emphasize the rhythm of the church year and the central themes of each Sunday.

The prospect of a new hymnal presents us with many options. In addition to the psalm tones and pointing schemes already found in *LW* and *LBW*, the new hymnal might include a psalter among its accompanying materials. This psalter would contain (at a minimum) all of the Psalms appointed for use in the lectionary. Such a resource could be revised and updated every four to five years with psalm settings and psalm indices. Examples of this include: *The Psalter—Psalms and Canticles for Singing*,[6] and *The New St. Paul Cathedral Psalter*, published by St. Paul Cathedral in London.

A psalter to accompany the new Lutheran hymnal might contain the following:

1) The hymnal's psalm tones used in responsive singing with antiphons for the choir and congregational participation. Choir verses could be presented in four-part harmony, or in two-part harmony with descants or alternate lower parts. Various organ accompaniments and intonations, such as Donald Rotermund's recent CPH resource, *Intonations and Alternative Accompaniments for Psalm Tones*,[7] could also be included. Some of these settings could have hand bell accompaniments.

2) Psalm settings for the choir set in Anglican chant form. Unlike the *New St. Paul Cathedral Psalter*, the music and text should not be separated.

3) Singing a four-part setting of the antiphon, as in *The Psalms for the Church Year*.[8] This series also contains psalm verses for the choir alternating with related hymns verses for the congregation.

4) Choir/cantor settings of Gelineau Psalms or Taizé settings with

---

[6]Association for Liturgical Resources, Presbyterian Church (U.S.A), *The Psalter—Psalms and Canticles for Singing* (Louisville: Westminster/John Knox Press, 1993).

[7]Donald Rotermund, *Intonations and Alternative Accompaniments for Psalm Tones* (St. Louis: CPH, 1997).

[8]Paul Thomas, *The Psalms for the Church Year*, 12 vols. (St. Louis: CPH, 1982).

refrains for the congregation.

5) Settings for cantor/congregation like those found in the GIA *Cantor/Congregation* series, or GIA's *Celebration* series,[9] or CPH's *17 Psalms for Cantor and Congregation*,[10] or Oregon Catholic Press' *Singing the Psalms*.[11]

6) Indices for suggested hymnic settings.

7) Index of choral settings recently published or currently available settings for choir.

Such a project would be ambitious. However, it would be a tremendous resource. If one cathedral like St. Paul's Cathedral can publish a Psalter, our Synod certainly has the resources to do the same.

---

[9] *Cantor/Congregation Series*, (Chicago: GIA Publications); *Celebration Series* (Chicago: GIA Publications).

[10] Alan Mahnke, *17 Psalms for Cantor and Congregation* (St. Louis: CPH, 1995).

[11] *Singing the Psalms* (Portland, Oreg.: Oregon Catholic Press).

Assisting Ministers

Serving at the Altar

Serving at the Altar Reconsidered

IN RECENT YEARS MANY CONGREGATIONS have adopted the practice of involving laypeople in the liturgy in the reading of Holy Scripture and distribution of the Sacrament. While greater participation of the laity is always desirable in the church, many of these changes have occurred without serious theological reflection. In its 1985 document, *The Role of Women in the Church,* the Synod's Commission on Theology and Church Relations raised several concerns related to this issue. More work needs to be done.

The following essays offer highly contrasting views on this topic. Again, it is important to note that the Commission on Worship has not reached a final position on this issue. Reflection similar to that which follows will be necessary, however, for the commission to complete work on the new hymnal.

Serving at the Altar
Retaining the Role of Assisting Minister as Defined in the Rubrics of *Lutheran Worship*

Mark A. Waldron

WHEN DISCUSSING THE ROLE OF ASSISTING MINISTERS IN THE LITURGY, one must first understand what the ministry is, and what is happening in worship. Yet, there has probably been more disagreement in the Lutheran Church over the years about the doctrine of the ministry than perhaps any other doctrinal issue. The debate continues to this day. While this essay brings nothing new to the debate, the role of assisting ministers in the liturgy must be considered in that larger context of the church's ministry. Similarly, the church also has been engaged in what some have termed, "worship wars," for the past two decades. Thus, we must at least seek common ground regarding the fundamentals of worship and what it is that Christians do when they gather on the Lord's Day.

This essay will endeavor to review, in a cursory way, a Lutheran understanding of the pastoral office in relation to the priesthood of all believers; to discuss what it means for the faithful to assemble each week around Word and Sacrament; and to suggest, in the light of these considerations, why the role of assisting ministers in the liturgy should be retained. Finally, it would be irresponsible to discuss the role of the laity at this point in history without addressing the issue of women's service in the worshiping community.

Over the past several years, there has been considerable debate in the LCMS concerning the relationship between the pastoral office and the priesthood of all believers. Much of the discussion has included such questions as these:

- Are there certain functions of the ministry that only pastors may or should perform; and if so, what are they?
- What implications does a priesthood of all believers have for lay members of the church?
- Are all Christians ministers? If so, what does this imply about the ministry of Christian women?

It is not within the scope of this essay to answer these questions completely, nor even to rehearse the church's debate. An effort will be made, however, to discuss what is most pertinent to the matter at hand.

Without question, Luther's teaching on the priesthood of all believers, on the basis of 1 Peter 2:9–10, is one of the great legacies of the Reformation. Its implications for a Lutheran understanding of the ministry could hardly be overstated. Luther writes:

> All Christians whatsoever really and truly belong to the religious class, and there is no difference among them except in so far as they do different work. The fact is that our baptism consecrates us all without exception and makes us all priests.[1]

And again, he writes:

> We are priests, and thus greater than mere kings, the reason being that priesthood makes us worthy to stand before God, and pray for others. For to stand before God's face is the prerogative of none except priests.[2]

Luther did not conclude, however, that, because all Christians are priests, all are pastors. He writes:

> For although we are all priests, this does not mean that all of us can preach, teach, and rule. Certain ones of the multitude must be selected and separated for such an office. And he who has such an office is not a priest because of his office but a servant to all the others, who are priests.... This is the way to distinguish between the office of preaching or the ministry, and the general priesthood of all baptized Christians.[3]

---

[1] Martin Luther, "An Appeal to the Ruling Class of German Nationality, 1520," in *Reformation Writings of Martin Luther*, ed. Bertram Lee Woolf, 2 vols. (London: Lutterworth Press, 1952), 1:113.
[2] Martin Luther, "The Freedom of a Christian, 1520," in *Reformation Writings*, 1:366.
[3] Martin Luther, *What Luther Says*, ed. Ewald M. Plass (St. Louis: CPH, 1959), 3:1139 f.

In the Lutheran Church, pastors are divinely called to the office of the holy ministry. In its 1981 report on *The Ministry: Offices, Procedures and Nomenclature,* the CTCR defines this ministry as "the divinely established office referred to in Scripture as 'shepherd,' 'elder,' or 'overseer.' This term is equivalent to 'the pastoral office.' Within this office are contained all the functions of the ministry of Word and sacrament in the church."[4] In order to consider properly the role of assisting ministers, the priesthood of all believers and the pastoral office must be kept in proper balance.

The propensity for contemporary churches to cast their pastors in managerial roles (like those of a corporate CEO) has led to much confusion regarding the pastoral office. One might wonder what has happened to the notion of the pastor as a caretaker of the Lord's church, in the way St. Paul describes in 1 Timothy 3:1 ff. A concerted effort is needed to instill in the people what it means for a man to be called to the pastoral office, and what the distinctive functions of that office are, namely, the absolving of sins, the preaching of the Gospel, the administration of the Sacraments, and the supervision of a flock entrusted to the pastor's care. However, in so doing, one dare not compromise the priesthood of all believers by unnecessarily diminishing the role of the laity simply for the sake of shoring up an understanding of and respect for the pastoral office.

Now must come a consideration of public worship because one's understanding of worship determines the way in which he regards the role of assisting ministers. A proper understanding of worship always begins with God. He comes to the church in Word and Sacrament and invites a response of faith. The liturgy is the manner in which the church receives God's grace and orders her response. In worship, the pastor presides over the liturgy, the distinctive functions of his role being the absolution of sin, the preaching of the Word, and presiding at the celebration of the Eucharist. While the pastor rightfully presides in these ways, the liturgy belongs to the whole assembly. Care must be taken not to imply

---

[4]Commission on Theology and Church Relations of The Lutheran Church—Missouri Synod, *The Ministry: Offices, Procedures, and Nomenclature* (St. Louis: The Lutheran Church—Missouri Synod, 1981), 12.

that worship is the work of the pastor while the assembly simply observes and makes appropriate responses. To go back to the days when only ordained clergy were present in the chancel would be eerily reminiscent of a time when only priests were worthy to approach God while the assembly watched. A Lutheran understanding of the priesthood of all believers dispels that heresy. Hence, the church must be careful not to compromise the legitimate role of the laity in worship by not allowing them to assist with the liturgy in ways that are neither forbidden nor discouraged in Scripture or the Confessions. When laypeople serve as assisting ministers in the liturgy, the worshiping community encounters a vivid demonstration of what God is doing in worship, namely, lavishing His grace upon all and eliciting a response of prayer, thanksgiving, and praise. The rubrics of *LW* summarize these points:

> The liturgy is the celebration of all who gather. Together with the pastor who presides, the entire congregation is involved. It is appropriate, therefore, that where it is considered necessary or desirable or both, lay persons fulfill certain functions within the service.[5]

The rubrics of *LW* and Appendix 1 of *Lutheran Worship: History and Practice* indicate what are the duties of the assisting minister(s):
- Kyrie
- Hymn of Praise
- Old Testament and Epistle
- Prayer of the Church
- Distribution of the cup
- Post-Communion Prayer

The more fully representatives of the worshiping community assist with these duties, the clearer it is that in this gathering God is at work in all His people. It is puzzling that any of these duties are argued by some to belong distinctively to the pastoral office. But the most prominent argument against the performance of these duties by the laity is that it may become a stumbling block for some (that is, for those who under-

---

[5]Commission on Worship of The Lutheran Church—Missouri Synod, *Lutheran Worship: Altar Book*, (St. Louis: CPH, 1982), 25.

stand these duties as functions of the pastoral office). But this argument, however well-intentioned, is dismaying. It serves better as a call for clearer and more intentional teaching of that which Scripture says about the church's ministry, the Lutheran understanding of the holy ministry and specifically the pastoral office. It is easy to avoid this fundamental issue by arguing that, because it might give offense or be misunderstood, the laity should not assist in the liturgy. In fact, offense is given whichever conclusion is reached in this debate. If we take seriously that Scripture is the sole authority in matters of faith and life, then we must be honest in hearing Scripture speak to this issue, in order to know what the church's practice ought to be.

Now, all of this begs the question, what should be the role of women in this aspect of the church's ministry? The answer is another question: if Scripture does not forbid it, may the church? It is simply not responsible, nor does it give people credit for the intelligence they possess, to argue that, because those functioning in these roles *may be perceived* as performing duties belonging to the pastoral office, the practice should be avoided. The solution to this mis-perception and offense is not avoidance, but again, the clear biblical teaching of the ministry, the priesthood of all believers, and the pastoral office.

Unfortunately, confusion in this area was compounded by the CTCR report, *Women in the Church: Scriptural Principles and Ecclesial Practice* (1985). In response to the question whether a woman may or should participate in public worship by the reading the Scriptures for the day, or by assisting with the formal liturgical service, the CTCR advised:

> All Christians have access to the Scriptures. . . . The reading of the Scriptures belongs to the priesthood of all believers, men and women. Moreover, there is no ceremonial law in the New Testament regarding the reading of Scripture in the context of public worship. Nor is there explicit apostolic prohibition of such reading by women. Nevertheless, it is the opinion of the CTCR that the reading of the Scriptures is most properly the function of the pastoral office and should therefore not ordinarily be delegated to a lay person, woman or man.[6]

---

[6]Commission on Theology and Church Relations of The Lutheran Church—Missouri Synod, *Women in the Church: Scriptural Principles and Ecclesial Practice* (St. Louis: The Lutheran Church—Missouri Synod, 1985), 45.

The report goes on to invoke the "possible misperception argument" as a reason for avoiding the practice of lay readers. It is at least confusing to state that Scripture does not prohibit such activity, but then that the CTCR does suggest its prohibition. In fact, this may itself be a sound argument for giving these roles to laypeople.

It may seem obvious, but it should nonetheless be stated, that the aforementioned duties of assisting ministers assume the appropriate talents and gifts. Congregations, under the guidance of their pastors, must take seriously the responsibility to discern who has received these talents and gifts, and must provide the necessary instruction and training of those who are thus gifted for the performance of their duties in a way that honors God and edifies the worshiping assembly. To this end, the Commission on Worship can provide an invaluable service to the church through educational and training materials.

Serving at the Altar Reconsidered
The Role of the Assisting Minister in *Lutheran Worship*

THOMAS M. WINGER

HISTORY
The Pedigree of *Lutheran Worship* (1982): Rationale

ONE SEARCHES IN VAIN FOR A DETAILED HISTORICAL OR THEOLOGICAL justification for the role of "Assisting Minister" given in *Lutheran Worship*. It is certainly new, finding no precedent in any of the service books preceding *LW* in the LCMS. Whatever immediate answer may be found lies in the materials produced by the ILCW prior to the publication of *LW*. The introductory rubrics of *Contemporary Worship 2*, in which the new rite for the chief service is introduced, seem to root the new practice in a "corporate" theology of worship:

> The service should never be led by one minister alone. The presiding minister is always ordained, but he should be assisted by others both clergy and laymen. Otherwise the symbolism of a truly corporate action is blurred. . . . If the parish has two pastors, one will assume some of the assistant's role. But in no case should this preclude lay participation. As a minimum, laymen should read the first and second lessons.[1]

Underlying this explanation is a definition of worship as an "action" rendered to God and for the church by the whole body. No portion of the body of Christ may be left out of this liturgical "action"; or, more to the point, functions that were restricted to clergy should be shared by the laymen *and* clergy. (No mention is made of the clergy receiving a share in the congregational portions of the liturgy.)

---

[1] Inter-Lutheran Commission on Worship, *Services: The Holy Communion*, Contemporary Worship Series, no. 2 (Minneapolis: Augsburg Publishing House, 1970): x.

The literary children of these introductory rubrics would be the "Notes on the Liturgy," of *LBW* and *LW*, respectively. First, from the earlier work:

> [In the Introduction:] An examination of the contents will reveal the several goals toward which the Commission worked in liturgy . . . to involve lay persons as assisting ministers who share the leadership of corporate worship. . . .[2]

Here the same "corporate" theology is adduced. Secondarily, the minister's role in the liturgy is defined as "leadership," a concept presupposing a body with essentially the same task as its leader. This in contrast to the traditional model of the liturgist as a "servant" to those who "are served." The notes go on to give a definition: "Leadership portions appropriate for laypersons are marked [A]=assisting minister."[3] There is no room here for two ordained pastors taking the "P" and "A" roles; "A" is specifically intended for "laypersons," in accordance with the stated objectives of the ILCW.

The *LW* notes, by contrast, offer a more helpful ambiguity: "Portions appropriate for either those ordained or non-ordained are marked [A]=assisting minister."[4] Here there is room for the assisting minister to be an ordained man; it is not a role specifically given to a "layperson," as in *LBW*. Nevertheless, when the entire context is read, a similar theological rationale is apparent:

> The liturgy is the celebration of all who gather. Together with the pastor who presides, the entire congregation is involved. It is appropriate, therefore, that where it is considered necessary or desirable or both, lay persons fulfill certain functions within the service. Portions reserved for pastors are marked [P]=presiding minister. Portions appropriate for either those ordained or non-ordained are marked [A]=assisting minister.[5]

Although a similar "corporate" theology is cited, there seems to be a certain hesitancy to "require" the use of laypersons in assisting roles. On

---

[2]*Lutheran Book of Worship: Ministers Desk Edition* (Minneapolis: Augsburg Publishing House; Philadelphia: Board of Publications, Lutheran Church in America, 1978): 12.

[3]*LBW Ministers Desk Edition*, 13.

[4]"Notes on the Liturgy," *Lutheran Worship: Altar Book* (St. Louis: CPH, 1982): 25. See also p. 11.

[5]Ibid.

the surface, one could read this as nothing more than pointing out those places where a non-ordained liturgist might appropriately serve.⁶

The Explanatory Resources

The brief theological rationale cited in these notes is fleshed out in the various companion resources produced to accompany the introductions of these two new hymnals. Frank Senn's *The Pastor as Worship Leader* offers a threefold rationale: First: "As a matter of principle, the presiding minister should not do everything in a service."⁷ This principle stems, apparently, from that "corporate action" theology which requires leadership by laymen. (Yet again, one notes a preoccupation with so-called "leadership roles," for no Lutheran service has ever been conducted apart from a congregation's participation!) Secondly, and significantly, Senn makes reference to the historical role of the deacon in the liturgy:

> Here we are restricting the use of the term ["assisting minister"] to those who function in the traditional diaconal capacity: i.e. to read the Gospel, lead the petitions of the intercessions, and administer the chalice at the communion.⁸

In other words, what deacons traditionally did now is given to laypersons. This is the crucial step that needs to be challenged below. Thirdly, Senn refers to a "work of the people" philosophy:

> While the pastor, as presbyter, presides over the liturgical assembly, the liturgy does not belong to the pastor. The very word *leitourgia* suggests that it is the "public work of the people," from *laos* (people) and *ergon* (work). Nor is the pastor the only minister of Christian worship. There are traditional liturgical roles for deacons, sub-deacons, lectors, acolytes, cantors, and other assistants who help to lead the worship of the people of God. But the pastor is the *presiding minister*, and that gives him ... a great deal of control over the character and style of the service.⁹

This too is a philosophy that must be questioned.

---

⁶One *might* be thinking only of vicars, field workers, or lay readers serving in the absence of a pastor.

⁷Frank Senn, *The Pastor as Worship Leader: A Manual for Corporate Worship* (Minneapolis: Augsburg Publishing House, 1977), 26.

⁸Ibid., 102.

⁹Ibid., 22–23. Emphasis original.

One final source, however, provides the clearest rationale for what the ILCW intended with the assisting minister role. The guide for introducing *LW* explains:

> At the time of the Reformation the low mass or the *missa cantata* (a sung low mass) was the normal pattern of worship in Western Europe. It was this mass that the Reformers knew and used for their model. This low mass was led by the celebrant, and the responses were said by the congregation, or in most cases by a single server. To have a single minister at the altar was the normal way the service was done. The Reformers of course understood that the congregation was not to consist of mere passive spectators. They encouraged participation by the people and understood worship to be a corporate action. But the low-mass model with which they worked called for a single minister at the altar, and the congregation.[10]

The corporate quality of worship is a concept that *LW* attempts to expand with the use of assisting ministers. Most Lutheran parishes have only one ordained pastor; therefore, the assisting minister role cannot be limited to ordained clergy. Most congregations would not be able to use the assisting minister sections if they were limited to ordained assisting pastors. Laymen are encouraged to assume the assisting minister role.

LW uses the model of the solemn high celebration of the Eucharist with, to continue in the same idiom, a deacon and a subdeacon. The model is not to be found in the shared leadership of many American Protestant denominations. The assisting minister role is not to give the people a chance to "play pastor," as if that were the really important part. Nor is the goal of *LW* a clericalization of worship by having more and more ministers, with less and less to do for the congregation. Rather, the rationale behind the use of assisting ministers is that we understand that each order (German: *Stand*) in the church has its office (*Amt*) to perform.[11]

The congregation has its service, its liturgy, its offering of prayer, praise, and thanksgiving to do. No one can take that liturgy from the people of God. The presiding minister (pastor) has his liturgy, or service, to render. He is called to preach the Gospel, absolve, and celebrate the Sacraments. That ministry is from God Himself, and the pastor is the

---

[10] *Guide to Introducing Lutheran Worship* (St. Louis: CPH, 1981), 23.
[11] Ibid.

representative of Christ in the midst of the people of God as the Sacraments are celebrated and the Gospel is preached. The assisting ministers reestablish the important diaconal ministry. They represent the people; as assisting ministers they lead in prayer, their essential task, and assist in the reading of the Word of God and in the distribution of the chalice at Communion.

Each has a liturgy to perform. None is complete without the other as they together form a symphony of praise to God.[12]

This introduction makes the remarkable claim that *LW* follows a different liturgical tradition than any Lutheran liturgical rite has ever followed before! And yet, it provides no rationale for making this change. What justification is there for the (apparent) repudiation of a Reformation liturgical model in favor of another?

Other Theological Commentary

Further theological rationalizing can be found in the *LBW Manual on the Liturgy:*

> Even in small congregations, at least one assisting minister should assist in the distribution. There is no reason why the pastor should do it alone. Assisting ministers need not be ordained. In fact, *laypeople should be appointed for this ministry on principle, for the presiding minister should be assisted by others whose ministries contribute to the whole work of worship.*[13]

These apparently "practical" comments are loaded with implications for a theology of worship. In this definition of worship as a "whole work," one hears echoes of both "corporate" theology and "work of the people." Furthermore, it implies a purely sacrificial definition of worship, even in those portions which are supposedly sacramental, for assisting ministers are used in roles that embrace both characteristics.

Unfortunately, the same theological confusion is evident in Robert Sauer's contribution to the *LW* handbook, *Lutheran Worship: History and Practice*:

---

[12]Ibid., 24. Presumably, much of this material was drawn directly from its *LBW* equivalent.

[13]Philip H. Pfatteicher and Carlos R. Messerli, *Manual on the Liturgy: Lutheran Book of Worship* (Minneapolis: Augsburg Publishing House, 1979), 244. Emphasis added.

> *Lutheran Worship* envisions laypeople serving as assisting ministers, as such representing the congregation as they lead in prayer, assist in the reading of the Word of God and in the distribution of the chalice at the Communion.... Such service is a visible picture of the priesthood of believers sharing a common response to God's truth.[14]

In this description, Sauer arbitrarily mixes sacramental and sacrificial elements of the liturgy. Certainly, a lay assistant represents the congregation when he offers up prayers on their behalf to God. One might even consider this a "picture of the priesthood of believers." But this cannot be said about the giving of God's Word and the blood of Christ. These are gifts from God to man. The reading of the Scriptures cannot be from the congregation to the congregation. Nor can giving the gift of the sacramental elements be considered a priestly response to God's truth. The Word and the blood are themselves God's truth, not a response to it. To assert the latter turns the Gospel into Law, the Sacrament into a sacrifice!

RESPONSE

We have already begun to formulate a response to the material in hand. But let us consider in sequence the various theological and historical reasons that have arisen from the preceding sources for using laypersons in "assisting minister" roles.

Restoring the Diaconate

There certainly is historical truth in what has been said about the diaconate. It is unclear what the role of the deacon was in New Testament times. In earliest pre-Constantinian times, the deacon's role seems to have been the administration of the church's goods and care for the poor. Nevertheless, liturgical functions developed quite early, and indeed focused on three duties: to read the Gospel, bid the Prayers, and give out the blood of Christ from the chalice.[15] In the earliest rites, the minor office of lector ("reader") exists, to whom the Epistle Reading was

---

[14] Robert Sauer, "Lutheran Worship (1982)," in *LWHP*, 136.

[15] The most helpful place to trace these duties is Paul F. Bradshaw, *Ordination Rites of the Ancient Churches of East and West* (New York: Pueblo, 1990).

given. The subdeacon assisted the deacon in his administrative work and also prepared the sacred vessels for the Sacrament. Later, the office of lector lost its liturgical functions, and the subdeacon took over the reading of the Epistle.[16]

When the ILCW materials speak of restoring the historic role of the deacon, therefore, one must ask precisely what this means. In giving the first Readings to the assisting minister and reserving the Gospel for the ordained presiding minister, they have departed from history and from the stated goal.[17] But more importantly, one must question how it is that giving the liturgical roles of the historic deacon to a *layperson* does anything to restore the diaconate. In the first place, it is decidedly imprecise to say that the deacon came from the people and represented them. Although in the earliest times and in some places this might have been true, it was also true at such times of the presbyterate and episcopate. Later, when the orders were more clearly defined, the deacons were chosen from the lower "clerical" orders.[18] Although the deacon did not consecrate the elements and rarely preached, he was ordained with the laying on of hands and tonsured. He was considered "clergy," even "major clergy" in the terminology of the Middle Ages. Although Lutherans may have trouble in speaking of a "clergyman" prohibited from the essential acts of a pastor, the church of that time did not by any means consider the deacon a layman.

One cannot simply give the liturgical responsibilities of a deacon to a layperson and claim the support of tradition. He does not become a deacon

---

[16]Interestingly, it became an honorable title given to those who were enrolled on the path to the priesthood. This emphasizes the connection between the lower orders and the office of the ministry.

[17]Although it is theologically sound for the *ipsissima verbi Christi* ("the very words Christ himself actually spoke") to be given to the man who represents Christ.

[18]One clear example of the order of advancement is given in the Georgian rite: "From layman to reader / from reader to subdeacon / from subdeacon to archdeacon / from archdeacon to presbyter / from presbyter to chorepiscopos / from chorepiscopos to bishop" (Bradshaw, 166). See also the Coptic rite: "The person who is to be brought as deacon shall be chosen from the clergy because they are trustworthy for this ministry" (Bradshaw, 143).

merely by doing what a deacon did, no more than a layman who consecrates becomes a pastor. If the diaconate is to be resurrected (as it is already being revived in the Lutheran Church–Canada), it ought to be done according to better precedent. Indeed, Luther once gave his opinion on the matter:

> In the papist church the man who reads the Gospel is a subdeacon. The distribution of goods and the care of the poor have been relegated to the hospices. The truth of the matter is that there ought to be chaplains [*Kapläne*, a German term for deacon] and common funds.... There ought to be deacons for the church—men who should be of service to the bishop and at his recommendation have control in the church in external matters.[19]

Of interest here is the fact that Luther cares little for the liturgical functions of deacons. He does wish, however, that deacons would take on their ancient role of caring for the poor. This is the wise judgment of a man who understands *Amt* and *Beruf*, office and vocation.

Low Mass versus High Mass

There have been Lutheran churches in which the diaconate continued to exist—and that with liturgical functions. It is not true that the Reformers knew only a service in which the *Priester* did everything; they did also know the so-called "high mass." The *Kirchenordnungen* edited by Sehling are a worthy resource for studying this—although it is a task that this author has only begun.[20] Even a brief preliminary survey of these *Ordnungen* has already yielded two examples of a "fuller" celebration of the mass. A 1533 order refers to pastors and deacons:

> And where the parish pastor has no deacon, he [himself] should administer the body of Christ to each person before he administers the chalice to each. Where, however, one has Levites, one of them may administer the chalice to each one who has received the body of Christ.[21]

---

[19]Martin Luther, "Lectures on 1 Timothy" (1528), trans. Richard J. Dinda, AE 28:295–96. Why he says that the *subdeacon* reads the Gospel is unclear, unless there were only two offices: subdeacon and archdeacon, as in the Georgian rite above.

[20]Emil Sehling, ed., *Die evangelischen Kirchenordnungen des 16. Jahrhunderts*, 15 vols. (vols. I–V, Leipzig: O.R. Reisland, 1902–13; vols. VI–XII, Tübingen: J.C.B. Mohn, 1955–63).

[21]"Und wo der pfarherr keinen diaconum hat, soll er den leib Christi raichen jederman, ehe er jemand den kelch raiche. Wo man aber leviten hat, mag derselben einer den Kelch raichen einem jeden der den leib Christi empfangen hat." From "Ordnung der

And the liturgy two hundred years later in J.S. Bach's Leipzig refers to the division of liturgical duties among more than one pastor:

> At this point the previously mentioned priest goes again to the altar and sings: *The Lord be with you.* ... After singing the Collect *another priest* goes to the lectern and sings the Epistle.... After the hymn the priest sings the Gospel at the altar.[22]

Thus, Lutherans did indeed know the diaconate and use deacons liturgically. Where proper (ordained) deacons were not in use, however, the pastor or pastors assumed those roles traditionally given to the deacons. There is certainly no precedence here for bestowing these roles upon laypersons.[23]

Λειτουργία as "Work of the People"

The supposed etymological definition of "liturgy" (λειτουργία) as "work of the people" has been a particular emphasis of the 20th-century liturgical movement, and it lies at the heart of all "corporate" talk. In response, one would do well to listen to modern linguistics, which dismisses the previous century's pre-occupation with etymologies and root meanings. For though a word may have originated from the composition of smaller parts and attained its meaning by adding them together, yet—over time and in differing contexts—the word's meaning changes. One may not trump the meaning of a word in one time and replace it with a meaning it supposedly had in another. Our theology of the liturgy does not come from an etymological dictionary.

Messe aus der Brandenburg-Nürnberger Kirchednordnung 1533," in Wolfgang Herbst, *Evangelischer Gottesdienst: Quellen zu seiner Geschichte*, 2nd ed. (Göttingen: Vandenhoeck & Ruprecht, 1992): 100. Author's English translation. In the early ordination rites, "Levites" is a term used typologically of deacons.

[22]"Hierauff gehet der vorige Priester wieder vor dem Altar und singet: Dominus vobiscum. ... Nach Absingung der Collecte gehet ein andrer Priester vor das Pult und singet die Epistel. ... Nach dem Liede singet der Priester vor dem Altar das Evangelium." From "Der Leipziger Gottesdienst zur Zeit Joh. Seb. Bachs," in Herbst, *Quellen*, 145. Emphasis added. Author's English translation. The prayers are bid from the pulpit after the Sermon—one presumes the preacher does this. No other mention is given of who does what.

[23]Thus far, this author has found only one possible exception. For Vespers on the evening before major festivals, the Dresden rite in the time of Heinrich Schütz (1662) specifies that a boy intone the Epistle from the choir. Otherwise, the priest reads the Psalm or other text from the altar. See Herbst, *Quellen*, 139.

Nevertheless, there is still a profit in debunking the quite untenable etymology of "liturgy" as "work of the people." Indeed, the constituent parts of the Greek word λειτουργία do stem from λήϊτος, "concerning the people or national community," and the verbal root ἐργ– pertaining to "work." But how are these two roots combined? In another context, one might ask, "what sort of genitive is it?" It is helpful, in this respect, to hear the greatest "etymologizer" of all, Kittel's *Theological Dictionary of the New Testament*:

> λειτουργεῖν is to do things which are related, not to private concerns, but to the national community as a political unity, or more briefly, to the body politic. More precisely, it is "to render service to the people (as a common political entity)" by discharging a true task for society. λειτουργεῖν is the discharge of the task, or "service to the nation."[24]

In ancient Greece, at least, λειτουργία was a term applied to a public service, not because it was done "*by* the people," but "*for* the people." In this case, the etymology corresponds with a Lutheran theology of worship.

That seems to be Melanchthon's thought, as well, when he appeals to the history and etymology of the word in the Apology:

> The Greeks call the Mass "liturgy," and this, they say, means "sacrifice." . . . But let us talk about the term "liturgy." It does not really mean a sacrifice but a public service [*publicum ministerium*]. Thus it squares with our position that a minister who consecrates shows forth the body and blood of the Lord *to* the [rest of the] people [*reliquo populo*], just as a minister who preaches shows forth the gospel *to* the people, as Paul says (1 Cor. 4:1), "This is how one should regard us, as ministers of Christ and dispensers [*dispensatores*] of the sacraments of God," that is, of Word and sacraments. . . . Thus the term "liturgy" squares well with the ministry.[25]

Melanchthon here rejects the sacrificial definition of liturgy, that is, as a work that is offered *by* the people (presumably *to* God). Rather, it is that which is done *to* or *for* the people *by* the minister who gives gifts *from* God. The concise German version of this paragraph is even more to the point:

> So heißt *liturgia* gräkisch eigentlich ein Amt, darinne man der Gemeine dienet; das schicket sich wohl auf unsere Lahr, daß der Priester da als ein

---

[24]H. Strathman, "λειτουργέω," in *TDNT*, 4:216.
[25]Ap XXIV:79–81. Tappert, 263–64. *BSLK*, 371–72. Note the Latin, *reliquo populo*, "to the *remaining* people"; the minister is that part of God's people which gives on His behalf to the others. Tappert fails to translate the word *reliquo*.

gemeiner Diener denjenigen, so communicieren wöllen, dienet und das heilige Sakrament reichet.

Thus *liturgy* actually means in Greek an office in which one serves the congregation; that corresponds well to our teaching, that the priest as a common servant serves those who wish to commune, and administers the Holy Sacrament.[26]

The liturgy is thus more properly termed a "service" or "ministry," rather than a "work."

The "Priesthood of Believers"

Another related issue is the claim that lay involvement through "assisting minister" roles appropriately exhibits the so-called "priesthood of believers" (a phrase that occurs nowhere in the Scriptures, nor in the Confessions, nor in Luther's writings). The precise meaning of this grossly misused teaching cannot be explored in the brief space of this essay.[27] However, a few points are in order.

What does St. Peter mean to say about Christians in 1 Peter 2:5 when he describes them as a "priesthood" (ἱεράτευμα)? Certainly, he is alluding to Exodus 19, in which God refers to Israel as a "kingdom of priests." With a catena of Old Testament terminology, Peter applies to the Christian church all the gracious names and promises that God had given to His people Israel. What Israel was, the church is. "Priesthood" is thus primarily a reference to the election of God, a term of grace and promise and gift. God gives to His New Testament Christians what He gave to His Old Testament people, what is primarily described in terms of "holiness"—"holy" (ἅγιος) being the adjective first coupled with "priesthood" (ἱεράτευμα).

Secondly, we must ask what this "priesthood" is to *do*, for there are certainly verbs attached to it in 1 Peter. On the one hand, they are "to offer up spiritual sacrifices" (2:5), and on the other hand, they are "to proclaim the wonderful deeds of the One who called you out of darkness" (2:9). The former activity is manifestly sacrificial; the latter is often

---

[26] *BSLK*, 373. Author's English translation.

[27] On this see Thomas M. Winger, "The Priesthood of All the Baptized: An Exegetical and Theological Investigation" (S.T.M. Thesis, Concordia Seminary, 1992).

understood quasi-sacramentally, that is, that the priesthood speaks God's Word to His people. But the text does not give the *indirect object* of the speaking or proclaiming. So, who is it *to whom* they declare the deeds of God? The answer is obtained by tracing Peter's language through the Old Testament from which it came. In short, it can be shown that very similar language appears in the LXX Psalms as a description for *offering praise to God*.[28] In fact, one praises God best when one tells Him what great things He has done for us (just as, e.g., the Gloria in Excelsis and the Te Deum are mostly "You-talk," praising God by referring to all the good things He does for us).

Thus, the scriptural teaching on the priesthood of the baptized cannot be used to justify the performance of ministerial, sacramental actions by the laity. For when Holy Scripture describes what this priesthood does, it speaks only in terms of sacrifice and praise. It's that sort of priesthood.

Sacrificial and Sacramental Aspects of Divine Service

The preceding comments will be helpful in reaching a conclusion. Melanchthon, it is well known, distinguishes in the Apology between two aspects of *Gottesdienst*. He does this most clearly in the following section, speaking specifically of a celebration of the Lord's Supper:

> This use of the *sacrament*, when faith gives life to terrified hearts, is the worship [*cultus, der rechte Gottesdienst*] of the New Testament, because what matters in the New Testament is the spiritual motivation [*motus*], dying and being made alive.... There is also a *sacrifice*, since one action can have several purposes. Once faith has strengthened a conscience to see its liberation from terror, then it really gives thanks for the blessing of Christ's suffering. It uses the ceremony itself as a praise to God, as a demonstration of its gratitude, and a witness of its high esteem for God's gifts. Thus the ceremony becomes a sacrifice of praise. The Fathers speak of a twofold effect, of the comfort for the conscience and of thanksgiving or praise; the first of these belongs to the nature of the *sacrament*, and the second to the *sacrifice*.[29]

---

[28]The older translations offer quite rightly that we declare His "praises" (KJV) or "excellencies" (RSV). See parallels in Psalms 9:15, 55:9, 70:15, 72:28, 78:13, 106:22 and 118:13, 26 (all LXX numbering), where this "proclamation" always takes place in God's house and toward Him.

[29]Ap XXIV, 71, 74–75; Tappert, 262–63. Emphasis added.

In the fullness of the *Gottesdienst*, these two elements are present in their proper relationship. The latter responds to the former, the sacrifice being called forth from the one who receives the gift of the Sacrament.

The justification for the use of lay assisting ministers arises in large part from a confusion of the sacrificial and sacramental elements. The whole body of Christ is indeed involved in the service: there are those who give and those who receive. Just as the one who bears the office of the ministry should not infringe upon the congregation's role in the liturgy, stealing their "Amen,"[30] so also the congregation should not step into a foreign office by taking on the unique roles God has given to the pastor.[31] The body is whole when each part does what is uniquely its own.

Speaking in terms of the distinction between sacrament and sacrifice helps to clarify these roles. What is *sacramental* in the liturgy, God's gracious giving to man, is properly given to the ordained man who holds the office of Christ. This would include the Absolution, the Scripture Readings, the Sermon, the Sacrament, and the Benediction. The *sacrificial* is a response of faith, and thus it is given for all the baptized to offer. Faith is created by the sacramental gifts. It is the first office of the laity, therefore, to receive these gifts. Then they give back to God in prayer, praise, and thanksgiving. Although traditionally the pastor has also functioned sacrificially, carrying these three sacrificial elements before God on behalf of the congregation (as indeed Christ Himself bears them to God on our behalf), certain of the sacrificial elements of the liturgy could be offered by designated laymen. The traditional Lutheran office of "Kantor" reflects such an approach. The Kantor functioned as a choir reduced to one, even as the choir itself represented the congregation (not the clergy). Such duties might also include bidding the prayers of the people, but would not include proclaiming the Word or giving out the body and the blood. In such a way, the practice of the liturgy would confess what is truly happening; and instead of tempting God's people to regard His work as their work, it will prompt them to receive, rejoice, and respond in faith.

---

[30]Hence the prohibition of private masses among Lutherans.

[31]Tertullian (*Prescription Against Heresies*, 40) describes this as a characteristic of the heretics, that they grant to the laity the functions of priests.

Miscellanea

Liturgical Texts

Holy Absolution

Confirmation

Boolean Worship

With time rather limited at the forum, several topics received only cursory consideration. Though brief, the essays in this section offer important insights into topics that will figure prominently in the new hymnal.

The first essay examines issues related to current English-language versions of the liturgy. As work on the hymnal proceeds, questions will have to be asked concerning the faithfulness and usefulness of these translations. The second essay invites us to consider the rich blessings of Private Confession and Absolution and to ponder how the reintroduction of this practice would benefit our Synod. The third essay examines the issue of confirmation and offers several suggestions on how this venerated practice in our Synod might be more appropriately grounded in the church's sacramental life. In the final essay, a concept advanced in recent anthropological studies is applied to worship. While we must always be cautious in the use of extra-biblical theories, the concept of liminality offers some intriguing explanations of the great paradoxes of the Christian faith.

Liturgical Texts
Ecumenical Translations and Doctrinal Concerns

ROBERT A.D. CLANCY

THE ASSIGNED QUESTION TO BE ADDRESSED IN THIS ESSAY WAS WORDED, "Liturgical texts: do we strive to adopt ecumenical translations even if it means using less-than-desired texts on occasion, or do we go with our own translations, striving for faithfulness and accuracy?" In response to which, this author initially wondered, "Am I really going to present a group of confessional Lutheran theologians with an argument against faithfulness and accuracy?" In court, a lawyer would object to the question on the grounds that it has already answered itself. But on second thought, this author has never been one to avoid a challenge.

The Case for Ecumenical Translations

In *The Lutheran Liturgy,* Luther Reed observes succinctly that "the liturgy is the product and possession of the universal church."[1] This statement applies in particular to the ordinary of the liturgy: the Kyrie, Gloria, Creed, Sanctus, Lord's Prayer, and Agnus Dei. Much of the surrounding material in the liturgy has varied from church to church and, within specific churches, from age to age. But these "six chief parts" (of the liturgy) have all been able to hold their place (though the Gloria in Excelsis is on the wane in many churches, where "This Is the Feast" has replaced it). Whatever differences exist—both liturgical and doctrinal—between various churches, these six texts are a tie that binds them together in worship.

---

[1] Luther D. Reed, *The Lutheran Liturgy: A Study of the Common Liturgy of the Lutheran Church in America,* revised ed. (Philadelphia: Muhlenberg Press, 1959), 21.

Would it not be desirable, therefore, for all those who share this liturgical heritage—whether they have retained it (as have the Lutherans and Roman Catholics), or whether they are just now recovering it (as are the Methodists and Presbyterians)—to have the texts of the ordinary in a common translation and form? To this end, in the 1970s, the International Consultation on English Texts (ICET) published *Prayers We Have in Common*—translations of these shared liturgical texts in more contemporary English. The main purpose of this work was to "expose the Church's visible unity."[2] In this way, whatever differences exist between churches, one could still perceive and celebrate a common heritage in the confession of commonly held words.

By the mid-1980s, one could observe a "widespread usage" of the ICET texts.[3] As Horace Allen notes, this was "a vital test for any liturgical text. It must be prayed, chanted, spoken, sung, printed, and memorized."[4] (Perhaps not surprisingly, the greatest divergence from ICET translations occurred in the case of the Lord's Prayer.)[5] Following the success of these efforts, the English Language Liturgical Consultation (ELLC) was formed with the hope that the liturgy might continue to provide a unifying bond between churches and thus bring together the ecumenical and liturgical movements.

The case for ecumenically-agreed-upon texts for the liturgy is built upon a solid foundation: these texts are part of a common heritage, which continues to bind the church universal into one, even though "by schisms rent asunder, by heresies distressed."[6] To this, one might also add a practical aspect. In a day and age when people no longer remain within a single congregation (or even a single church body) for the majority of their lives, but move from place to place (and communion to communion), it is perhaps desirable for churches to share a common translation of their liturgical core.

---

[2]Horace T. Allen, Jr., "Vienna Consultation on Liturgical Texts," *Mid-Stream* 23 (January 1984): 133.
[3]Ibid., 134.
[4]Horace T. Allen, Jr. "Forum: Common Texts Revisited," *Worship* 60 (March 1986): 173.
[5]"Vienna Consultation," 134
[6]"The Church's One Foundation," *TLH* 473:4.

While Luther would object to the "church of the moment" mentality, the goal of common texts is one he would likely approve. Concerning his paraphrase of the Lord's Prayer in the *German Mass* (*Deutsche Messe*) of 1526, he wrote:

> I would . . . like to ask that this paraphrase or admonition follow a prescribed wording or be formulated in a definite manner for the sake of the common people. We cannot have one do it one way today, and another way tomorrow, and let everybody . . . confuse the people so that they can neither learn nor retain anything. What chiefly matters is the teaching and guiding of the people.[7]

In many ways, the use of common liturgical texts is an effort to apply Luther's advice in a contemporary, ecumenical context.

The ELLC Revisions: The Case Weakens

One of the first tasks undertaken by the ELLC was a revision of the ICET liturgical texts. It may be wondered why it was felt that a revision was necessary a mere decade after the new translations had been published. The guidelines for revision (adopted in 1985) offer a clue:

1. In order to avoid pastoral disruption, only necessary changes should be made.
2. Sensitivity should be shown to the need for inclusive language.
3. The revision should be made bearing in mind that these texts are for use in the liturgical assembly. The ease with which they can be said, heard, and sung is an essential element of the revision.
4. The revision should use language that is contemporary and suited to the present version of the ICET texts.[8]

Apparently, the desire for inclusive language was squarely behind the revision. How is this apparent? If one is trying to avoid "pastoral disruption," producing a revision so soon after the original version would seem to be counterproductive. Moreover, the rhythm and cadence of the ICET texts remained essentially unaltered in the ELLC revision, *Praying Together*, which would indicate that the "ease" of liturgical usage was not a real issue. And if the need for more contemporary language had been

---

[7]Martin Luther, *The German Mass and Order of Service, 1526;* trans. by Augustus Steimle, rev. Ulrich S. Leupold. AE 53:80.

[8]English Language Liturgical Consultation, *Praying Together* (Nashville: Abingdon Press, 1988), 7.

a major stumbling block with the ICET texts, then why didn't the ELLC insist on changing such archaisms as "hallowed" in the Lord's Prayer? It is significant to note that at the Vienna Consultation in 1983, inclusive language was deemed "to be largely a North American preoccupation."[9] Thus, it appears that the large number of North American churches which became involved in the ELLC turned this preoccupation into a priority in revision.

All of this is not to say that inclusive language is wrong *per se*. The reality of the contemporary American dialect of the English language is that "man" is no longer universally accepted as a generic term for "human." People today tend to hear "man" with an exclusively masculine denotation. Consequently, to say that Christ was incarnate "for us men" might (and does) imply to many women that they are not included. To avoid a similar misperception, *LW* altered the hymn, "Hark! the Herald Angels Sing" (stanza 3), replacing "Born to raise the sons of earth" with "Born to raise each child of earth."[10] Charles Wesley, when he wrote the hymn, surely did not intend "sons of earth" to exclude women; but that is how many would perceive it today. So, inclusive language is not inherently wrong and is sometimes necessary.

However, should inclusive language involve a change in the way we reference God? The ELLC recognized that "male-oriented language referring to God presents greater problems. ELLC considered that the removal of all masculine forms would take the texts beyond the process of translation and into the realm of theological reinterpretation."[11] Nevertheless, the ELLC did reduce the number of masculine pronouns referring to God, "without compromising fidelity to the original texts."[12]

Ultimately, the ELLC revision weakens the argument for having a common text, for there is an agenda apparent in the push for revision— one that is not universal even to all those countries speaking English, let alone all churches within the consultation. Allen recognized the situa-

---

[9]"Vienna Consultation," 134.
[10]*LW*, no. 49.
[11]*Praying Togethe*r, 7.
[12]Ibid. This begs the question, to put it mildly.

tion from the outset: "The more these matters are negotiated the clearer it becomes that the English-speaking churches are, in our time, caught in a difficult tangle of ecumenical and linguistic priorities."[13]

All of this becomes evident when one examines the responses to a survey on the use of the ELLC texts among the various churches involved in the Consultation on Common Texts (CCT). These responses varied widely, but no church indicated a use of the ELLC texts exclusively or without alteration (the United Methodist Church showed the greatest adherence). Most indicated a preference either for the traditional translations used in their church or for the ICET translation. The United Church of Christ made the most significant objection—that the inclusive language did not go far enough: "Although there is not full consensus in the United Church of Christ about monarchical, exclusively masculine and/or three-tiered cosmology language, it is honest to say that these concerns make some of the texts unusable to many of our members."[14] In a summary "reflection" on the responses to the survey, members of the CCT observed:

> Inclusive language as it relates to ways of addressing and referring to God in liturgical texts has become increasingly important in North American Christianity. On this topic there is evident tension, not only in differing positions between the Churches but also in the give and take within individual Churches. The issue is made only more complex by the common belief of these Churches that we worship a Trinitarian God, the Second Person of whom preexisted creation, became incarnate as a human person, and in his humanity died and rose to glory.[15]

---

[13]"Forum: Common Texts," 175. On p. 172, he even goes so far as to subtitle his article, "Is English One Language?"

[14]Thomas E. Dipko, "Brief Response to the ELLC Survey on Common Liturgical Texts" (April 18, 1995, photocopied).

[15]Consultation on Common Texts, "Reflections on the Responses of the Member Churches of the CCT to the ELLC Texts," Document No. 2 (December 1996, photocopied), 2. The interesting choice of language in this paragraph seems to imply that the incarnation causes problems for inclusive language referring to God, which begs the question: which should we abandon, the doctrine of the incarnation or inclusive language referring to the Second Person of the Trinity?

They further note that "it is perhaps over this ongoing issue of God language that the Churches' commitment to the common liturgical texts will be most tested."[16] And in their final reflection they admit that

> Solid and long-lived solutions to the tensions that arise from the accompanying responses do not seem yet at hand. The Consultation on Common Texts has had difficulty in its own discussions of these matters arriving at proposals that seem satisfactory even to a fair number of its participants.[17]

It is with this confession/concession that the case falls apart for adopting "ecumenical translations even if it means using less-than-desired texts on occasion."

A Responsible Response

The notion is a good one, that all English-speaking churches might share a common translation of those texts that are at the heart of our liturgical heritage. That situation would be desirable in many ways. But it needs to be remembered that liturgical language is, by its very nature, theological. The words chosen to render a liturgical text in one's own language express a particular confession, and no church—no matter where they are on the theological spectrum—will willingly abandon its own confession for the sake of ecumenical liturgical consensus. Thus the response of the CCT churches to the ELLC texts.

It is not true, however, that "ecumenical translations" are always "less-than-desired texts." In fact, the ELLC translations often do reflect a greater faithfulness and accuracy to the original texts than many of our currently-used translations, as well as a greater clarity of expression.[18] Even in the area of inclusive language, the ELLC translations at least suggest places where sensitivity ought to be employed.

Consider, for example, the Nicene Creed. In two lines, 13 and 16, the term "men/man" has been abandoned by the ELLC. Line 13 reads, "for us

---

[16]Ibid.

[17]Ibid, 3.

[18]Compare, for instance, the ELLC translation of the line 24 of the Nicene Creed, "and his kingdom will have no end," with *LW*'s ambiguous "whose kingdom shall have no end" (i.e., whose kingdom—Christ's or the living and the dead's?).

and for our salvation." Here, the Greek word ἀνθρώπους remains untranslated. Line 16 reads, "and became truly human." In this case, an alternative translation of the Greek ἐνανθρωπήσαντα was sought to replace "man." In each case, inclusive language is the primary issue. But should our response to both revisions be the same?

True, the easy response is simply to reject inclusive language *in toto*. But in doing so, we would also reject those individuals who believe that speaking only of "men" excludes them from the discourse—and the doctrine. It is easier, then, but neither pastorally nor theologically responsible. After all, ἄνθρωπος is the generic word for "human," as opposed to the gender-specific ἀνήρ ("man"). Perhaps one could find a richer way of translating line 13 than a bare "us," as even the ELLC concedes.[19] But if using "men" causes part of Christ's body to feel excluded, then by all means let us translate in a way that preserves the universal scope of Christ's redemption without seeming to exclude some of those who are very much included.

Line 16 is another issue. One may concede that "became truly human" is an adequate translation, perhaps in some ways even superior to the traditional "and was made man" (again, the universal ἄνθρωπος is used, not the gender-specific ἀνήρ). Yet, here we are no longer speaking of all humanity, but confessing the singular fact of the incarnation. And Christ was incarnate as a *man*. The very polysemy of the word, "*man*," is here advantageous: He was man, as in male; and as such, He was man, as in a member of the human race.

The Nicene Creed moves from people-talk in line 13 to God-talk in line 16. That, in itself, could and perhaps should influence our decision regarding the translation of the latter text. As in the previous section, God-talk is a divisive issue because of current political and theological agendas. In such a case, Article x of the Formula of Concord seems to apply: "When a clear-cut confession of faith is demanded of us, we dare not yield to the enemies in such indifferent things" (FC Ep x, 6).[20] Given the challenge to the incarnation in current theological discourse, it is

---

[19] *Praying Together*, 25.
[20] Tappert, 493.

inadvisable to yield any ground that might stage a battle over such a fundamental doctrine.

Conclusion

Ultimately, in answer to the question posed at the beginning of this study, it must be said that ecumenicity is not sufficient reason to adopt objectionable translations of liturgical texts (especially when no one else is using them intact, which leads one to wonder how ecumenical they really are). Accuracy of translation and fidelity to both the original texts and our confession of the faith must remain primary.

Nonetheless, the ELLC revisions of the ICET texts might serve as a starting-point for the discussion of how liturgical texts should be translated in the next hymnal. Moreover, many of the ELLC guidelines for revision could serve as sound tools for use in the process of arriving at faithful, accurate, and useful translations. Above all, the principle of making only necessary changes should be heeded for the sake of God's people, for whom familiarity with the words of the liturgy is so important. Robert Taft, a Jesuit liturgist, seems to echo Luther's advice in the *German Mass*, when he writes, "I think it is time we liturgists came out strongly against [a] school-play approach to the awesome worship of God, and returned to the people the tradition that is theirs, not just ours."[21]

---

[21]Robert Taft, "Response to the Berakah Award: Anamnesis," *Worship* 59 (July 1985): 320–321.

Holy Absolution
Extolling and Rejoicing in the Gift

BRENT W. KUHLMAN

"WHAT IS CONFESSION?" SO READS THE QUESTION OF THE SMALL Catechism, in much the same way as the other two questions: "What is Baptism?" and "What is the Sacrament of the Altar?" But the answer is somewhat different. Here the Catechism responds with a breakdown of the activity itself. "Confession has two parts. First that we confess our sins, and second, that we receive Absolution, that is, forgiveness, from the pastor as from God Himself, not doubting, but firmly believing that by it our sins are forgiven before God in heaven." Then follows instruction as to which sins should be confessed: "Before God we should plead guilty of all sin, even those we are not aware of, as we do in the Lord's Prayer; but before the pastor we should confess only those sins which we know and feel in our hearts." The next question asks, "Which are these?" And the answer is found in the examination of one's place in life according to the Ten Commandments. Finally, Luther's liturgical formula is provided as an example of how one may confess to the pastor. The point is this: the concern of the Small Catechism is that sins be confessed, in order to be absolved.

We confess what the Lord has given. What He has instituted is for the existence and well-being of His church. What the Lord has given to His church is certain and sure. He has given Holy Baptism for washing and regeneration. He has given the Holy Supper for eating and drinking. He has given the Office of the Keys for loosing and binding sin.

> Jesus therefore said to them again, "Peace be with you; as the Father has sent Me, I also send you." And when He had said this, He breathed on them, and said to them, "Receive the Holy Spirit. If you forgive the sins of any, their sins have been forgiven them; if you retain the sins of any, they have been retained" (John 20:21–23; see also Matt. 16:19; 18:18–20).

Consequently, the Augsburg Confession states that "through these, as through means, He gives the Holy Spirit, who works faith, when and where He pleases, in those who hear the Gospel" (AC v, 2). Pastoral care is most concerned with faith, justifying faith, faith that receives the forgiveness of sins, God's grace, and the righteousness of Christ. "The highest worship in the Gospel is the desire to receive forgiveness of sins, grace, and righteousness" (Ap IV, 310). Faith receives what is given. Indeed, it is called into existence as it receives the Gospel and the Sacraments.

When the Small Catechism asks, "What is Confession?", it has arrived at the apex of pastoral care: faith, which clings to the *viva vox Christi* ("the living voice of Christ") in the Absolution. That is how Luther extols it. And that is how one seminary professor describes it:

> In private absolution there occurs the application of the universal promise of grace to anyone at all separately, so that whoever has been absolved can and should claim with certainty that Christ surely has forgiven him his sins because He has announced it to him with His own voice through the minister's absolution, no differently from how He did in the case of the paralytic: "My son, be of good cheer. Your sins are forgiven you," Matt. 9.[1]

Philip Melanchthon described Luther's reformation as the evangelical teaching and restoration of Confession and Absolution.[2] And Theodor Kliefoth (1810–95) likewise maintained that the Reformation was essentially the restoration of Confession and Absolution.[3] Melanchthon and Kliefoth were correct.

Confession and Absolution are anchored in the life of Holy Baptism (repentance = contrition and faith) and flow into the Lord's Supper. That is the arrangement of the Small Catechism, which confesses the truth of Holy Scripture. The Fifth Chief Part on Confession is sandwiched between the Fourth Chief Part on Holy Baptism and the Sixth Chief Part on the Sacrament of the Altar. These mark the life of a sinner who is justified by grace through faith.

---

[1] David Chytraeus, *A Summary of the Christian Faith (1568)*, trans. Richard Dinda (Decatur, Ill.: Repristination Press, 1994), 137.

[2] Martin Luther, *Widder das wuetende urteyl der Pariser Theologisten, 1521*, WA 8:311.

[3] Theodor Kliefoth, "Die Beichte und Absolution," in *Liturgische Abhandlungen* (Schwerin: Verlag der Stiller'schen Hof-Buchhandlung, 1856), 2:125.

Likewise, witness the order of the articles in the Augsburg Confession. Article II: Original Sin. Article III: The Son of God. Salvation is accomplished in the crucified, risen, and ascended Jesus. The articles that follow confess the delivery of this salvation through the Son of God. Article V: The Office of the Ministry. Articles VII–VIII: The Church. Article IX: Baptism. Article X: The Lord's Supper. Articles XI–XII: Confession and Repentance. Article XIII: The Use of the Sacraments. "The doctrine of penitence and the doctrine of justification are very closely related" (Ap XII, 59). In Holy Absolution, the words of Christ have their locatedness (the "when" and "where" of Article V), as they also do in Holy Baptism and the Lord's Supper. Consequently, "It is taught among us that private absolution should be retained and not allowed to fall into disuse" (AC XI, 1). And again, "We keep confession, especially because of the absolution, which is the Word of God that the power of the keys proclaims to individuals by divine authority (*quae est verbum Dei quod de singulis auctoritate divina pronuntiat potestas clavium*). It would therefore be wicked to remove private absolution from the church. (*Quare impium esset ex ecclesia privatam absolutionem tollere.*)" (Ap XII, 99–100).

Note too the order of the Smalcald Articles in Part III. Sin (Article I) revealed by the Law (Article II) is confessed (Article III) and forgiven by the Gospel (Article IV). The Gospel is the spoken and external word of forgiveness delivered in Baptism (Article V), the Sacrament of the Altar (Article VI), the Keys and Confession (Articles VII–VIII), and the mutual conversation and consolation of the brethren according to Matthew 18:20. Here Luther teaches that justification by grace through faith is not a mantra, cliché, theory, concept, slogan, or human reflection. It is a divine fact, a reality, the enactment of God on behalf of the sinner through the Word and the sacramental Word of the Divine Service. Accordingly, "We should and must constantly maintain that God will not deal with us except through his external Word and sacrament (*äußerlich Wort und Sakrament*). Whatever is attributed to the Spirit apart from such Word and sacrament is of the devil" (SA III, VIII, 10).

Suppose a member of the high-school debate team stands at the podium and says, "I'm here to debate. I must stand here. I must speak to the issue at hand. I have 15 minutes in which to speak. I cannot call my opponent dirty names." Has he spoken falsely? No. But has he debated? No. He has recited the rules of the debate, but he has not debated. Similarly, when a pastor says that "justification is by grace through faith," has he forgiven anyone's sins? No. Has he said anything which is false? No. Has he recited the rules of theological grammar? Yes. But simply stating the guidelines and boundaries of theological syntax is not a proclamation of the Gospel.

Our theological grammar should be correct. We are rightly concerned with sound doctrine. But we are also concerned that "orthodoxy" not degenerate into empty sloganeering, that orthodox teaching not be divorced from its right practice. We correctly teach that we are saved by grace through faith. But if this grace and faith are detached from the preached and sacramental Gospel, we may wake up like Rip van Winkle to discover that we are living and breathing in a totally different world— the world of mere assurances, of promises and decisions, of biblical principles for healthy and wealthy living, happy lives, and moral values. All of this might seem like common sense. It might appear to be religious, pious, and devout. But strictly speaking, such a life is not that which lives in and through the Gospel. Dietrich Bonhoeffer writes of a similar situation in his day. His discernment is appropriate for the theological climate in which we live.

> Cheap grace is the deadly enemy of our Church. We are fighting today for costly grace. Cheap grace means grace sold on the market like cheapjacks' wares. The sacraments, the forgiveness of sin, and the consolations of religion are thrown away at cut prices. Grace is presented as the Church's inexhaustible treasury, from which she showers blessings with generous hands, without asking questions or fixing limits. Grace without price; grace without cost! The essence of grace, we suppose, is that the account has been paid in advance; and, because it has been paid, everything can be had for nothing. Since the cost was infinite, the possibilities of using and spending it are infinite. What would grace be if it were not cheap? Cheap grace means grace as a doctrine, a principle, a system. It means forgiveness of sins proclaimed as a general truth, the love of God taught as the Christian "conception" of God. An intellectual assent to that idea is held to be of itself sufficient to secure remission of sins. The Church which holds the correct doctrine of grace has, it is supposed, *ipso facto* a part in that grace. In such a Church the world finds a cheap covering for its sins; no contrition is required, still less any real desire to be delivered from sin. Cheap

Holy Absolution

grace therefore amounts to a denial of the living Word of God, in fact, a denial of the Incarnation of the Word of God. Cheap grace means the justification of sin without the justification of the sinner. . . . Cheap grace is the grace we bestow on ourselves. Cheap grace is the preaching of forgiveness without requiring repentance, baptism without church discipline, Communion without personal confession. Cheap grace is grace without discipleship, grace without the cross, grace without Jesus Christ, living and incarnate.[4]

Justification by grace through faith is intimately bound to the preached Word and the Sacraments. When these, which God has joined together, are separated, one arrives in the land of American Protestant Enthusiasm. But rather, Gottfried Martens, pastor of St. Mary Lutheran Church, Berlin, Germany, explains justification this way:

It is self-evident, but nevertheless very important to say that in the Lutheran Confessions justification is throughout proclaimed and confessed as an act of the Triune God happening to sinful man, which continually comes to pass in Word and Sacrament, that is, in baptism, in the sermon, in holy communion, and *especially in the sacrament of holy absolution.* Justification . . . is a sacramental deed which is concertized [sic] in the worship service of the Christian congregation. It is an action in which God executes the sinner, and absolves him; in which God kills him, and raises him from the dead to a new life. . . . The Lutheran Confessions . . . teach that in preaching, in the absolution, and in the eucharist the Christian is led back to the saving act of God in baptism, which remains the decisive reality in his new life.[5]

Even psychologists are aware of this truth. A licensed psychologist from Wauwatosa, Wis., Dr. Beverly Yahnke states: "Holy Absolution is the divine miracle of God's grace given to a soul parched for mercy and pardon. . . . I had the sacred privilege of receiving Christ's personal acquittal from my sin."[6]

---

[4]Dietrich Bonhoeffer, *The Cost of Discipleship*, revised and unabridged ed. (New York: Macmillan Publishing Company, 1959), 45–47.

[5]Gottfried Martens, "Sola Fide—Do Lutherans Still Agree on What Is Meant?" Typed doc. (paper presented at the 13th Annual Symposium on the Lutheran Confessions, Concordia Theological Seminary, Fort Wayne, Ind., January 1990), 2–3. Emphasis added.

[6]Beverly Yahnke, "An Extravagance of Grace: One Penitent's Response to Individual Confession and Absolution," *For the Life of the World* 1 (December 1997): 9.

Why did Luther and the Lutheran Confessions extol Private Confession and Absolution? Why did the various church orders in Europe after the Reformation provide for its use in the church? Precisely because this is one of the ways and means whereby God justifies the sinner graciously for Christ's sake. Confession and Absolution, in particular, Private Confession and Absolution, is not only where justification by grace through faith is kept pure in the church; it is also one of the places where justification by grace is operative in the life of the believer.

Justification dare not be regarded as an abstract doctrine to which we assent intellectually, doff our hat, and then bid adieu with our practice. God justifies the sinner by terrifying and killing him with His Law, then raising the new man to an abundant life of faith in Christ. Existentially speaking, justification "happens." It happens by means of the Word and Sacrament, in which God graciously justifies the sinner and faith receives what God does and gives. To quote Martens again:

> For the Lutheran Confessions justification is essentially understood on the background of the sacramental practice of confession and absolution. . . . "When I admonish you to go to confession, I do nothing else than to admonish you to be a Christian," Luther says in the Large Catechism. To evoke this insight in the congregation would be an appropriate object for a renewal in Missouri, for this could contribute to the realization of justification as the fundamental act of God.[7]

Absolution is the spoken Gospel (Ap IV, 271). It is the true voice of the Gospel (Ap XII, 39). It is a great help against sin and a tormented conscience. It brings reconciliation, delivery from the wrath of God. It is the enactment of justification by grace, to be received in and with faith. "When we are baptized, when we eat the Lord's body, when we are absolved, our hearts should firmly believe that God really forgives us for Christ's sake" (Ap XIII, 4).

The achievement of salvation happened at a particular place and time: in the body of Jesus outside of Jerusalem on the tree, *circa* A.D. 33. So also do the delivery and bestowal of salvation happen in a particular place and time. Justification happens in space and time, the particular space and time where and when God puts Himself: the waters of

---

[7]Martens, "Sola Fide," 12

Holy Absolution

Baptism applied to the body; the sound waves of preaching, vibrating in the ear and convicting the heart; the body and blood of the Supper consumed with the mouth; a word from the tongue and vocal chords of a brother or sister in Christ, or from the pastor, entering the ears of a penitent. Just as there is necessarily a specific time and place for Baptism, preaching, and the Supper, so is there a need for the specific time and place of Confession and Absolution.

While many search desperately for the key to effective preaching, the key to courageous ministry, the key to exciting youth work, the key to inspiring teaching and celebrative worship, the key to growth, the key to stopping back door losses, the key to more efficient restructuring, the key to this, the key to that—the Lord has given His church the Office of the Keys. Every believer, by virtue of his Baptism, is privileged to forgive his neighbor and thus to exercise the Office of the Keys, each within his own particular station in life. How much more, then, should the man who has been entrusted with the office of the holy ministry use the Keys to unlock or shut tight heaven!

How often are the Keys employed in Christian families or in the many and various places that Christians live and work? Far more often what happens is grudge-holding, grounding, a cold shoulder, the silent treatment, or sleeping on the couch. Rarely, one suspects, is there any straightforward practice of Confession and forgiveness, but rather explanations and excuses. And probably a lot of this talk: "I said I'm sorry." "I promise I'll never do it again." "That's okay." "Don't worry about it." Then again, how often do the members of a congregation forgive each other with the words, "I forgive you," or "Jesus forgives you"? One is more likely to find resentment, discontent, gossip, and murmuring. But Christ would not have His Keys to rust and crumble from such disuse. Thus, He has also provided a public office in which men are put under a stole with orders to forgive the repentant (and to withhold forgiveness from the unrepentant, so long as they do not repent).

As the LCMS Commission on Worship prepares for a new hymnal, the issue of Confession and Absolution is its *proprium*. Do we baptize *en masse*? Do we eat the Lord's Supper like some Protestants who pass around bread and grape juice among themselves in their theater chairs?

No. The Lutheran pastor deals with each person individually. "I baptize you (singular)." "The body of Christ for you (singular). The blood of Christ for you (singular)." "*Ego absolvo te*" ("I forgive you") is how the Latin rite speaks forgiveness to the individual. Thus the penitent is asked, "Do you believe that my forgiveness is God's forgiveness?"

Does this rule out the use of a Corporate or General Confession and Absolution? Not necessarily. There are many in our congregations who cling to the Corporate Absolution. We dare not take that away. Osiander at Nürnberg was advised by the Wittenberg faculty that a General Confession and Absolution could be used. But he was to remember that the norm was Private Confession and Absolution, and that it be continued. Unfortunately, Pietism and Rationalism sounded the death knell for Private Confession and Absolution, so highly extolled by Luther and the Confessions, so that in our day, the addendum has replaced the norm.

We do not question the content of the General Absolution. There are questions to be raised, however: is the General Confession and Absolution the best way to deliver the gift? Does it extol the *proprium* of Holy Absolution? Is it the wrong tool at the wrong time? Are we casting pearls before swine in some cases? Is it a proper distinction of the Law and the Gospel when a pastor absolves people without any knowledge of their life and confession? And what about the binding key? Wilhelm Loehe maintains that

> absolution will be worth more if there is also excommunication. Comfort will be treasured if it is not given in every situation. In fact the entire institution of confession will be ridiculed if men know in advance that everyone will be comforted and absolved.... The church certainly does not carry out its responsibility in the care of souls if it does not use the key that binds. Easy care of souls is worthless; its very love is to be doubted. There is no such thing as care of souls without training and discipline. Gentleness works for fathers only when they also know the proper time to be strict with their children, just as severity in a man makes the right impression only if he is able to be gentle when the good of others requires it.[8]

How impoverished have we become since one of the ordinary ways of pastoral care, Private Absolution, has been relegated to the extraordi-

---

[8] Wilhelm Löhe, *Three Books About the Church*, trans. James L. Schaaf (Philadelphia: Fortress Press, 1969), 176.

nary or emergency situation? What has been lost? In 1859, two officials of the Northern District, Ottomar Fuerbringer (1810–92) and Friedrich Lochner (1822–1902), maintained that to deprive a congregation the benefits of Private Confession and Absolution would harm the congregation, the Synod, those outside the Synod, our children and our posterity.[9]

In 1522, Dr. Luther allowed the Wittenbergers to receive the Lord's Supper under one kind, even though it was not the proper evangelical understanding or reception of that gift. First there had to be the proclamation of God's Word before the inappropriate old forms would fall away. In a similar fashion, it would be hasty to make such a bold change as to remove the General Confession and Absolution from the hymnal. Preaching and teaching—and the receiving of Holy Absolution individually by the pastors themselves—these will be the means to win the hearts of the people. The General Confession and Absolution may be used in the church. It is not unchristian. The Gospel, in and of itself, is a general Absolution.[10] But it should be used along with a lively and ongoing use of Private Confession and Absolution in our congregations. C.F.W. Walther gives this advice:

> In an evangelical way, through instruction and exhortation, and through praising it, [the pastor should] work toward the goal that [Private Confession] be diligently used in addition to general confession and that, where it is possible and advisable, it be finally reintroduced as the exclusive custom and that it be properly preserved where it exist."[11]

This will be quite a task! Humanly speaking, it is impossible. But not with the Lord. As Loehe rightly observes:

> All other methods of individual care of souls have proved unsatisfactory and often impracticable substitutes for private confession. . . . The reintroduction will not be so difficult as one might think. There are examples to prove that it may be successful. Of course, we must be ready and willing to take some trou-

---

[9]Carl S. Meyer, ed., *Moving Frontiers: Readings in the History of The Lutheran Church—Missouri Synod* (St. Louis: CPH, 1964), 241.

[10]Martin Luther, "Luther, Bugenhagen, Justus Jonas, Melanchthon und Kaspar Cruciger an den Rat zu Nürnberg," *WA Br* 6:529, 62, notes: "Also ist das Evangelium selbs eine gemeine Absolution."

[11]C.F.W. Walther, *Pastoral Theology*, trans. and abridged by John M. Drickamer from the 5th ed., 1906 (New Haven, Mo.: Lutheran News Inc., 1995), 120.

ble to get accustomed to something new. The more we become accustomed to it, the more its blessing will be apparent.[12]

The Lord has put you at a specific place to be the steward of His mysteries (1 Cor. 4:1). The Holy Spirit creates faith when and where it pleases Him in those who hear the Gospel. So, dear brother pastors, happy preaching and teaching. Happy confessing. Happy forgiving. All heaven will break loose! And with that, the joy of all the angels over the sinner who repents!

---

[12] Löhe, *Three Books*, 174–175.

Confirmation
Living and Rejoicing in the Sacramental Life

Kent J. Burreson

LITURGICAL REVISION IS UNQUESTIONABLY A RISKY MATTER. LITURGICAL rites and hymnody are the most formative elements in the shaping of theology and piety among the people of God. Confirmation is one process and rite that has indelibly shaped Lutherans, including Missouri Synod Lutherans. Many Lutherans treasure their confirmation (which they should)—but perhaps even as highly as the Sacraments of Holy Baptism, Holy Absolution, and the Lord's Supper. (For the Lutheran confession of Holy Absolution as a Sacrament, see LC IV, 74; Ap XIII, 4.) Yet, the high esteem in which confirmation is held often overshadows the benefits and gifts that are offered in the means of forgiveness. This betrays the reality that the church has done a poor job of deriving confirmation's purpose from the Sacraments.

The catechetical process and liturgical rite of confirmation is a rite in search of a meaning, a rite desperately seeking a theology. The ambiguity inherent in confirmation is rooted in its checkered liturgical history prior to the 16th century, the diverse responses of the Lutheran reformers to confirmation's liturgical aspects, and the one-time celebration of the rite in association with first communion. Any liturgical revision of confirmation within the Missouri Synod should attempt to alleviate this catechetical and liturgical ambiguity by locating confirmation—with both its catechetical and liturgical aspects—within the broader sacramental life of the church. The means of forgiveness provide the *raison d'être* for confirmation; its purpose must always be to support and strengthen the church's sacramental life. Every aspect of confirmation, catechetically and liturgically, should serve this purpose.

A Lutheran Understanding of Confirmation: The Catechetical Element

Studies of Lutheran confirmation demonstrate that, for the Lutheran reformers, the catechetical instruction preceding the rite is at its center. The foundation for this instructional process is the baptismal mandate of Christ in Matthew 28:19–20, "Go therefore and make disciples of all nations, baptizing them in the name of the Father and of the Son and of the Holy Spirit, teaching them to observe all things that I have commanded you; and lo, I am with you always, even to the end of the age" (NKJV). Each Christian, at his or her Baptism, is blessed with the gift of the Holy Spirit, the teacher *par excellence* in St. John's trinitarian theology (see John 14 and 16; 1 John 2). Baptism immerses the Christian into the life of the Holy Spirit, who, in turn, continually immerses the Christian in the Word and Sacraments.

Likewise, the New Testament often links the Greek words for Holy Baptism with those for teaching, learning, and knowing. St. Paul uses a relatively rare Greek word to convey the uniqueness of Christian instruction in the content of the faith, the word from which we derive the term, "catechesis." This catechesis—instruction in the Word, or immersion in Christ—is a constant way of life for the baptized people of God. A Lutheran understanding of confirmation will take this scriptural perspective seriously. It will not allow confirmation to be viewed as a one-time educational ministry of the church. It will affirm, instead, that confirmation is at heart a lifelong process of instruction and immersion in the Word (in Christ), a continuation of the baptismal life.

The inclusion of Dr. Martin Luther's Large and Small Catechisms among the confessional corpus of the Lutheran Church affirms a Lutheran understanding of confirmation as a lifelong catechetical process. The Preface to the Large Catechism, for example, stresses the lifelong nature of catechetical instruction. It is this emphasis on lifelong catechesis that places confirmation firmly within the context of the church's sacramental life. For this catechesis bears the Christian from Baptism to first communion, and from the daily remembrance of Baptism to the regular hearing of the Holy Absolution and the weekly reception of the Lord's Supper. Immersion in the Word is the baptismal current that bears the Christian from one sacramental celebration to another, while unfolding the depths of meaning in those sacramental celebrations.

In a sense, for three Lutheran reformers, Martin Luther, Johannes Bugenhagen, and Johann Brenz, confirmation (as lifelong catechesis) becomes a post-baptismal catechumenate paralleling the pre-baptismal catechumenate of the early church—one that prepares a person for reception of the Lord's Supper. All three reformers stressed that if confirmation was to be retained by the church, then it must be conceived as a catechetical enterprise, a repetitive catechesis at that. Each time a communicant, whether a young child or an adult, prepares to receive the Lord's Supper, he or she becomes a catechumen once again. The catechesis, including Individual Confession and Absolution, was intended to insure that the recipient would receive the benefits of the Lord's Supper. Which is to say, that post-baptismal catechesis prepares for a worthy reception of the Lord's Supper.

In a monumental study of Lutheran confirmation, Arthur Repp termed this, among his five types of confirmation, the "catechetical type." This type, which subsequently shaped nearly all Lutheran confirmation rites, did not necessarily include any ritual act at all. By focusing upon examination and instruction in the chief parts of the catechism—the Ten Commandments, the Creed, the Lord's Prayer, and the three means of forgiveness—this catechetical type immerses the catechumen in Christ, not through a ritual act of confirmation, but through the proclamation of scriptural, Christ-bearing words and through the ritual act of Confession and Absolution. A Lutheran understanding of confirmation will emphasize that confirmation is, first and foremost, a process of being taught by the Holy Spirit through lifelong catechesis in preparation for regular reception of the Lord's body and blood. Any rite of confirmation should serve to buttress this lifelong confirmation process.

A Lutheran Understanding of Confirmation: The Liturgical/Ritual Element

Although the Lutheran reformers thought of confirmation as a lifelong catechetical process, what they inherited from the medieval western church was a ritual act that had developed out of Baptism. The reformers—Luther and Martin Chemnitz, in particular—denounced medieval confirmation, that is, the bishop's anointing of the confirmand with chrism ("oil," understood theologically in many circles as a completion of the grace given in Baptism), which they regarded as a blasphemy against the efficacy of Baptism and against Christ who instituted Baptism. As Chemnitz and modern authors have shown, the medieval sacrament of confirmation developed out of various post-baptismal ceremonies, such as the laying on of hands and anointing with oil, which were intended to portray the rich benefits bestowed on the newly-baptized in Baptism. However, in the western church, the laying on of hands and the administration of oil was eventually reserved to the bishop as a sign of his personal involvement in the Baptism of the catechumens, whether he was personally present for the Baptism or not. As it became more common for this episcopal rite to be separated in time from the actual Baptism, the term, "confirmation," was employed to convey its distinctiveness. Eventually, this separation of the rites—both in practice and in terminology—resulted in the definition of confirmation as a Sacrament intended to complete what Baptism supposedly failed to provide: the fullness of the Holy Spirit, His graces and benefits.

Attempting to steer completely away from any understanding that would undermine Baptism, the Lutheran reformers adopted a number of different approaches to the rite of confirmation. They sought to affirm the statement of Philipp Melanchthon in the Apology of the Augsburg Confession that confirmation was a rite received from the Fathers (Ap XIII, 6). Arthur Repp categorized the various approaches of the different church orders into types, many of which shared features in common with one another. These types included the catechetical type previously mentioned; the hierarchical type, which focused on a profession of faith and a vow of obedience to the church; the sacramental type, centered in the laying on of hands with prayer; and the traditional type, which preserved many elements of medieval confirmation.

Although these types emphasize different ritual elements, they all in some way confirm the catechetical process conducted prior to the rite (often with a profession of faith), and they all make reference to or affirm each catechumen's Baptism. Central, therefore, to a Lutheran

Confirmation

understanding of confirmation, is what might be called ritual or liturgical parallelism. That is to say, the rite of confirmation parallels as closely as possible the texts—and potentially also the ceremonies—of Holy Baptism. Confirmation, as a result, has no independent ritual existence. It functions, instead, much like Confession and Absolution, as a return (by faith) to the promises made by the Lord at an individual's Baptism. The Lord speaks again the words of promise given in Baptism, reminding the catechumen of his or her continuing, lifelong benefit. This is most concretely the case with the profession of faith. Here the individual repeats the same threefold confession of the Apostles' Creed in the same question and answer format as at Baptism. This affirms that the individual has been immersed in the same faith from the time of Baptism until this affirmation of Baptism.

The liturgical parallelism need not stop with the profession of faith. As with most of the current Lutheran confirmation rites, the parallelism might include the laying on of hands with prayer. This practice, adopted by many 16th-century rites of Baptism, follows the apostolic custom of intercessory prayer, identifying that prayer for a particular individual through the laying on of hands. In such cases, the prayer ought to recall the prayer spoken over the catechumen at his or her Baptism. This consciously links confirmation to Baptism, in order to immerse the catechumen once again in the Lord's promises given at Baptism.

The liturgical parallels with Baptism might also include a rekindling of the baptismal candle, a signing of the cross with the appropriate text, and perhaps even anointing with oil. Admittedly, the re-introduction of anointing at Baptism and confirmation would have to be done with great pastoral sensitivity. No one should be led to believe that anointing somehow completes Baptism. Nevertheless, it seems that most people, removed from the controversies of the 16th century, would not draw such conclusions today. The anointing at Baptism, with an appropriate text, would remind the baptized that in the waters of Baptism, they have been anointed with the Holy Spirit in Christ and sealed with the cross of Christ forever. An anointing at confirmation would then also recall the significance of the anointing in Baptism. Of course, the addition of ceremonies in Baptism and confirmation has the potential to obscure the sacramental washing of the water with the Word. The means to prevent such obfuscation lies in the preparation of texts that clearly and repeatedly lead the baptized back to that Word and those waters of Holy Baptism.

One other way to lead the baptized back to the waters of their Baptism would be through the use of a baptismal/confirmation vow. Such vows in confirmation are not foreign to the Lutheran tradition, having found their way into Lutheran confirmation rites through the liturgical example of Martin Bucer. In the 16th century, such vows included a profession of loyalty to the faith, to the baptismal covenant, to Christ, to church discipline, to Christian living, and to a regular reception of the means of grace.

The problem with such vows is the way they can give the false impression that a person participates somehow in the Lord's work of conversion and justification. Furthermore, in order for a vow at confirmation to be most beneficial, particularly as a way of recalling Baptism, a similar vow would have to be included in the baptismal rite, as well, which Lutherans have been very reticent to do. These obstacles may be overcome through the use of what might be called a "passive vow." Although not necessarily worded in the passive voice, such a vow would be theologically passive; in other words, it would be made clear that the vow will be kept—not by the individual—but by Christ, who lives in and through the individual. A passive vow of this kind would afford the opportunity to inculcate a proper Lutheran understanding of sanctification in which the perfecting of the individual in holiness is (like justification) a monergistic work of the Lord, a work begun in Baptism and continued through Holy Absolution and the Lord's Supper. To this end, such vows would begin by emphasizing that Christ will live through the individual by leading him or her continually to the Sacraments from which the rest of the Christian life flows. And these vows would clearly reference Baptism as the foundation and source of Christ's presence within the individual. And as such, as one scholar has noted, all such vows would follow the Baptism proper.

Given that a Lutheran understanding of confirmation affirms a lifelong process of catechization into the sacramental life, including a continuous return to the Lord's promises in Baptism, perhaps it would be best to adopt a name significant of this reality: such as "Confirmation of Baptism" or "Affirmation of Baptism." In this way, the rite could be seen as something repeatable throughout the Christian life, especially as a means of marking passages in human life, such as a return to the church's sacramental life, or as a conclusion to periods of intense catechization. This would include the traditional period of confirmation instruction employed in most LCMS congregations (near the beginning of puberty). However, the repetitive and continual aspects of a "Confirmation of Baptism" would challenge Lutherans to consider additional times and ways of offering intense catechization, particularly in the late-teenage and early-adult years. This would allow the sacramental life to play a formative role in the shaping of an individual at a time of personal self-realization and soul searching.

Practicing the repetitive nature of confirmation in both its catechetical and liturgical aspects will be possible only if confirmation is weaned from its one-time use as a preparation for first communion and membership in a local Christian congregation. The means to this end is to celebrate a "Confirmation of Baptism" at the conclusion of *all* intense periods of catechization, including that period leading to first communion.

Freeing first communion from a one-time practice of confirmation (but not from a repeatable "Confirmation of Baptism") would also allow a discussion of the appropriate age at which a child might be communed to be pursued on its own right in relation to Christ's mandate and institution of the Lord's Supper. The reformers (as witnessed by the church orders) engaged this question not in terms of age, but in terms of individual readiness. Thus, children were introduced to the Lord's Supper at various ages. The concern of the reformers was that children participate in the Sacrament in a worthy manner, partaking of the body and blood of Christ to their benefit, using it in faith. On the basis of the four records of the institution narrative, as well as Mark 10:13–16 and 1 Corinthians 11:17–32, the reformers clearly express that faith, with regard to the Lord's Supper, includes a cognitive, intellectual component. This entails the ability to understand and take to heart the words of promise given in the institution narrative with regard to the signs of the Sacrament, Christ's body and blood.

Yet, most of the church orders indicate that individual readiness to participate in the Supper will be apparent prior to the age of 12 and usually around the age of 7 or 8 years. In most cases, this would be prior to the age of abstract reasoning, that is, the ability to comprehend and distinguish the bodily presence of Christ in the Supper and the benefits offered in the Supper. What type of cognitive ability is entailed in a worthy reception of the Sacrament? Does it mean simply the ability to recite by heart the chief parts of the catechism, especially the Words of Institution? Or does it imply the ability to explain reasonably the use and benefits of the Lord's Supper?

The ambiguity of this issue encourages a continued examination of the institution narrative, first of all, as the interpretive foundation for the Lord's Supper, in order to determine when a person may participate in the Supper. The passages from Mark 10, 1 Corinthians 11, and John 6 would also help to formulate an answer to the question. Might it be possible that the institution narrative indicates that worthy participation is determined relative to the cognitive abilities particular to each of the various stages of human life? Thus, the mandate of Christ to "do this in remembrance of Me"—that is, to partake and receive the benefits of the Supper in faith—requires that one do so with whatever cognitive abilities are appropriate to one's stage of human development. Thus, young children, even though incapable of abstract reasoning, would nevertheless be able to participate worthily in the Lord's Supper according to their own stages of cognitive development.

The word of the Lord in Mark's record of the institution narrative, "This is My blood of the covenant which is shed for *many*," seems to imply this possibility. A cursory examination of the word, "many," as it is used in the New Testament, suggests that it usually refers to all the baptized. In addition, the fact that some of the reformers, including Bugenhagen, referred to Mark 10:14 as a basis for inviting young children to the Supper, would also support the possibility of worthy participation on the part of young children prior to the ability of abstract reasoning. As the congregations of the Synod move to commune children when they are ready, most often at younger ages, the possibility of communing young children will continue to be raised. It is a question that must continually be engaged, even if the Synod continues to affirm the historic, 600-year tradition of *not* communing infants or very young children.

Where does that leave us with regard to confirmation? The questions we should be asking are these: how can a ritual of "Confirmation (or Affirmation) of Baptism" best inculcate the lifelong catechetical process that flows from Baptism? How can such a rite best affirm the sacramental life of the Christian—in particular, a continual return to the promises of Baptism? How can ceremonial elements be used properly in both Baptism and confirmation so as to extol the blessings of Baptism without obscuring its benefits? Could a baptismal and/or confirmation vow serve the "Affirmation of Baptism" in a way that promotes a true Lutheran understanding of sanctification and does not imply a form of works righteousness? How might confirmation be separated from first communion while still maintaining an intimate connection with the Sacrament of the Altar? What should determine a worthy participation in the Lord's Supper according to the Words of Institution? Do the Lord's words allow the possibility of worthy participation on the part of infants and very young children? Answering these questions will help to insure that "Confirmation/Affirmation of Baptism" leads the people of God to live and rejoice in the sacramental life.

Boolean Worship

Jay S. Lemanski

We will need to deal with particular issues regarding worship and liturgy. But before we can deal with specifics of the service, such as the Salutation and the lectionary, we must first have a clear understanding of the broader issue, that is, the setting and context of worship itself. To that end, a logical category formulated over the past two decades among anthropologists may be helpful in better understanding our theology and our liturgy. That logical category is "liminality."

"Liminality" and its adjective, "liminal," are derived from the Latin word *limen*, which means "threshold." The term was used extensively by anthropologist Victor Turner in his study of rites of passage. Turner noted that in many rituals of movement from one state or status into another, there is a point where the subject enters a "neither/nor" state. For example, before becoming a man, a boy is brought to the threshold that borders the mutually exclusive states of boyhood and manhood. The subject thus enters a "liminal" state. This "neither/nor" point may be described as "exclusive liminality."

Other anthropologists, such as Paul Friedrick and G.S. Kirk, have used liminality in the study of mythological characters. They note that certain characters exhibit contrary qualities, such as Aphrodite, who is both promiscuous and yet referred to as "virgin." This kind of liminality embraces two mutually exclusive categories completely, without qualification or quantification. Characters possessing such characteristics are called liminal *personae*. This "both/and" existence may be described as "inclusive liminality."

The concept of inclusive liminality is applicable not only to anthropological studies but also to theology. There are many "both/and" elements in Christian doctrine. One example is the two natures of Christ.

Boolean Worship

The liminal nature of Jesus is expressed by Ignatius in his letter to the Ephesians: "There is one Physician, who is both flesh and spirit, born and yet not born, who is God in man, true life in death, both of Mary and of God, first passible and then impassible, Jesus Christ our Lord" (Ign. to Eph. 7:2). Here Ignatius lists a series of liminal pairs, also called "binary oppositions" (mutually exclusive states), and he defines Jesus as the embodiment of both. Examples of other liminal doctrines include the doctrine of the real presence in the Lord's Supper and the anthropological doctrine of *simul iustus et peccator*.

Examples of exclusive liminality are also found in Christian theology. Thus, when Paul calls the Christians "sons of God" in his letter to the Galatians, he defines the nature of that sonship with a list of liminal pairs: "There is neither Jew nor Greek, there is neither slave nor free man, there is neither male nor female; for you are all one in Christ Jesus" (Gal. 3:28). Unlike the passage from Ignatius, Paul lists these liminal pairs exclusively, which is to say, that "sonship" transcends earthly categories. As sons of God in Christ, we are neither male nor female; that is, we are liminally exclusive. Consequently, for example, when we examine the issue of inclusive language, we must ask ourselves: when Paul refers to "sons of God" or "brothers," is he employing the masculine gender as a linguistic convention for a mixed audience, or is he using these terms theologically? Is Paul referring to a gender, or is he referring to our "Christness"—a liminal state that excludes the normal categories of gender, race, and social status?

With these and other liminal concepts identifiable in our theology, it is no surprise that liminality should also find an application to Christian worship. In studying the liturgy from this perspective, one finds liminal features in various aspects. For consideration, let us reflect upon three of those aspects: the liminal office of the pastor, the spatial liminality of the worship setting, and the temporal liminality of the worship setting.

In dealing with the office of the pastor, it is important to note, first of all, that the pastor is not a liminal *persona*, as if he were liminal in and of himself. Jesus is a liminal *persona*, embodying the mutually exclusive states of Creator and creature. The pastor occupies a liminal *office*, which is the office of Christ. As an ἀπόστολος (lit. "sent one"), the pastor is sent to exercise the liminal role of Christ. By virtue of that office, within the confines of that office, he embodies the faithful to God *and* God to the faithful.

The liminal nature of the pastoral office is best illustrated by the sacramental and sacrificial elements of the service. In the sacramental elements, the pastor speaks and acts in the stead of God; in the sacrificial elements, the pastor embodies all of the faithful before the throne of God in offering their praises and petitions.

The one element of the liturgy that cannot be categorized as either sacramental or sacrificial is the Salutation. At that point, the pastor does not embody God to the faithful, nor the faithful to God, but he addresses the congregation as himself. By stepping out of his liminal role with the Salutation, the pastor marks transitions between the major parts of the service, specifically, immediately prior to the most sacrificial and sacramental acts in the service.

Historically, the service began with psalmody: the Introit, the Kyrie, and the Gloria in Excelsis. In this portion of the service, the whole body of believers joins in the praise of God. In the Service of the Word, however, beginning with the Collect and including the Readings and Sermon, the pastor assumes his liminal role in the service. It is significant, therefore, that the Salutation marks the boundary between the psalmody and the Service of the Word.

Similarly, the Salutation marks the boundary between the Service of the Word and the Service of Holy Communion. It is also used to mark the closing of the service just prior to the Benediction. In each of these cases, the Salutation immediately precedes a sacrificial or sacramental function.

In light of these observations, it would seem that the Salutation is actually a reaffirmation of the pastor's liminal office—that office which gives him the authority to perform his role in the liturgy. If so, then the congregation's response to the Salutation is not a means of including the pastor as one of their number; rather, by these words, the faithful set the pastor apart from themselves, distinguishing him as the one who holds the liminal office of Christ.

In addressing the *place* of worship, the liminal pair of heaven and earth comes into view. Scripture sometimes defines "heaven" as God's dwelling in His full glory. Thus, for example, Deuteronomy 26:15 calls heaven God's "holy habitation"; Jesus, in the Sermon on the Mount, calls heaven God's throne (Matt. 5:34); and in his prayer, Solomon bids God, "Hear from heaven, Your dwelling place, and when You hear, forgive" (1 Kings 8:30). The clear dichotomy is that God's dwelling is in heaven, man's on earth.

Yet, Scripture also describes the temple, God's dwelling, as a union of heaven and earth. In fact, the Hebrew term הֵיכָל means both "temple" and "palace," indicating that the temple is the palace of God. Thus, Psalm 65:5 refers to the temple as "God's house." And Psalm 11:4 declares, "Yahweh is in His holy temple; Yahweh is on His heavenly throne." The throne here is the ark of the covenant. This same function of the ark is likewise reflected in the reference to God in 1 Samuel 4:4, "Yahweh Sabaoth, who is enthroned between the cherubim," that is to say, between the cherubim on the ark of the covenant. The temple, then, was a liminal reality, both heaven and earth, the dwelling of God in a dwelling of man.

This liminal mode of divine presence did not end with the establishment of the new covenant. While there is no more a temple of stone and mortar, the New Testament professes that the temple of God still exists, a temple of flesh and blood. In his letter to the Ephesians, St. Paul writes:

> Consequently, you are no longer foreigners and aliens, but fellow citizens with God's people and members of God's household, built on the foundation of the apostles and prophets, with Christ Jesus Himself as the Chief Cornerstone. In Him the whole building is joined together and rises to become a holy temple in the Lord. And in Him you too are being built together to become a dwelling in which God lives by His Spirit (Eph. 2:19–22, NIV).

In similar vein, St. Peter writes in his First Epistle, "You also, like living stones, are being built into a spiritual house to be a holy priesthood, offering spiritual sacrifices acceptable to God through Jesus Christ." (1 Pet. 2:5).

The theology of the church as a "living temple" is reflected in the service itself, especially so in the parousia imagery of the liturgy. By way of example, the angelic Sanctus hymn incorporates the words of the Palm Sunday crowds: "Hosanna to the Son of David, blessed is He who comes in the name of the Lord" (Matt. 21:1). This coming of Jesus into Jerusalem was treated by the crowd as a parousia, the visitation of a king.

So do these same words in the liturgy proclaim the coming of Jesus among His people as their King, as they witness His enthronement in their midst.

A further example is the canticle, "Worthy Is the Lamb: This Is the Feast," based on Revelation 4 and 5. In the words of this canticle, the congregation enters the heavenly throne room with St. John. The people join the hymn of the four beasts and the elders as Jesus, the Lamb, assumes His throne. As the old television show was titled, "You Are There."

When the faithful of God are gathered around the Lamb in His Word and Sacrament, they are the living stones that form the temple of God, the "threshold" between heaven and earth. This is a liminal reality: heaven and earth come together in this time and place. In the worship of the church on earth, the people of God stand at the threshold of the heavenly throne room.

This liminal union of heaven and earth in worship is a proleptic fulfillment of the final union of heaven and earth in the parousia of Christ. As St. John reports in Revelation 21:

> I saw a new heaven and a new earth; for the first heaven and the first earth passed away.... And I heard a loud voice from the throne, saying, "Behold, the tabernacle God is among men, and He shall dwell among them, and they shall be His people, and God Himself shall be among them" (Rev. 21:1, 3, NIV).

In dealing with proleptic fulfillment and eschatology, one broaches the issue of temporal liminality. However, in this case, one is not dealing with binary oppositions but rather with tertiary oppositions, the mutually exclusive states of past, present, and future. And it is here suggested that the historic liturgy reflects a liminal understanding of time.

In the Sanctus, for example, the coming of Christ Jesus into Jerusalem on Palm Sunday, the coming of Christ to His faithful people in the Sacrament, and the future coming of Christ in His glory are all caught up together into one liminal moment. Past, present, and future are bound together by the sacramental act of God.

The Sacrament itself is temporally liminal: though Christians gather at the Lord's Table to receive His body and blood in the present, they are also transported to the past; though they do not re-sacrifice Jesus, they are returned to the singular sacrifice of Christ on the cross. But the church is also transported into the future, as in this meal she receives a "foretaste of the feast to come," a participation in the marriage feast of the Lamb in His kingdom. The Lord's Supper, then, has one foot in the present, one in the past, and yet another in the future—all true, all at the same moment.

The logical categories with which most people are normally acquainted may be quite helpful for their mundane existence. In dealing with God and His activities, however, one is often confronted with new realities, realities that defy an Aristotelian view of the universe. The concept of liminality offers another category with which to understand better the truths of the faith, and thus provides a helpful means of expressing those truths in our worship.

The liminal reality of the faithful, of the pastoral office, and of the temporal and spatial settings of the liturgy has a bearing on such issues as inclusive language, the Salutation, the role of assisting ministers, the lectionary, and eucharistic prayer. Hopefully, this essay will be constructive to that end.

Ending

Unified in Act and Song

THERE IS NO SIMPLE WAY TO SUM UP THE ESSAYS IN THIS BOOK. Certainly, more could have been written, both on these topics and on many others that will be examined as the new hymnal is prepared.

What these essays demonstrate, beyond the scholarship and insights they contain, are the manifold blessings that God has showered on our Synod. We have been given gifted pastors and musicians whose knowledge is matched by pastoral sensitivity in the way they address issues related to worship, music, and theology. Their gifts, and those of many others, will be vital to the work of the Commission on Worship as it prepares a Lutheran hymnal for the 21st century.

Soli Deo Gloria

Unified in Act and Song

Ronald R. Feuerhahn

Momentous Event

THE ORIGINAL PRESENTATION OF THESE ESSAYS TO THE COMMISSION ON Worship—now also their publication to the Synod—is a momentous event. In substance, but also in significance. Not only the splendid essays and the discussion they engender; not only the scholarship and commitment they reflect, the churchmanship and pastoral concern; but also what all of this means for the Lutheran Church in our time. The Commission on Worship and all of those involved recognize that we are embarking on a most excellent task, one already favored by the blessings of God.

Problem

We know the problem. When those who are old enough to remember observe that the troubles of 20 years ago are here again, and even worse, we can concur. The problem may be different, but it is more pervasive and threatening.

The fundamental problem is becoming more and more clear. In a paper delivered a few years ago at the Liturgical Symposium of Concordia Theological Seminary in Fort Wayne, Indiana, this author described the problem as a loss of faith—a loss of faith in the words and promises of God in His means of grace. We have come to a day in which there is no trust in those words and promises, but instead a compulsion to add something. Our Confessions call this the *extra Christum*—something added to Christ, "Christ plus something." That is a great evil in our midst.

But we who work with the Commission on Worship—who have written these fine essays—we have our own problems; or, at least, we are also in great danger. The problem is not only outside, but within. So we pray that God would spare us from arrogance, from that attitude which says, "We know all about the liturgy, and no one else does; therefore. . . ." We pray that God would spare us from triumphalism, from that attitude which puts others down and condemns them. We pray that God would spare us from sinful anger in response to a neglect and mistreatment of both the Divine Service and the doctrines of the church. We pray that God would spare us from despair, from that great sin which lies on the verge of faithlessness (as Luther might describe it). For we do, at times, despair that the church will ever come to face the issues involved in these so-called "worship wars." And we despair too when we see the faithful champions of a sacramental, means-of-grace churchmanship being put down.

We are called to a renewed churchliness. There was a time when "churchman" seemed to mean a church politician or official; it was a negative designation. But that is the wrong impression. To be churchly is to be catholic (among other things) and to have a high regard for the tradition.

Holy Scripture is surely the foundation of all our doctrine, theology, and practice; but the tradition of the church should also be regarded. Otherwise we fall into the error of Zwingli and Calvin, who rejected the medieval church as church. Luther properly regarded the medieval church as such, and he received its traditions (wherever possible) in a godly manner. He understood the gift in such traditions: "So then, brethren, stand firm and hold to the traditions which you were taught, whether by *word of mouth* or by letter from us" (2 Thess. 2:15). Thus the description of Lutheranism as "catholic in substance, evangelical in principle."[1]

This also serves to remind us that the liturgy is not our property—not the property of any one pastor, nor a single congregation, nor even the entire LCMS—not ours to do with as we please. The liturgy belongs to the church in the broadest sense, and we too are gifted by that tradition. For the liturgy was not formed by a man, but by those men who live together as saints in the church.

---

[1]Jaroslav Pelikan, *Obedient Rebels: Catholic Substance and Protestant Principle in Luther's Reformation* (New York: Harper & Row, Publishers, 1964).

Blessings

We are pleased to recall the blessings of our own church's history. We are grateful that Dr. Walther restored the heritage of the rhythmic chorale. We are grateful for the great churchly musical heritage of Concordia, River Forest, and Concordia, Seward. We are grateful for our "church musicians" and "Kantors," who have been sorely abused and neglected. These precious resources for the church have been grossly squandered by a pastorate that was never trained to appreciate, make use of, depend upon, or rejoice in such a treasury of talent.

We are grateful for the phenomenal contribution over the past 25 years of Kramer Chapel at Concordia Theological Seminary, Fort Wayne. One can only begin to appreciate that blessing when he has experienced it or encountered its product in that faithful, remarkable team which is today's Commission on Worship—under the guidance of a leader with truly remarkable vision and theological gifts. We rejoice in the Commission's single-mindedness of principle and purpose.

We rejoice in our teachers, those who have come from our Concordia Colleges to serve the church as music leaders. They too have been misused and even abused. "They have no clout!" But they have, in spite of that, served so well, so faithfully, often exhibiting a finer grasp of the Divine Service and its theology than their pastors.

And we rejoice in those words that have been given to us, over and over again, as a refrain throughout these essays. It is sometimes observed that only in the poetry of hymns are words remembered from one generation to the next . . . and even beyond. But these words of prose will surely survive beyond our day and for many days to come:

> Our Lord speaks and we listen. His Word bestows what it says. Faith that is born from what is heard acknowledges the gifts received with eager thankfulness and praise.[2]

May these words remain our litany and our refrain as we embark upon the task before us.

Now, as we have heard, there is a "new division"—reinforcements on the horizon. There are many others in the church, as well, who might

---

[2]*LW*, 6.

also have contributed essays like those published here. They are there, in great service to and in appreciation for the liturgy. They understand what it means to serve in and through the liturgy, thereby to be in service to the church. For through the liturgy, the Gospel is honored, the people of God are taught, and the pastor is guided.

Meanwhile, the demise of the church's liturgy continues. This can give us doubts about the church and even about the Lord. One of the most threatening doubts is the doubt of justice. How can this happen? How can God allow this to continue in His church? But here we also find comfort in the means of grace. For we too can be guilty of a lack of faith in God's promises to and for His church. When threatened by discouragement or even despair, remember those who have contributed these essays, as well as the many others who support the same efforts. But far more importantly, turn again to the promises of God in those very means that are served in the ministry of the Divine Service.

Let us conclude with a hymn (which should, of course, be sung)—a hymn that has brought so much encouragement to so many, not least to Hermann Sasse, who ended so many essays with it:

> *Lord Jesus Christ, will You not stay?*
> *It is now toward the end of day.*
> *Oh, let Your Word, that saving light,*
> *Shine forth undimmed into the night.*
>
> *Rekindle for this end-time stress*
> *Faith's ancient strength and steadfastness*
> *That we keep pure till life is spent*
> *Your holy Word and Sacrament.*
>
> *Restrain, O Lord, the human pride*
> *That seeks to thrust Your truth aside*
> *Or with some man-made thoughts or things*
> *Would dim the words Your Spirit sings.*
>
> *The cause is Yours, the glory too.*
> *Then hear us, Lord, and keep us true,*
> *Your Word alone our heart's defense,*
> *The Church's glorious confidence.*
> (LW 344:1-2, 5-6)*

*Copyright © 1982 Concordia Publishing House. Reprinted by permission.

Bibliography

THE FOLLOWING BIBLIOGRAPHY includes significant works for further reading and study, categorized according to the various subheadings below. Not all of the works cited in the footnotes of this book have been included in this bibliography, and a number of works have been included here which were not cited in the notes to the chapters. Although there may be some crossover from category to category, sources below have been listed only once and under the category for which they seemed most appropriate.

This bibliography should be considered "representative" of the categories listed but by no means "exhaustive." It is hoped that this bibliography (and volume) will serve as a stimulus in our Synod to pastor, musician, student, and scholar alike to pursue further study and discussion of these and other matters pertaining to worship.

General

Baumler, Gary and Kermit Moldenhauer, eds. *Christian Worship: Manual.* Milwaukee, Wis.: Northwestern Publishing House, 1993.
Brunner, Peter. *Worship in the Name of Jesus.* Trans. M.H. Bertram. St. Louis: Concordia Publishing House, 1968.
Danielou, Jean. *The Bible and the Liturgy.* Ann Arbor, Mich.: Servant Books, 1956.
Dix, Gregory. *The Shape of the Liturgy.* London: A & C Black, 1993.
Elert, Werner. *Eucharist and Church Fellowship in the First Four Centuries.* Trans. N.E. Nagel. St. Louis: Concordia Publishing House, 1966.
Giertz, Bo. *Liturgy and Spiritual Awakening.* Trans. Clifford Ansgar Nelson. Rock Island, Ill.: Augustana Book Concern, 1950.
Jones, C., G. Wainwright and E. Yarnold, eds. *The Study of Liturgy.* New York: Oxford University Press, 1992.
Jungmann, Joseph A. *The Mass of the Roman Rite: Its Origins and Development.* 2 vols. Trans. Francis A. Brunner. Westminster, Md.: Christian Classics Inc., 1986.
Koenker, Ernest B. *Worship in Word and Sacrament.* St. Louis: Concordia Publishing House, 1959.
Lang, Paul H.D. *Ceremony and Celebration.* St. Louis: Concordia Publishing House, 1965.

Leaver, Robin A. *The Theological Character of Music in Worship.* Church Music Pamphlet Series, ed. Carl Schalk. St. Louis: Concordia Publishing House, 1989.

Löhe, Wilhelm. *Three Books About the Church.* Trans. James L. Schaaf. Philadelphia: Fortress Press, 1969). (See especially pp. 173–176.)

Luther, Martin. *Luther's Works: Liturgy and Hymns* (AE 53), ed. Ulrich S. Leupold. Philadelphia: Fortress Press, 1965

Maxwell, Lee A. *The Altar Guild Manual.* St. Louis: Concordia Publishing House, 1996.

Muller, Karl F. and Walter Blankenburg, eds. *Leiturgia: Handbuch des evangelischen Gottesdienstes; mit einem Geleitwort der Lutherischen Liturgische Konferenz Deutschlands.* 5 vols. Kassel: Johannes Stauda-Verlag, 1954–70.

Precht, Fred L., ed. *Lutheran Worship: History and Practice.* St. Louis: Concordia Publishing House, 1993.

Reed, Luther D. *The Lutheran Liturgy: A Study of the Common Liturgy of the Lutheran Church in America.* Revised ed. Philadelphia: Muhlenberg Press, 1959.

Sasse, Hermann. *We Confess.* Trans. Norman Nagel. St. Louis: Concordia Publishing House, 1984–86.

Sehling, Emil, ed. *Die Evangelischen Kirchenordnungen des 16. Jahrhunderts.* 15 vols. Vols. I–V. Leipzig: O.R. Reisland, 1902–13. Vols. VI–XII. Tübingen: J.C.B. Mohr, 1955–63.

Senn, Frank C. *Christian Liturgy: Catholic and Evangelical.* Minneapolis: Augsburg Fortress, 1997.

Thompson, Bard. *Liturgies of the Western Church.* New York: World Publishing, 1962.

Vajta, Vilmos, *Die Theologie des Gottesdienstes bei Luther.* Berlin: Evangelische Verlagsanstalt, 1958. English translation, abridged: *Luther on Worship. An Interpretation.* Trans. U.S. Leupold. Philadelphia: Muhlenberg Press, 1958.

Van Loon, Ralph R. and S. Anita Stauffer. *Worship Wordbook: A Practical Guide for Worship.* Minneapolis: Augsburg Fortress, 1995.

Wainwright, G. *Doxology. The Praise of God in Worship, Doctrine and Life.* London: Epworth, 1980.

White, James F. *Introduction to Christian Worship.* Rev. ed. Nashville: Abingdon Press, 1990.

Beginning

Barry, A.L. *The Unchanging Feast: The Nature and Basis of Lutheran Worship.* St. Louis: The Lutheran Church—Missouri Synod, 1995.

Cwirla, William M. "The Law, The Gospel, The Liturgy." *Modern Reformation* 5 (Jan.–Feb. 1996): 22–27.

Herrlin, Olof. *Divine Service: Liturgy in Perspective.* Trans. Gene J. Lund. Philadelphia: Fortress Press, 1966.

Nagel, Norman E. "Whose Liturgy Is It?" *Logia* 2, no. 2 (April 1993): 4–8.

Piepkorn, Arthur Carl. *What the Symbolical Books of the Lutheran Church Have to Say about Worship and the Sacraments.* St. Louis: Concordia Publishing House, 1952.

Pless, John T. "Toward a Confessional Lutheran Understanding of Liturgy." *Logia* 2, no. 2 (April 1993): 9–12.

Pittelko, Roger. "Worship and the Community of Faith." In *Lutheran Worship: History and Practice*, ed. Fred L. Precht, 44–57. St. Louis: Concordia Publishing House, 1993.

Lectionary

Adam, Adolf. *The Liturgical Year: Its History and Its Meaning after the Reform of the Liturgy.* Trans. Matthew J. O'Connell. New York: Pueblo Publishing Company, 1981.

Allen, Horace T., Jr. "Common Lectionary: Origins, Assumptions, and Issues." *Studia Liturgica* 21 (1991): 14–30.

⸻. "Emerging Ecumenical Issues in Worship." *Word & World* 9 (1989): 16–22.

⸻. "Lectionaries—Principles and Problems: A Comparative Analysis." *Studia Liturgica* 22 (1992): 68–83.

Barrois, Georges. *Scripture Readings in Orthodox Worship.* Crestwood, N.Y.: St. Vladimir's Seminary Press, 1977.

Bieritz, Karl-Heinrich. "The Order of Readings and Sermon Texts for the German Lutheran Church." *Studia Liturgica* 21 (1991): 37–51.

Boehringer, Hans. "The Revised Common Lectionary." *Bride of Christ* 27 (Advent 1992): 5–7.

Boon, Rudolf. "Bringing the Old Testament to Its Legitimate Place and Function in the Church's Liturgical Reading of the Scriptures." *Studia Liturgica* 17 (1987): 19–25.

Brauer, James L. "The Church Year." In *Lutheran Worship: History and Practice*, ed. Fred L. Precht. St. Louis: Concordia Publishing House, 1993.

Briner, Lewis A. "A Look at New Proposals for the Lectionary." *Reformed Liturgy and Music* 17 (Summer 1983): 126–29.

Bugnini, A. *The Reform of the Liturgy, 1948–1975.* Collegeville, Minn.: Liturgical Press, 1990.

Calendar and Lessons for the Church's Year, The. A Report submitted by the Church of England Liturgical Commission. London: S.P.C.K., 1969.

Davies, J.G., ed. *The New Westminster Dictionary of Liturgy and Worship.* Philadelphia: Westminster Press, 1986. S.v. "Lectionary."

Dienst, K. *Die Religion in Geschichte und Gegenwart.* 3rd edition. Tübingen, 1961. S.v. "Perikopen."

Evanson, Charles J. "The Lectionary." Unpublished paper, 1990.

Gray, Donald. "The Contribution of the Joint Liturgical Group to the Search for an Ecumenical Lectionary." *Studia Liturgica* 21 (1991): 31–36.

Gundert, Wilhelm. "Das neue katholische Meßlektionar." *Lutherische Monatsheft* 8 (1969): 595–99.

Hultgren, Arland J. "Hermeneutical Tendencies in the Three-Year Lectionary." In *Studies in Lutheran Hermeneutics*, ed. John Reumann, 145-73. Philadelphia: Fortress Press, 1979.

Inter-Lutheran Commission on Worship. *The Church Year: Calendar and Lectionary.* Contemporary Worship Series, no. 6. Minneapolis: Augsburg Publishing House, 1973.

Joint Liturgical Group. *A Four Year Lectionary (JLG 2)*, ed. Ronald Jasper. Oxford: Oxford University Press, 1967.

_____. *The Calendar and Lectionary: A Reconsideration*, ed. Ronald Jasper. London: Oxford University Press, 1967.

_____. *The Word in Season: Essays by Members of the Joint Liturgical Group on the Use of the Bible in the Liturgy*, ed. Donald Gray. Norwich: Canterbury Press, 1988.

Jones, Douglas R. "Corporate Attention to the Whole Word of God." *Theology* 70 (April 1967): 146–52.

Kirchenleitung der Vereinigten Evangelisch-Lutherischen Kirche Deutschlands. *Lektionar für Evangelisch-Lutherische Kirchen und Gemeinden mit Perikopenbuch*. Hannover: Lutherisches Verlagshaus, 1985.

Kunze, Gerhard. "Die Lesungen." In *Leiturgia: Handbuch des evangelischen Gottesdienstes*. Vol. 2:87–180 (See full bibliographic reference under "General" above.)

Langford, Andy. "The Revised Common Lectionary 1992: A Revision for the Next Generation." *Quarterly Review* 13 (1993): 37–48.

Lutherische Liturgische Konferenz Deutschlands. *Neue Lesungen für den Gottesdienst*. Hamburg: Lutherisches Verlagshaus, 1972.

Nelson, Richard D. "Reading Texts in Lectionary Pairs." *Dialog* 21 (Spring 1982): 95–101.

Ramshaw, Gail. "The First Testament in Christian Lectionaries." *Worship* 61 (November 1990): 494–510.

Reed, Luther D. *The Lutheran Liturgy: A Study of the Common Liturgy of the Lutheran Church in America*. Revised ed. Philadelphia: Muhlenberg Press, 1947.

Reumann, John H.P. "History of Lectionaries: From the Synagogue at Nazareth to Post-Vatican II." *Interpretation* 31 (1977): 116–30.

Revised Common Lectionary 1992: The Report from the Consultation on Common Texts, The. Nashville: Abingdon Press, 1992.

Seitz, Christopher R. "The Lectionary as Theological Construction." In *Inhabiting Unity: Theological Perspectives on the Proposed Lutheran-Episcopal Concordat*, ed. E. Radner and R.R. Reno. Grand Rapids, Mich.: W.B. Eerdmans Publishing Co., 1995.

Shelly, Tom. "The Revised Common Lectionary." *Bride of Christ* 19 (Pentecost 1995): 5–7.

Sloyan, Gerard S. "Some Suggestions for a Biblical Three-Year Lectionary." *Worship* 63 (1989): 521–35.

Stookey, Lawrence H. "Marcion, Typology, and Lectionary Preaching." *Worship* 66 (1992): 251–62.

Storley, Calvin. "Reclaiming the Old Testament." *Lutheran Quarterly*, n.s. 1 (1987): 487–94.

Talley, Thomas J. *The Origins of the Liturgical Year*. 2nd (emended) ed. Collegeville, Minn.: The Liturgical Press, 1991.

West, Fritz. "An Annotated Bibliography of the Three-Year Lectionaries. Part I: The Roman Catholic Lectionary." *Studia Liturgica* 23 (1993): 223–44.

_____. "An Annotated Bibliography of the Three-Year Lectionaries. Parts II–IV." *Studia Liturgica* 24 (1994): 222–48.

_____. *Scripture & Memory: The Ecumenical Hermeneutic of the Three-Year Lectionaries*. Collegeville, Minn.: The Liturgical Press, 1997.

Bibliography

Eucharistic Prayer

Bates, W.H. "Thanksgiving and Intercession in the Liturgy of St. Mark." In *The Sacrifice of Praise*, ed. Bryan D. Spinks. Rome: C.L.V., 1981.

Bergsma, Johannes. *Die Reform des Meßliturgie durch Johannes Bugenhagen.* Hildescheim: Kevelaer, Butzon & Bercker, 1966.

Bergsma, Joop. "The Eucharistic Prayer in the Non-Roman Catholic Churches of the West Today." *Studia Liturgica* 11 (1976): 177–85.

Botte, Bernard. *Le Canon de la Messa Romaine.* Louvain: Abbaye du Mont Cesar, 1935.

Bouyer, L. *Eucharist.* English translation. Notre Dame, Ind.: E. Quinn, 1968.

Brand, E. "Luther's Liturgical Surgery." In *Interpreting Luther's Legacy*, ed. Fred W. Meuser and Stanley D. Schneider, 108–19. Minneapolis: Augsburg Publishing House, 1969.

Bridge, Donald and David Phypers. *The Meal that Unites.* London: Hodder and Staughton, 1981.

Brilioth, Y. *Eucharistic Faith and Practice, Evangelical and Catholic.* Trans. G. Hebert. London: S.P.C.K., 1930.

Buszin, Walter E. "Luther on Music." *Musical Quarterly* 32 (1946): 80–97.

Casel, Odo. *The Mystery of Christian Worship, and Other Writings,* ed. Burkhard Neunheuser. Westminster, Md.: Newman Press, 1962.

Chemnitz, Martin. *Examination of the Council of Trent.* Trans. Fred Kramer. 2 vols. St. Louis: Concordia Publishing House, 1978. (See especially Part II.)

Couratin, A.H. and E.C. Ratcliff. "The Early Roman Canon Missae." *Journal of Ecclesiastical History* 20 (1969): 211-24.

Cuming, G.J. *He Gave Thanks: An Introduction to the Eucharistic Prayer.* Grove Liturgical Study, no. 28. Bramcote: Grove Books, 1981.

Davis, J.G. *A Dictionary of Liturgy and Worship.* S.v. "Liturgies: Lutheran." London: S.C.M., 1972.

Fendt, Leonhard. *Der lutherische Gottesdienst des 16. Jahrhunderts: Sein Wesen und sein Wachsen.* Munich: Verlag von Ernst Reinhardt, 1923.

Feuerhahn, Ronald R. "Luther's Mass: Origin, Content, Impact 1521–1529." M.Phil. Thesis, University of Cambridge, 1980.

Horn, Edward T. "Luther on the Principles and Order of Christian Worship." *Lutheran Church Review* 10, no. 3 (1892): 217-56.

Jasper, R.C.D., et al. *Prayers of the Eucharist: Early and Reformed.* New York: Oxford University Press, 1980.

Jensen, Robert. "A 'Great Thanksgiving' for Lutherans?" *Response* 15, nos. 2–3 (1975): 52–60.

Keifer, Ralph A. "The Unity of the Roman Canon: An Examination of Its Unique Structure." *Studia Liturgica* 11 (1976): 39–58.

Krodel, Gottfried G. "The Great Thanksgiving of the Inter-Lutheran Commission on Worship: It Is the Christians' Supper and Not the Lord's Supper." *The Cresset.* Occasional Paper 1. Valparaiso, Ind.: Valparaiso University Press, 1976.

Krueger, J.F. "Liturgical Worship in Wittenberg from 1520–1530." *Lutheran Church Quarterly* 4 (1931): 292–303

Lietzmann, Hans. *Mass and Lord's Supper: A Study in the History of the Liturgy.* Trans. Dorothea H.G. Reeve. Leiden: E.J. Brill, 1979.

Luther, Martin. "An Order of Mass and Communion for the Church at Wittenberg, 1523," ed. Ulrich S. Leupold. Trans. Paul Zeller Strodach. AE 53:15–40.

———. "The Abomination of the Secret Mass, 1525," ed. and trans. Abdel Ross Wentz. AE 36:307–28.

———. "The German Mass and Order of Service, 1526," ed. Ulrich S. Leupold. Trans. Augustus Steimle. AE 53:51–90.

Nagel, Norman E. "Holy Communion." In *Lutheran Worship: History and Practice*, ed. Fred. L. Precht, 290–323. St. Louis: Concordia Publishing House, 1993.

Olson, Oliver K. "Contemporary Trends in Liturgy Viewed from the Perspective of Classical Lutheran Theology." *Lutheran Quarterly*, o.s., 26 (1974): 110–57.

———. "Liturgy as 'Action.'" *Dialog* 14 (1975): 108–13.

———. "Luther's 'Catholic' Minimum." *Response* 11 (1970): 17–31.

Pelikan, Jaroslav J. "Luther and the Liturgy." In *More About Luther*. Martin Luther Lectures. Vol. 2. Decorah, Iowa: Luther College Press, 1958.

Quill, Timothy C.J. *The Impact of the Liturgical Movement on American Lutheranism.* Drew Series in Liturgy, no. 3. Lanham, Md. and London: The Scarecrow Press Inc., 1997.

Reim, E. "The Liturgical Crisis in Wittenberg, 1524." *Concordia Theological Monthly* 20 (April 1949): 284–92.

Richter, Aemilius L., ed.. *Die evangelischen Kirchenordnungen des sechzehnten Jahrhunderts: Urkunden und Regesten zur Geschichte des Rechts und der Verfassungder evangelischen Kirche in Deutschland.* Weimar: Landindustriecomptoir, 1846.

Rorem, Paul. "Luther's Objections to a Eucharistic Prayer." *The Cresset* 38 (March 1975): 12–16.

Sasse, Hermann. "Luther and the Word of God." In *Accents in Luther's Theology*, ed. Heino O. Kadai, 47–97. St. Louis and London: Concordia Publishing House, 1967.

Senn, Frank C. "Liturgia Svecanae Ecclesiae: An Attempt at Eucharistic Restoration during the Swedish Reformation." *Studia Liturgica* 14 (1980–81): 20–36.

———. "Luther's German Mass—A Sixteenth Century Folk Service." *Journal of Church Music* 18 (October 1976): 2–6.

———. "Martin Luther's Revision of the Eucharistic Canon in *Formula Missae* of 1523." *Concordia Theological Monthly* 44 (1973): 101–18.

Spinks, Bryan. *Luther's Liturgical Criteria and His Reform of the Canon of the Mass.* Bramcote: Grove Books, 1982.

———. "Mis-shapen: Gregory Dix and the Four-Action Shape of the Liturgy." *Lutheran Quarterly*, n.s., 4 (1990): 161–77.

Talley, T.J. "The Eucharistic Prayer of the Ancient Church according to Recent Research: Results and Reflections." *Studia Liturgica* 11 (1976): 138–58.

Torrance, T.F. "The Paschal Mystery of Christ and the Eucharist." In *Theology in Reconciliation: Essays towards Evangelical and Catholic Unity in East and West.* London: Geoffrey Chapman, 1975. Reprint, Grand Rapids, Mich.: Eerdmans Publishing Company, 1976.
Vajta, Vilmos. "The Theological Basis and Nature of the Liturgy." *Lutheran World* (December 1959): 234–46.
Wainwright, G. *Eucharist and Eschatology.* London: Epworth, 1971.
White, James F. *Christian Worship in North America, A Retrospective: 1955–1995.* Collegeville, Minn.: The Liturgical Press, 1997.
Willis, G.G. *Essays in Early Roman Liturgy.* London: Alcuin/SPCK, 1964.
Yelverton, Eric E. *The Mass in Sweden. Its Development from the Latin Rite from 1531 to 1917.* London: Harrison, 1920.

Hymnals and Hymnody

Apel, Willi. *Harvard Dictionary of Music.* 2nd ed. Cambridge: The Belknap Press of Harvard University Press, 1972.
Brauer, James L. "The Hymnals of The Lutheran Church—Missouri Synod." S.T.M. Thesis, Concordia Seminary, 1967.
Brown, Edgar S. *Liturgical Reconnaissance: Papers Presented at the Inter-Lutheran Consultation on Worship,* February 10–11, 1966, Chicago, Illinois. Philadelphia: Fortress Press, 1968.
Evanson, Charles J. "*Lutheran Worship* at 'Midlife.'" *Lutheran Forum* 27, no. 4 (1993): 25–27.
Grime, Paul and Joseph Herl, eds. *Hymnal Supplement 1998 Handbook.* St. Louis: The Lutheran Church—Missouri Synod, 1998.
Halter, Carl, and Carl Schalk, eds. *A Handbook of Church Music.* St. Louis: Concordia Publishing House, 1978.
Lang, Paul H.D. *Liturgy, Theology, and Music in the Lutheran Church,* ed. Mandus A. Egge. Minneapolis: S.P.A. Inc. for International Choral Union, 1959.
Leaver, Robin. "Renewal in Hymnody." *Lutheran Quarterly,* n.s., 6 (1992): 359–383.
Precht, Fred L. *Lutheran Worship: Hymnal Companion.* St. Louis: Concordia Publishing House, 1992.
_____. "Worship Resources in Missouri Synod's History." In *Lutheran Worship: History and Practice,* ed. Fred L. Precht, 77–116. St. Louis: Concordia Publishing House, 1993.
Resch, Richard C. "Hymnody as Teacher of the Faith." *Concordia Theological Quarterly* 57 (July 1993): 161–76.
Sauer, Robert and Fred L. Precht. "*Lutheran Worship* (1982)." In *Lutheran Worship: History and Practice,* ed. Fred L. Precht, 117–45. St. Louis: Concordia Publishing House, 1993.
Schalk, Carl F. *God's Song in a New Land.* St. Louis: Concordia Publishing House, 1995.
_____. *Source Documents in American Lutheran Hymnody.* St. Louis: Concordia Publishing House, 1996.

———, ed. *Key Words in Church Music: Definition Essays on Concepts, Practices, and Movements of Thought in Church Music.* St. Louis: Concordia Publishing House, 1978.

———. *Music in Lutheran Worship.* Church Music Pamphlet Series, ed. Carl Schalk. St. Louis: Concordia Publishing House, 1983.

Van Loon, Ralph R., ed. *Encountering God: The Legacy of Lutheran Book of Worship for the 21st Century.* Minneapolis: Kirk House Publishers, 1998.

Vieker, Jon D. "C.F.W. Walther, Editor of Missouri's First and Only German Hymnal." *Concordia Historical Institute Quarterly* 65, no. 2 (1992): 53–69.

Liturgy, Music and Culture

Bunjes, Paul G. "The Music of *Lutheran Worship.*" In *Lutheran Worship: History and Practice,* ed. Fred. L. Precht, 536–55. St. Louis: Concordia Publishing House, 1993.

Crowe, Jerome. *From Jerusalem to Antioch: The Gospel Across Cultures.* Collegeville, Minn.: The Liturgical Press, 1997.

Deiss, Lucien. *Springtime of the Liturgy: Liturgical Texts of the First Four Centuries.* Collegeville, Minn.: Liturgical Press, 1979.

Evanson, Charles J. *Evangelicalism and the Liturgical Movement and Their Effects on Lutheran Worship.* ALCM Pamphlet Series. St. Louis: MorningStar Music Publishers, 1990.

Grothe, Jonathan F. "A Missionary in Fellowship with the Church." *Lutheran Theological Review* 2 (Spring/Summer 1990): 7–14.

Just, Arthur A. "Liturgical Renewal in the Parish." In *Lutheran Worship: History and Practice,* ed. Fred L. Precht, 21–43. St. Louis: Concordia Publishing House, 1993.

Kleinig, John W. "Witting or Unwitting Ritualists." *Lutheran Theological Journal* 22 (May 1988): 13–22.

———. *The Function of Hymnody in Its Cultural Context.* Ft. Wayne, Ind.: Concordia Theological Seminary, 1998. Audiocassette.

Liturgy Digest 3, no. 2 (1996). (A whole issue devoted to liturgy and culture.)

Marquart, Kurt E. *"Church Growth" as Mission Paradigm: A Lutheran Assessment.* A Luther Academy Monograph. Houston, Tex.: Our Savior Lutheran Church, 1994.

———. "Corporate Worship of the Church: Liturgy and Evangelism." In *Lutheran Worship: History and Practice,* ed. Fred L. Precht, 58–76. St. Louis: Concordia Publishing House, 1993.

———. "Law/Gospel and 'Church Growth.'" In *The Beauty and the Bands: Papers Presented at Congress on the Lutheran Confessions, Itasca, Illinois, April 20–22, 1995.* John R. Fehrmann, Daniel Preus, Bruce Lukas, eds. Crestwood, Mo.: Luther Academy; Minneapolis: Association of Confessional Lutherans, 1995.

———. *Liturgy and Culture.* Ft. Wayne, Ind.: Divine Service Institute, St. Paul Lutheran Church, 1996. Audiocassette.

Bibliography

Masaki, Naomichi. "The Evangelist: The Sacramental Shape of the Church's Mission to the Japanese." A paper delivered at the Congress on the Lutheran Confessions, Itasca, Illinois, 10–13 April 1996.
⎯⎯⎯⎯. "Confessing Christ: Office and Vocation." *Logia* 7 (Holy Trinity 1998): 5–11.
Nagel, Norman E. "Medicine of Immortality and Antidote against Death." *Logia* 4 (Reformation/October 1995): 31–36.
Pless, John T. "Six Theses on Liturgy and Evangelism." *Concordia Theological Quarterly* 52 (January 1988): 41–52.
Resch, Richard C. "Church Music at the Close of the Twentieth Century: The Entanglement of Sacred and Secular." *Logia* 2 (April 1993): 21–27.
Roeske, Todd E. "Christian Worship in a Cross-Cultural Setting." *Missio Apostolica* 5 (May 1997): 19–33.
Scaer, David P. "*Cum Patre et Filio Adoratur*: The Holy Spirit Understood Christologically." *Concordia Theological Quarterly* 61 (Jan.–April 1997): 93–112.
⎯⎯⎯⎯. "Matthew as Catechist." Unpublished manuscript, 1995.
Schöne, Jobst. *The Christological Character of the Office of the Ministry and the Royal Priesthood*. Cresbard. S.Dak.: Logia Books, 1996.
Senkbeil, Harold L. *Sanctification, Christ in Action: Evangelical Challenge and Lutheran Response*. Milwaukee: Northwestern Publishing House, 1989.
Stamoolis, James J. *Eastern Orthodox Mission Theology Today*. Minneapolis: Light and Life Publishing Company, 1986.
Weinrich, William C. "Evangelism in the Early Church." *Concordia Theological Quarterly* 45 (Jan.–April 1981): 61–75.
Wenthe, Dean O. "Entrance into the Biblical World: The First and Crucial Cross-Cultural Move." *Logia* 4, no. 2 (1995): 19–24.
Westermeyer, Paul. *Te Deum: The Church and Music: A Textbook, A Reference, A History, An Essay*. Minneapolis: Fortress Press, 1998.
⎯⎯⎯⎯. *The Church Musician*. Rev. ed. Minneapolis: Augsburg Fortress, 1997.
Yeago, David S. "Messiah's People: The Culture of the Church in the Midst of the Nations." *Pro Ecclesia* 4 (Spring 1997): 146–171.

Variety

Association for Liturgical Resources, Presbyterian Church (U.S.A.). *The Psalter—Psalms and Canticles for Singing*. Louisville: Westminster/John Knox Press, 1993.
Bobb, Barry L. Bobb Hans Boehringer, eds. *Proclaim: A Guide for Planning Liturgy and Music*. 2nd ed. St. Louis: Concordia Publishing House, 1994.
Buttrick, George Arthur, ed. *The Interpreter's Dictionary of the Bible*. New York: Abingdon Press, 1962. S.v. "Psalms, Book of."
Cantor/Congregation Series. Chicago: GIA Publications. (Various composers' settings. Each setting published individually.)

Celebration Series. Chicago: GIA Publications. (Various settings in 7 volumes by composers from the "Catholic folk-mass tradition.")
Creative Worship for the Lutheran Parish. St. Louis: Concordia Publishing House, 1988– .
Dawn, Marva. *Reaching Out Without Dumbing Down*. Grand Rapids, Mich.: William B. Eerdmans Publishing Company, 1995.
Gaddy, C. Welton. *The Gift of Worship*. Nashville: Broadman Press, 1992.
Gelineau, Joseph. *The Grail/Gelineau Psalter—150 Psalms and 18 Canticles*. Chicago: GIA Publications, 1972.
Held, David and Edward Klammer. "Planning Corporate Worship." In *Lutheran Worship: History and Practice,* ed. Fred. L. Precht, 556–65. St. Louis: Concordia Publishing House, 1993.
Lettermann, Henry L. "Make it New: *Lutheran Worship* 1982." *Lutheran Education* 117 (Jan.–Feb. 1982): 158–159.
Mahnke, Alan. *17 Psalms for Cantor and Congregation*. St. Louis: Concordia Publishing House, 1992.
Rotermund, Donald. *Intonations and Alternative Accompaniments for Psalm Tones*. St. Louis: Concordia Publishing House, 1997.
Scott, John, ed. *The New St. Paul's Cathedral Psalter*. Norwich: Canterbury Press, 1997.
Singing the Psalms. Portland: Oregon Catholic Press, 1995. (Various contemporary settings for cantor/choir singing verses, congregation singing refrains.)
Thomas, Paul. *The Psalms for the Church Year*. 12 vols. St. Louis: Concordia Publishing House, 1982.

Assisting Ministers

Bradshaw, Paul F. *Ordination Rites of the Ancient Churches of East and West*. New York: Pueblo, 1990.
Henry R. Percival, ed. "Excursus on the Minor Orders of the Early Church." In *A Select Library of the Nicene and Post-Nicene Fathers of the Christian Church*. 2nd series. Reprint, Grand Rapids, Mich.: William B. Eerdmans Publishing Company, 1988. (See pp. 144–47).
Herbst, Wolfgang. *Evangelischer Gottesdienst: Quellen zu seiner Geschichte*. 2nd ed. Göttingen: Vandenhoeck & Ruprecht, 1992.
Lutheran Book of Worship: Ministers Desk Edition. Minneapolis: Augsburg Publishing House; Philadelphia: Board of Publications, Lutheran Church in America, 1978.
Osborne, Kenan B. *Priesthood: A History of the Ordained Ministry in the Roman Catholic Church*. New York: Paulist Press, 1989.
Pfatteicher. Philip H. and Carlos R. Messerli. *Manual on the Liturgy: Lutheran Book of Worship*. Minneapolis: Augsburg Publishing House, 1979.
Roles in the Liturgical Assembly: The Twenty-Third Liturgical Conference of Saint Serge. Trans. Matthew J. O'Connell. New York: Pueblo Publishing Company, 1981.

Bibliography

Senn, Frank. *The Pastor as Worship Leader: A Manual for Corporate Worship.* Minneapolis: Augsburg Publishing House, 1977.

Winger, Thomas M. "The Priesthood of All the Baptized: An Exegetical and Theological Investigation." S.T.M. Thesis, Concordia Seminary, 1992.

Liturgical Texts

A Liturgical Psalter for the Christian Year. Prepared and edited by Massey H. Shepherd Jr. with the assistance of the Consultation on Common Texts. Minneapolis: Augsburg Publishing House; Collegeville, Minn.: Liturgical Press, 1976.

Allen, Jr., Horace T. "Forum: Common Texts Revisited." *Worship* 60 (March 1986): 172–75.

Kumpf, Eric. "Liturgical Diction in a Lutheran Paradigm Shift." *Dialog* 30 (1991): 296–299.

Commission on Theology and Church Relations of The Lutheran Church—Missouri Synod. *Biblical Revelation and Inclusive Language.* St. Louis: The Lutheran Church—Missouri Synod, 1998.

Commission on Worship of the Lutheran Church of Australia. "Principles Governing the Use of Language in the Liturgy of the Church." Available from http://www.lca.org.au/cwst13.htm. Internet.

Consultation on Common Texts. "Reflections on the Responses of the Member Churches of the CCT to the ELLC Texts." Document No. 2. December 1996, photocopied.

Dipko, Thomas E. "Brief Response to the ELLC Survey on Common Liturgical Texts." 18 April 1995, photocopied.

English Language Liturgical Consultation. *Praying Together.* Nashville: Abingdon Press, 1988.

International Consultation on English Texts. *Prayers We Have in Common: Agreed Liturgical Texts Proposed by the International Consultation on English Texts.* Enlarged and rev. ed. Philadelphia: Fortress Press, 1972.

McHugh, John. "On Englishing the Liturgy: An Open Letter to the Bishop of Shrewsbury." 25 March 1983, photocopied.

Taft, Robert. "Response to the Berakah Award: Anamnesis." *Worship* 59 (July 1985): 305–25.

Confession and Absolution

Bennethum, D. Michael. "Private Confession: An Evangelical Perspective." *Bride of Christ* 5 (St. Michael and All Angels, 1981): 8–17.

Bonhoeffer, Dietrich. *Life Together.* Trans. John W. Doberstein. New York: Harper & Row Publishers, 1954. (See especially pp. 110–22.)

―――. *Spiritual Care.* Trans. Jay C. Rochelle. Philadelphia: Fortress Press, 1985. (See especially pp. 60–69.)

_____. *The Cost of Discipleship.* Revised and unabridged ed. New York: Macmillan Publishing Company, 1959.
Boumann, Walter. "Confession-Absolution and the Eucharistic Liturgy," *Lutheran Quarterly,* o.s., 26 (May 1974): 204–20.
_____. "Private Confession and Absolution: A Word to Pastors." *Una Sancta* 18 (St. Mark the Evangelist, 1961): 9–15.
Chytraeus, David. *A Summary of the Christian Faith (1568).* Trans. Richard Dinda. Decatur, Ill.: Repristination Press, 1994. (See especially pp. 136–37.)
Conroe, Jon W. "A Historical Survey of the Office of the Keys as Confessed in the Missouri Synod's 'Explanation of the Fifth Chief Part of Luther's Small Catechism' from 1912–1986." *Concordia Student Journal* 16 (Easter 1993): 21–32.
Dudley, Martin and Geoffrey Rowell, eds. *Confession and Absolution.* Collegeville, Minn.: The Liturgical Press, 1990.
Elert, Werner. *The Christian Faith: An Outline of Lutheran Dogmatics.* Trans. Martin H. Bertram and Walter R. Bouman. Typed manuscript (photocopy). Fuerbringer Memorial Library, Concordia Seminary, St. Louis, 1974. (See especially pp. 306–308.)
Enger, Kurt N. "Private Confession in American Lutheranism: A Study of Doctrine, History, and Practice." Th.D. diss., Princeton Theological Seminary, 1962.
For The Life of the World 1 (December 1997). (A whole issue devoted to Private Confession and Absolution.)
Fousek, Marianka S. "Theological-Historical Perspectives of Private Confession and Absolution for the Lutheran Pastor Today." In *Essays on Private Confession and Absolution.* New York: Commission on Worship, Lutheran Church in America, 1969.
Girgensohn, Herbert. *Teaching Luther's Catechism.* Trans. John W. Doberstein. 2 vols. Philadelphia: Muhlenberg Press, 1960. (See especially 2:62–86.)
Hardt, Tom G.A. "The Means of Grace According to The Confessions of the Evangelical Lutheran Church." *Confessional Lutheran Research Society Newsletter,* no. 1 (Advent 1985): 1–9.
Jungkuntz, Theodore. "Private Confession: A 20th-Century Issue Seen from a 16th-Century Perspective." *Concordia Theological Monthly* 39 (February 1968): 106–15.
Kliefoth, Theodor. "Die Beichte und Absolution." *Liturgische Abhandlungen.* Vol. II. Schwerin: Verlag der Stiller'schen Hof-Buchhandlung, 1856.
Koehler, Walter. *Counseling and Confession: The Role of Confession and Absolution in Pastoral Counseling.* St. Louis: Concordia Publishing House, 1982.
Korby, Kenneth F. "A Suggested Program for the Reintroduction of Private Confession and Absolution in Our Parishes," English District Pastoral Conference of Greater Detroit. Toledo, Ohio, April 19, 1966.
_____. "C.F.W. Walther on Confession & Absolution." Unpublished manuscript, February 2, 1964.
_____. "Naming and Healing the Disorders of Man: Therapy and Absolution." In *Confession and Congregation,* ed. David G. Truemper. *The Cresset.* Occasional Paper III. Valparaiso, Ind.: Valparaiso University Press, 1978.

Bibliography

———. "The Theology of Pastoral Care in Wilhelm Löhe: With Special Attention to the Function of the Liturgy and the Laity." Th.D. diss., Concordia Seminary in Exile in Cooperation with Lutheran School of Theology, 1976.

Krispin, Gerald S. "*Propter Absolutionem:* Holy Absolution in the Theology of Martin Luther and Philipp Jacob Spener: A Comparative Study." Th.D. diss, Concordia Seminary, 1992.

Lang, Paul H.D. "Private Confession in the Lutheran Church." *Una Sancta* 22 (Resurrection 1965): 18–40.

Leske, Elmore. "Another Look at Luther's Indulgence Theses in the Context of a Study of Luther's Progress towards His Radical Understanding of Repentance." In *And Every Tongue Confess: Essays in Honor of Norman Nagel on the Occasion of His Sixty-fifth Birthday,* ed. Gerald S. Krispin and Jon D. Vieker, 61–85. Dearborn, Mich.: Nagel Festschrift Committee, 1990.

Loehe, Johann Conrad Wilhelm. "The Sacrament of Repentance." Trans. Delvin E. Ressel. *Una Sancta* 10, no. 2 (1951): 1–9; and 10, no. 3 (1951): 10–23.

Luther, Martin. "The Sacrament of Penance" (1519), AE 35:3–22.

———. "The Holy and Blessed Sacrament of Baptism" (1519), AE 35:23–44.

———. "A Discussion on How Confession Should Be Made," (1520), AE 39:23–47.

———. "An Instruction to Penitents Concerning the Forbidden Books of Dr. Martin Luther" (1521), AE 44:218–29.

———. "The Eighth Sermon, March 16, 1522, Reminiscere Sunday," at Wittenberg, AE 51:97–100.

———. "Instructions for the Visitors of Parish Pastors in Electoral Saxony (1528), AE 40:263–320.

———. "A Short Order of Confession Before the Priest for the Common Man" (1529), AE 53:116–18.

———. "The Keys" (1530), AE 40:321–77.

———. "How One Should Teach Common Folk to Shrive Themselves" (1531), AE 53:119–21.

———. "Table Talk, No. 4362" (1539), AE 54:334.

———. "Table Talk, No. 5176" (1540), AE 54:394.

Lutheran Forum 31, no. 3 (Una Sancta, Fall 1997). (A full issue devoted to Holy Absolution.)

Martens, Gottfried. "Sola Fide—Do Lutherans Still Agree On What Is Meant?" Fort Wayne, Ind.: 13th Annual Symposium on the Lutheran Confessions, Concordia Theological Seminary, Fort Wayne, Ind., January 1990. Typed document.

Mueller, Norbert H. and George Kraus, eds. *Pastoral Theology.* St. Louis: Concordia Publishing House, 1990 (See especially pp. 118–124.)

Nagel, Norman E. "Christ on the Rainbow." Unpublished paper, n.d.

Piepkorn, Arthur C. "Christ Today: His Presence in the Sacraments." In *The Church: Selected Writings of Arthur Carl Piepkorn,* ed. Michael P. Plekon and William S. Wiecher. Delhi, NY: ALPB Books, 1993.

———. "The Lutheran Church: A Sacramental Church." In *The Church: Selected Writings of Arthur Carl Piepkorn,* ed. Michael P. Plekon and William S. Wiecher. Delhi, N.Y.: ALPB Books, 1993.

Pittelko, Roger. "Confessional Perspectives on the Practice of Confession." *Bride of Christ* 5, no. 4 (St. Michael and All Angels 1981): 5–7.

Pless, John T. "The Lutheran Confession on Individual Confession and Absolution: An Approach for Today." *Bride of Christ* 4, no. 3 (Pentecost 1980): 10–17.

Precht, Fred L. "Changing Theologies of Private and Public Confession and Absolution." Th.D. diss., Concordia Seminary, 1965.

———. "Confession and Absolution: Sin and Forgiveness." In *Lutheran Worship: History and Practice,* ed. Fred L. Precht, 322–86. St. Louis: Concordia Publishing House, 1993.

Richter, Stephan. *Metanoia: Christian Penance and Confession.* New York: Sheed and Ward, 1966.

Rogness, Alvin. *Forgiveness and Confession. The Keys to Renewal.* Minneapolis: Augsburg Publishing House, 1970.

Sawyer, J. Richard. "Preliminary Thoughts on Restoring Confession and Absolution." *Bride of Christ* 22, no. 2 (1998): 12–19.

Schattauer, Thomas H. "Announcement, Confession, and Lord's Supper in the Pastoral-Liturgical Work of Wilhelm Löhe: A Study of Worship and Church Life in the Lutheran Parish at Neuendettelsau, Bavaria, 1837–1872." Ph.D. diss., University of Notre Dame, 1990.

Schöne, Jobst. *Ich bekenne, Eine Beichthilfe für evangelisch–lutherische Christen.* Ülzen: FesteBurg Verlag, 1963.

Senkbeil, Harold L. *Dying To Live: The Power of Forgiveness.* St. Louis: Concordia Publishing House, 1994. (Especially pp. 70–90.)

Stumpf, Eric D. "Private Confession: A Call for Restoration in Pastoral Care." *Concordia Journal* 19 (July 1993): 218–33.

Telfer, W. *The Forgiveness of Sins.* London: SCM Press, 1959.

Tentler, Thomas N. *Sin and Confession on the Eve of the Reformation.* Princeton, N.J.: Princeton University Press, 1977.

Walther, C.F.W. "Duties of an Evangelical Lutheran Synod." In *Essays for the Church.* Vol. II. Trans. Everette W. Meier. St. Louis: Concordia Publishing House, 1992. (Especially Thesis III, point c., pp. 42–45.)

———. *Pastoral Theology.* Trans. and abridged John M. Drickamer from the 5th ed., 1906. New Haven, Mo.: Lutheran News Inc., 1995. (Especially pp. 120–29.)

———. *The Proper Distinction Between Law and Gospel.* Trans. W.H.T. Dau. St. Louis: Concordia Publishing House, 1929. (Especially pp. 127–210.)

Wittenberg, Martin. "Wilhelm Löhe and Confession: A Contribution to the History of Seelsorge and the Office of the Ministry within Modern Lutheranism." Trans. Gerald S. Krispin. In *And Every Tongue Confess: Essays in Honor of Norman Nagel on the Occasion of His Sixty-fifth Birthday,* ed. Gerald S. Krispin and Jon D. Vieker, 113–52. Dearborn, Mich.: Nagel Festschrift Committee, 1990.

BIBLIOGRAPHY

Ylvisaker, S.C. "On Absolution." In *Grace for Grace: A Brief History of the Norwegian Synod.* Christian Anderson; and G.O. Lillegard, eds. Mankato, Minn.: Lutheran Synod Book Company, 1943.

Confirmation

Andrén, Carl-Gustaf. "Die Konfirmationsfrage in der Reformationszeit." In *Zur Geschichte und Ordnung der Konfirmation in den Lutherischen Kirchen,* ed. Kurt Frör, 36–57. Munich: Claudius Verlag, 1962.

Benze, Charles T. "The Liturgical History of Confirmation." In *Memoirs of the Lutheran Liturgical Association.* Vol 3. Pittsburgh: Lutheran Liturgical Association, 1907.

Boehme, Armand J. "Sing a New Song: The Doctrine of Justification and the *Lutheran Book of Worship* Sacramental Liturgies." *Concordia Theological Quarterly* 43 (April 1979): 96–119.

Boehringer, Hans. "Baptism, Confirmation and First Communion: Christian Initiation in the Contemporary Church." In *Christian Initiation: Reborn of Water and Spirit,* Institute Of Liturgical Studies Occasional Papers, no. 1, ed. Daniel C. Brockopp, Brian L. Helge, and David G. Truemper. Valparaiso, Ind.: Institute of Liturgical Studies, 1981.

Brand, Eugene L. "New Rites of Initiation and their Implications in the Lutheran Churches." *Studia Liturgica* 12:2–3 (1977): 151–65.

Burreson, Kent J. "The United Methodist *Book of Worship*: A Prod to the Revision of Lutheran Baptismal Rites." *Bride of Christ* 21, no. 4 (1997): 12–16.

Cartford, Gerhard. "Rethinking the Eucharistic Liturgy with Children in Mind." *Cross Accent: Journal of the Association of Lutheran Church Musicians* 3 (January 1994): 16–23.

Debard, Jean Marc. "La première Communion dans la principauté luthérienne de Montbéliard du XVIue au XVIIIue siècle." In *La première Communion,* ed. J. Delumeau. Paris: Desclee de Brouwer, 1987.

Deffner, Donald L. "Confirmation." In *Lutheran Worship: History and Practice,* ed. Fred L. Precht, 387–400. St. Louis: Concordia Publishing House, 1993.

Erling, Bernhard. "Rites of Christian Initiation." *Lutheran Quarterly,* o.s., 25 (August 1973): 254–69.

———. "Rites of Christian Initiation." *Lutheran Quarterly,* o.s., 25 (August 1973): 254–69.

Evangelical Lutheran Church in America. *The Use of the Means of Grace: A Proposed Statement on the Practice of Word and Sacraments.* Chicago: Evangelical Lutheran Church in America, 1996.

Fisher, J.D.C. *Christian Initiation, The Reformation Period: Some Early Reformed Rites of Baptism and Confirmation and Other Contemporary Documents,* 159–260. Alcuin Club Collections, No. 51. London: SPCK, 1970.

Frör, Kurt. "Confirmation: A Lutheran World Federation Seminar." *Lutheran World* 8 (Spring 1961): 174–81.

———. "Die Ordnung der Konfirmation in der lutherischen Kirche." In *Zur Geschichte und Ordnung der Konfirmation in den Lutherischen Kirchen*, ed. Kurt Frör, 122–42. Munich: Claudius Verlag, 1962.

———. "Theologische Grundfragen der Konfirmation Versuch einer Interpretation." In *Confirmatio: Forschungen zur Geschichte und Praxis der Konfirmation*, ed. Kurt Frör, 75–117. Munich: Evangelischer Presseverband für Bayern, 1959.

———. "Zur Interpretation der Kasseler Konfirmationsordnung von 1539." In *Reformatio und Confessio: Festschrift für Wilhelm Maurer*, ed. Friedrich W. Kantzenbach and Gerhard Müller, 113–29. Berlin: Lutherisches Verlagshaus, 1965.

Hareide, Bjarne. "Die Konfirmation in den Kirchenordnungen der Reformationszeit." In *Zur Geschichte und Ordnung der Konfirmation in den Lutherischen Kirchen*, ed. Kurt Frör, 58–82. Munich: Claudius Verlag, 1962.

Heinecken, Martin J. "Confirmation in Relation to the Lord's Supper." *Lutheran Quarterly* 15, o.s., (Fall 1963): 22–28.

Holeton, David. "Children and Communion: A Gift to the Community." *Cross Accent: Journal of the Association of Lutheran Church Musicians* 3 (Jan. 1994): 4–14.

———. *Infant Communion—Then and Now*. Bramcote: Grove Books, 1981.

Holmes, Urban. *Young Children and the Eucharist*. 2nd edition. New York: Seabury Press, 1982.

Jagger, Peter J. *Christian Initiation, 1552–1969: Rites of Baptism and Confirmation Since the Reformation Period*. London: S.P.C.K., 1970.

Johnson, Maxwell E., ed. *Living Water, Sealing Spirit: Readings on Christian Initiation*. Collegeville, Minn.: The Liturgical Press, 1995.

Klos, Frank W. *Confirmation and First Communion*. Minneapolis: Augsburg Publishing House; Philadelphia: Board of Publication of the Lutheran Church in America; St. Louis: Concordia Publishing House, 1968.

Knowles, James W. "Confirmation in the Lutheran Tradition: Toward Redefinition and Renewal." Ph.D. diss., Andover Newton Theological School, 1986.

Lutheran World Federation. *Confirmation Ministry Study: Global Report*. LWF Documentation, no. 38. Geneva: Lutheran World Federation, 1995.

Maurer, D. Wilhelm. "Geschichte von Firmung und Konfirmation bis zum Ausgang der lutherischen Orthodoxie." In *Confirmatio: Forschungen zur Geschichte und Praxis der Konfirmation*, ed. Kurt Frör, 9–38. Munich: Evangelischer Presseverband für Bayern, 1959.

Nagel, Norman E. "Holy Baptism." In *Lutheran Worship: History and Practice*, ed. Fred L. Precht, 262–89. St. Louis: Concordia Publishing House, 1993.

Pfatteicher, Philip H. *Commentary on the Lutheran Book of Worship: Lutheran Liturgy in Its Ecumenical Context*, 67–76. Minneapolis: Augsburg Fortress, 1990.

Repp, Arthur C. "Theological Implications of Confirmation." *Concordia Theological Monthly* 31 (March 1960): 165–73 and (April 1960): 227–35.

———. *Confirmation in the Lutheran Church.* St. Louis: Concordia Publishing House, 1964.
Senn, Frank C. "Confirmation and First Communion: A Reappraisal." *Lutheran Quarterly,* o.s., 23 (May 1971): 178–91.
Spinks, Bryan D. "Luther's Timely Theology of Unilateral Baptism." *Lutheran Quarterly,* n.s., 9 (Spring 1995): 23–45.
Stone, Glenn C. "Confirmation—The Problem Still Unsolved" [review article]. *Una Sancta* 22, no. 4 (1965): 53–57.
Sturm, Wilhelm. "Aus dem Gespräch über Ursprung und Frühgeschichte der Konfirmation." In *Confirmatio: Forschungen zur Geschichte und Praxis der Konfirmation,* ed. Kurt Frör, 39–42. Munich: Evangelischer Presseverband für Bayern, 1959.
Truemper, David G., ed. *The Grace-full Use of the Means of Grace: Theses on Worship and Worship Practices.* Valparaiso, Ind., 1994.
Turner, Paul. *Confirmation: The Baby in Solomon's Court,* 36–56. New York: Paulist Press, 1993.
———. *The Meaning and Practice of Confirmation: Perspectives from a Sixteenth Century Controversy.* American University Studies, series 7: Theology and Religion, vol. 31. New York: Peter Lang, 1987.
Volz, Carl A. "Review of Recent Literature on Confirmation." *Word & World* 11 (Fall 1991): 408–14.
Von Schenk, Berthold. "First Communion and Confirmation." *Concordia Theological Monthly* 42 (June 1971): 353–60.
Wiencke, Gustav K. "Confirmation in Historical Perspective." *Lutheran Quarterly,* o.s., 7 (May 1955): 99–113.

Liminality

Friedrich, Paul. *The Meaning of Aphrodite.* Chicago: University of Chicago Press, 1978.
Kirk, G. S. *Myth: Its Meaning and Functions in Ancient and Other Cultures.* Sather Classical Lectures, no. 40. Cambridge: Cambridge University Press, 1970.
Levi-Strauss, Claude. *The Raw and the Cooked.* Mythologiques, vol. 1. Trans. John and Doreen Weightman. Chicago: University of Chicago Press, 1969.
Turner, Victor. *The Ritual Process: Structure and Antistructure.* Ithaca: Cornell University Press, 1969.